AMERICAN CULTURE - WHAT THEY'RE SAYING
ABOUT *CONFESSIONS OF A GOOD KID*

"The story of a horse and the boy who loves him . . . what?
There's no horse? How about a dog? No dog? Crap! Well . . .
it's probably pretty good anyway - MacArthur hated it!" -
Dwight D. Eisenhower

"A splendid chronicle of the idiocy of infancy and the folly of
youth." - Ambrose Bierce

"Look out, Dreiser - this book, carefully designed and
smoothly written, with no puerile clichés in it and no maudlin
moralizing, makes *An American Tragedy* look like an
American tragedy" - H. L. Mencken

"The book stops here . . . just kidding." - Harry S. Truman

"Reminds me of my boyhood, although I was much more
talented and I never had a pet lizard. " - Mickey Rooney

"It was great, although I am troubled by the fact that he never
had a dog. Every boy needs a dog. Hell, I was around at the
time. I could have intervened. It haunts me - along with the
fact that I named names for that bastard McCarthy - the two
major regrets of my life. " - Lassie

READ IT FOR YOURSELF AND SEE WHAT THE
EXCITEMENT IS ALL ABOUT!

# confessions of a good kid

william fogg

Published by BHC Books

This is a memoir, but names have been changed in some cases. To anyone who might find fault with the accuracy of my narrative, I offer an apology, as well as encouragement to write an alternate version. I will be the first to buy a copy!

Thank you to Joan, Sheryl, Thurlene, Mike, Brian and Sherri.
All contents copyright 2018 by William Fogg
Cover illustration and BHC logo by William Fogg

ISBN 978-1-54394-946-9

"Part of my plan has been to try to pleasantly remind adults of what they once were themselves, and of how they felt and thought and talked, and what queer enterprises they sometimes engaged in.
-Mark Twain, Adventures of *Tom Sawyer*

"Of course it's true!  It's all true!" - Alan Hale in *Adventures of Don Juan*

# 1

# In the Beginning

When I was a baby, I swallowed a cigarette butt. My parents called the doctor, and were told to have me drink warm salt water to induce vomiting. They anticipated a struggle, but I surprised them by ingesting the water without resistance. I further surprised them by refusing to vomit. They called the doctor again, this time being told not to worry, that things would take care of themselves. They then had to endure several hours of anxiety and frustration, waiting and wondering if their brand new child had sustained any damage. They were relieved when it was finally evident that I was unscathed, but also resentful that I had put them through such an ordeal.

My mom told me this story when I was a teenager, making the point that, although sometimes amusing, my behavior was often "difficult." I told her that I understood, but felt that it might equally illustrate the quality of medical service available in Hermosa Beach circa 1953. This just seemed to reinforce her position. Of course I had not understood what I was doing when I ate the butt, nor was I willfully refusing to disgorge it. It was a perfectly innocent act, and at the time it was probably understood as such. But, innocent or not, it seemed to be an indication of things to come.

I was raised in Southern California, and spent my first two plus years in Hermosa Beach, which was one of many coastal "small towns" of the era. Most of my memories of that time are innocuous fragments - sitting at a small kitchen table with a red and white checkered table cloth, in front of a window with Venetian blinds, contemplating a bowl of Campbell's alphabet soup, or playing with other kids my age on an overcast day, in the sand box at the nearby preschool. I had a friend named Stevie who was slightly older, and we would sometimes be allowed to mess with wagons and tricycles on the sidewalk just outside my front yard. He was a very grubby kid, complete with untied shoelaces, uneven cuffs, partially tucked t-shirts, uncombed hair, and stains of all kinds, including, but not limited to, mud, grass, and grape juice. Despite his rather unprepossessing appearance, he was a good companion for me. We got along well and kept ourselves occupied without too much parental supervision.

Although these early years were apparently enjoyable ones for our family, there were a few events which, along with the cigarette butt incident, gave my parents pause. I recall riding my little tricycle inside the Hermosa Beach duplex, stopping to vomit over the handlebars onto the hardwood floor, and then continuing my journey through the puddle undismayed. My mom was very dismayed, but handled it well. She was also annoyed when Stevie and I took the orange halves she had given to us as healthy snacks, and used them to polish the front door. It was a hot day, and we created a sticky mess involving flies and slightly discolored wood, but no major repairs were required.

When I was about two and a half years old, we started taking trips to Long Beach to watch our new house being built, and on one of those visits I was allowed to ride the bulldozer while the pool was being excavated. It was all very exciting. When we actually moved into the Long Beach house in 1956, everything seemed fresh and clean. There were more vacant lots than homes, and the asphalt streets were smooth and traffic free. Our area was an upper middle class development called Park Estates, and it was only one of many areas of the city that were experiencing rapid expansion. Long Beach was a wonderful place to grow up at that time. It was a large city characterized by post-war suburban housing and business developments, as well as a new state college and one of the first major shopping malls.

We celebrated my third birthday at the new house, on the patio by the built-in pool, with all of my friends from the Peter Pan Nursery School. It was a wonderful party, and I received a lot of cool presents. I was enjoying a glorious childhood, and appeared to be an exemplary young citizen most of the time, but there were still little incidents that contradicted that image and tried the patience of my parents. My mother, who had been quite tolerant of my earlier transgressions, was not such a good sport when I put our cat into the washing machine. Fortunately, I couldn't turn it on, at least not before I was caught in the act. When I deliberately rode my hybrid tricycle- tractor into the pool at the new house, I was spanked. The punishment seemed appropriate at the time, and a small price to pay for the thrill of pedaling full blast over the edge and into the water.

In 1957, my parents decided to take a trip to Las Vegas. I don't remember the trip itself, but my impression at the time was one of a few glittering hotels amidst a lot of rundown, tacky businesses. There was a little racetrack concession on one of the main streets where customers could pay to drive Micro-midget race cars. These were miniature race cars, and they could move at a good clip. I really wanted to drive one, and my dad consulted the man at the admission gate, but at four years old I probably did not look like a good prospect. However, a compromise was reached. One of the track employees was to stand on the racer at the back while I drove, in order to insure my safety. He must have had his feet on a bumper or platform of some kind, but I can't recall how he was positioned. I didn't care - I just wanted to drive.

As soon as everything was set, the car was started, and I was cautioned to be careful because it was "not a toy." Of course - that was why I was so excited. So, although I listened attentively, and solemnly promised to go slow, as soon as the guy behind me tapped my shoulder and said, "OK," I floored it. He immediately lost his grip and fell off. I could feel the warm air as it riffled my hair and made my eyes water. My hands felt good on the steering wheel, and the accelerator under my foot was very responsive. It was all quite intoxicating, and I ripped around the track several times before I became aware of the frantically signaling adults on the sidelines.

When I coasted in, there were some raised voices, but even though my mom had been horrified, my dad seemed amused. Not only did I not get in trouble, but the folks at the track gave me a little plastic trophy. In retrospect, it seems possible that my dad may have slipped somebody a few bucks. This was ultimately regarded as one of those "boys will be boys" incidents, the slight element of danger merely making it a better anecdote for parents to relate to friends and relatives.

A more serious incident took place when I figured out that the prongs of a corkscrew that was kept in a kitchen drawer would probably fit into the electrical outlet near the sink. I was just tall enough to get into the drawer, grab the corkscrew and reach the outlet. I remember trying to insert the prongs quite a few times without success, and that this went on over a period of several days. I don't know if I was deliberately working when my

4

parents weren't around, or if it was just a coincidence that they didn't catch me. However, there was a moment when I managed to achieve my goal, and a huge jolt of electricity knocked me off of my feet and into the cabinets opposite the sink. It was loud and scary, and the only thing that saved me was the wooden handle of the corkscrew. I wasn't hurt, or even very upset, probably because I was slightly stunned and had no idea of how close I had come to frying myself, but I never did it again.

In January of 1958, my parents brought home a baby brother. I found him mildly interesting at first, but until he was able to walk and talk I had very little to do with him, and would tend to leave the room whenever there was any talk of changing diapers. I did notice that I was getting less attention from mom and dad, who seemed thoroughly preoccupied, but this didn't bother me much, because I now knew many of the neighbor kids, and enjoyed the opportunity to get out of our baby-infested house to play with them. My friends and I had a fair degree of autonomy within the territorial limits of our block, where there was always a parent nearby in case of emergency. We were usually left to our own devices unless we made too much noise or were suspiciously quiet.

Since there was hardly any automobile traffic in our area, we were allowed to walk or ride tricycles to each other's houses. The many vacant lots were great places to explore. The wild grass would grow tall enough so that we could yank it out of the ground, and attached to the roots would be a big clod of damp earth. We would hold the clump of grass, swing it around, and launch it into the air, usually at another kid. These clumps were referred to, in the neighborhood vernacular, as "hairy boys," and provided excellent ammunition for suburban trench warfare. We had plenty of battles, and would arrive at our homes afterwards covered with dirt and a few scratches, scrapes, and bug bites, but no one was ever seriously injured.

These lots would sometimes yield unexpected treasures. A friend and I found a small stack of trading cards (phony ads) and two frozen ice cream cups which had been stashed by a couple of young girls. Naturally we confiscated the goods. Another friend was with me when we discovered hundreds of ladybugs clustered around some bushes. We soon had our cupped hands full of them - yellow, orange, red, and spotted. It seemed like something out of a fairy tale. One afternoon we encountered a pile of large ripe tomatoes, which ultimately provided ammunition for an excellent skirmish with some other kids. I loved the lots.

In July there was a pool party for my fifth birthday. Although we enjoyed the ice cream and cake, we were a bit distracted by my mom and the other mothers, who kept talking to us and to each other about how things would change when kindergarten began in the fall. I had attended a play school in Hermosa Beach, and my parents had immediately enrolled me in the Peter Pan Nursery School when we moved to Long Beach, so I was accustomed to finding my way in new social environments. I enjoyed making new friends and getting involved in activities like digging a hole to catch the devil in the garden, and jumping off of the swings in midflight. I had made some good friends at Peter Pan. Guy shared my interests in pirates, Superman, and plastic cavalry soldiers, and Conn told me stories about his older brothers beating him up. So the idea of a new school experience was not particularly intimidating in and of itself, but we knew that this would be different. It was real school! My friends and I alternated between excitement and dread, and compared information gleaned from older brothers and sisters, as well as some of the "big kids" in the neighborhood. These mature and sophisticated individuals ranged from six to eight years of age, and delighted in scaring the hell out of us with stories about whippings from teachers and beatings from bullies. We had two long months until school started, and most of that time was spent swimming, playing, and running around, but we continued to speculate as to what the near future might hold.

The day finally arrived, and my mom walked with me to the nearest school bus stop, which was only three blocks away. Other moms were providing the same protective escort services for their own children, and there were some big kids who arrived alone or with friends. The classic yellow bus pulled up and we rode off to Minnie Gant elementary school, which turned out to be terrific. No whippings, no beatings, just a bunch of new to kids to make friends with, and nice teachers with fun things to keep us constructively occupied. The rumors had been false! I was too young to speculate upon why so many people had gone to such lengths to frighten us about the future. All I knew was that everything had turned out fine. Life was good!

And yet - I still managed to create a few ripples in the kindergarten cosmos. One morning I brought my Mattel Fanner Fifty cap pistol for show and tell. While waiting at the bus stop, I fired a few shots at a small black poodle who didn't want to play guns, and promptly bit my leg. There was a little blood, a doctor visit, heated phone conversations between my parents and the dog owner, and a warning about where and when it was OK to shoot caps.

There was another bus stop incident later that year, when I got into a fight with my friend Curt. I don't remember what it was about, but we were rolling around in the dirt, surrounded by cheering kids, when the bus pulled up. The driver, a burly woman named Mrs. Brown, pulled us apart and made us sit in the back of the bus until we arrived at school. She then escorted us to our respective classrooms and informed our teachers of the scuffle. I don't know what happened to Curt, but I had to lie down quietly on a mat until class began. It wasn't exactly a punishment, but I did find it humiliating, and I hated humiliation more than being spanked.

When I brought my gopher snake to school for another show and tell session, my classmates were thrilled, but my teacher was not. She wouldn't let me take him out of the jar, or even take off the lid. She would only admit that it was "interesting" to know that we fed him live mice. I didn't get into any trouble for bringing my snake to school, though I was vaguely aware that I had not quite followed the rules somehow. When I told my dad about it, he thought it was pretty funny, which mystified me even more. Although I remained confused, I found that I could live with confusion as long as there was no punishment involved. Besides, my popularity soared as the word got around that we fed the snake on Saturdays. Quite a few kids came over to witness the spectacle - even some girls!

My father was the ultimate arbiter of justice in our household. When I was young, he frequently exhibited a sense of humor relative to my escapades, and I believe that he genuinely tried to be fair, but sometimes his temper got the best of him. He was very fair when I stole an Easter egg from the neighbor's kitchen. I had gone over to play with the girls, and finding an unlocked door and no one home, had taken one candy egg and eaten it. I was assailed by guilt, and confessed to my dad, who admonished me for stealing, but praised me for telling the truth. End result - no punishment.

It was a different story on a hot Spring day when I was playing in the pool. I came up for air to find him out of his lounge chair, screaming at someone who must have been directly behind me in the water. I turned around, but there was no one there. In fact, there was no one else in the pool. I turned again to look at my dad, whose face was very red at this point. "Yes, YOU!" he yelled, directly at me. I was so surprised and confused that I didn't know what to think. "Out of that pool!" I climbed out, and was promptly grabbed by the arm, given several solid swats, and told to go inside to my room. I never figured out what I might have done to set him off, but it could have been any one of a number of things.

There were many rules associated with the pool. I knew that they were intended to protect us from harm, but it was difficult to keep all of them in mind all of the time. Don't run on the wet pool deck, be careful in the deep end, don't go in without an adult present, wait at least thirty minutes after eating to avoid stomach cramps, wait at least thirty minutes after chlorination, don't horse around – you get the idea. Sometimes I got caught up in the moment and forgot to be careful, resulting in three stitches when I turned around while jumping into the water and whacked the concrete edge with my chin, and a severely lacerated leg when I jumped off the diving board into a plastic boat and crashed right through the bottom. So I had to admit to myself that it was entirely possible that I had been careless again, thereby justifying my dad's outburst.

Of course, these incidents, and others like them, took place at irregular intervals during my infancy and early childhood. I was not creating havoc every minute of every day. In fact, I was generally regarded as a "good kid" by the adults and other children around me. I was talkative, friendly, reasonably obedient, and received good reports from teachers. I also evidently looked like a good kid. By that, I mean that there was something about my appearance or general demeanor that seemed to inspire confidence in adults. Even when I was clearly guilty of misbehavior, they were frequently reluctant to be harsh with me. "Why did you do that?" they would ask, trying to understand my reasoning. But I usually had no idea myself, and even though I was articulate for my age, my attempts at explanation were not particularly enlightening. However, I was beginning to understand a few things about life as a suburban child in sunny California.

Kids were divided into three categories. There were little kids, like my brother, who were not worth bothering about, kids more or less my age who could be friends or enemies, and big kids who were to be considered dangerous until proven otherwise. The grownups ran everything and set the rules, and there were a lot of rules. Usually they were clearly defined, but there were some grey areas in which we were simply expected to "know better." There were consequences to breaking the rules, usually involving spankings or restrictions, and when a spanking was warranted I got one. On a few occasions I got one for no apparent reason, like the pool incident, and once in a while I expected one and didn't get it, but I usually understood what was going to happen and why. I also knew that an angry grownup was a dangerous grownup, and I had a pretty good working knowledge of the forces that seemed to govern my existence. But I realized that despite my wisdom, grownups could be tricky. In fact, the whole world was kinda tricky.

# 2
## Broken Arrow

My education in the arts and sciences of bad behavior was undertaken by a congenial delinquent named Gary Scott. Gary was a Bad Boy, and he embraced his calling with admirable devotion. He would cheerfully lie, cheat, and steal, with a bravado that was breathtaking to witness. If an object was not to be touched, his mission was to break it. If a street was not to be crossed, he would traverse it relentlessly. Any evidence of adult authority was an irresistible invitation to defiance. But Gary was sophisticated enough to understand that with that defiance came the responsibility of escaping consequences. He was a master of subterfuge and obfuscation. No matter what he had done, regardless of the evidence against him, Gary was always ready with a reasonable explanation, or a sincere apology, or both. He could look an angry parent in the eye, and tell the most outrageous story with absolute conviction. He could even muster tears if necessary. In short - he was gifted!

I don't recall the circumstances of our first meeting, or the formal establishment of my apprenticeship, but I was deeply flattered by his willingness to share his wisdom with me. I was six years old and he was eight, so I naturally bowed to his seniority. We would meander through the neighborhood, exploring the vacant lots and construction sites, and Gary would shine the light of his authority upon the dangers that surrounded us.

I was already aware of the big, ugly Jerusalem crickets, which we called potato bugs. They were rumored to have a ferocious bite. The huge, black, noisy bumblebees, or motor bees, which sometimes dive bombed us on the pool deck, supposedly had a sting like a gunshot. The black widow spiders that we sometimes stumbled across were known to be deadly. Once I even saw a tarantula in our garage, so I knew that I had to be careful. But according to Gary, there were many other, spookier threats out there. For example, there were black panthers hiding in the trees and bushes. This was in 1959, so it's safe to assume that he was not referring to militant African-Americans, but whatever they were, I sure didn't want to meet 'em face to face. Gary would point and whisper, "See - there it is!" And although I sometimes thought I heard the leaves rustle, I never actually saw a panther. I did see the dragonflies, however, and I gave them a wide berth because now I knew that they could zoom in and sew up my mouth. I also stayed away from the deepest and darkest of the vacant lots because, according to Gary, there were Older Boys lurking there, just waiting to capture a young kid like me. They would strip me, tie me to a tree, and write bad words all over my body with lipstick. Even though I took most of this very seriously, I usually felt pretty confident that I could navigate around such perils, except on the days when the Santa Ana winds blew through the neighborhood, sucking all of the moisture out of the air and sending tumbleweeds and dust skittering down the streets. There was something about those winds that made me feel more cautious than usual.

Gary was very generous with his knowledge, but he could be a bit prickly if I asked too many questions. I was pretty sure that he got most of his information from his older brother, Butch, who was a genuine bully, and would never allow a punk like me to interview him. So, although I was sometimes uncertain about the accuracy of Gary's observations, I held my tongue, for it was a dangerous world and I was very fortunate to have such a benevolent mentor.

Looking back on certain events with an adult awareness, I am stunned by the audacity and cunning that were the hallmarks of Gary's personality. As a child, however, I was often puzzled by the things that he did. There was a tantalizing quality of perversity that I found fascinating, but I wondered why he took such chances. On one occasion, I was sitting at the kitchen table with my paper and crayons when he arrived. Gary immediately sat down to join me, and as soon as my mom left the room, he proceeded to render an exquisite penis and testicles. This was not a crude, childish drawing – the strokes of the crayon were fluid and graceful. I was astounded not only by the subject, but the finesse of the execution as well. When my unsuspecting mother returned, he casually turned the paper over and started working on a battleship. When she left again, he folded the drawing and put it in his pocket, confident that he could dispose of it at his leisure.

A few days later, we were sitting on the curb in front of my house, drinking Seven-ups. My father had already admonished us to be careful with the bottles. This was a standard parental dictum, as soda bottles were then made of glass rather than plastic. They were breakable, but they were also refundable. Once Gary and I had quenched our respective thirsts with a whole seven ounce serving of Seven-up, we could count on trading in the bottles at Paul's Market for three cents each - candy money. Gary had other ideas, however. He took both of the empties, placed one on the curb, and smashed it with the other. He then began carefully picking up the bright green shards and casually tossing them into the street.

I was immediately gripped by several emotions simultaneously – disappointment at the loss of potential revenue, astonishment at Gary's audacity, and fear of what might lie ahead. As I attempted to regain my composure, I heard our front door slam, and turned around to see my father heading in our direction. Evidently, some unidentified blip had cropped up on his parental radar screen, and investigation was in order. This was going to be dicey.

Gary didn't miss a beat. "Oh, hi Dr. Fogg. We had an accident. I was trying to throw the pieces into the ivy here, but some of them went into the street. I'll go get 'em."

"Well . . . I think you two better go inside and get the dustpan and broom." Clearly not satisfied, yet unwilling to pounce on such a cheerfully polite young man who exhibited not the slightest trace of guilt, my father surveyed the perimeter of his domain, his eyes darting back and forth between the pile of shattered glass on the curb and the scattered pieces gleaming like emeralds on the asphalt. He stood there for what seemed like several minutes, certain that we had been up to no good, but unable to establish our guilt beyond a reasonable doubt, then trudged back into the house with an air of defeat. It was a typical adult response to such brilliant deceitfulness.

My father had an ambivalent attitude regarding Gary. Earlier that year, Gary had traded a bag of stale Halloween candy for my toy rifle. It had seemed like a good deal to me - I liked candy, and I didn't use the rifle very often. When he saw me with the bag of candy, my father was curious, but when I told him the circumstances of its acquisition, he was outraged. He took the bag and went to Gary's house, returning with the rifle, and the familiar admonition that I should have known better. He knew that Gary was a devious little con artist, and yet was still willing to have a pleasant conversation with him as to whether *The Time Machine* was a movie worth seeing. If he had known the depth of Gary's commitment to malfeasance, I doubt that he would have let him anywhere near me.

Just a few days after the Seven-up incident, Gary and I were hanging around the kitchen as my mother was beginning to plan dinner. She also had some reservations about Gary, and pointedly told me not to "spoil my appetite" by eating candy. She was looking directly at him as she said this, and as a result Gary immediately decided that we should take a little walk. The walk took us to Paul's Market, a small corner grocery store several blocks away. When we arrived, Gary handed me a dime and told me to buy two candy bars, preferably Three Musketeers, as they were the biggest. I bought them, and shortly thereafter was surreptitiously chowing down while hidden in a nearby lot. Although I loved candy, two Three Musketeers bars were almost more than I could handle. But I didn't want to let Gary down – after all, he had invested a whole dime of his own money in the project, and a dime was major coin for any kid at that time. I was close to gagging, but I had to admire Gary's commitment to sabotage. It was always beautifully orchestrated, the obvious manifestation of a deeply felt personal philosophy. I never ate another Three Musketeers bar, though.

One of the hallmarks of Gary's academic program was instruction in the proper pronunciation and application of bad words. Some, like "hell" and "damn," were pretty easy to remember, and were frequently and inadvertently reviewed for me by my father, especially when he was driving. But there were other words that were more sophisticated and sinister, with implications of devilish magic about them. These were the words that the Big Boys used on the playground to establish their power and authority, and I was about to enter their ranks.

"You need to learn this one – it's really bad!"

"OK," I replied.

"OK, this is really bad!"

"OK."

Gary scoured the area in just the same way the soldiers in the movies we watched searched the trees for snipers, assuring himself that what he was about to say would not be overheard. He paused for a second, letting the drama build, then leaned in close to my ear.

"Bastard," he whispered, "Now you say it."

"Bastard . . . bastard." I savored it – solid, pronounceable, two whole syllables. And it really sounded bad. Cool!

"What does it mean?" I asked.

"It's really bad."

"OK."

"Just be careful, OK?"

"OK."

Not long after my vocabulary lesson, I found myself exploring the untrammeled corners of one of the many overgrown lots around the block from my house. I had initially planned to visit my friend, Curt. We were still buddies despite our little dust up at the bus stop, but Curt was turning out to be a strange kid. He had recently attempted to demonstrate how his new football helmet could protect him from anything by pedaling his bike at full speed into a parked car. The helmet had not lived up to his expectations, and Curt was obviously injured and embarrassed by the outcome. He ran screaming across the street and into his house, slamming the door behind him. I wheeled his bent bicycle to the front door and rang the bell, but when no one answered I left it there and walked home.

Today, however, the doorbell was answered by the housekeeper, who politely but firmly informed me that Curt was not available. "In trouble again," she sighed, advising me to try tomorrow. Curt's home was bordered on both sides by undeveloped housing sites, but the one on the right was much more interesting, with big trees and bushes. So, having time on my hands and no particular itinerary, I elected to do some reconnaissance, and maybe climb a tree or two.

I was considered a good tree climber, at least by neighborhood standards. This meant that I was able to get pretty high, and also find my way back down without assistance. Of course, the real secret to tree climbing was in the selection process - many a talented arborialist had met with failure simply through making bad pre-climb decisions. I prided myself on my ability to do a good, solid check before committing, looking for thorns, rough bark, nasty bugs, and of course the dreaded panthers, or any other thing that might add unnecessary difficulty or danger to the ascent. There were several likely prospects, but some childish intuition led to me to choose the tallest, so I jumped up to grab the first branch with a familiar sense of exhilaration and adventure.

Everything went smoothly as I moved swiftly but carefully upward. As the branches began to get smaller I slowed down a bit, testing some before trusting them with my full weight. I was fairly high now, and I could scan the entire lot and the street beyond through the leaves. Looking for the best route to continue, I noticed something unusual – it looked like an arrow imbedded in the wood several feet above my head. An arrow!

Under normal circumstances, I would have considered heading back down. I could see that it was going to be difficult to continue my ascent. However, if there really was an arrow up there, I would never forgive myself for missing it. I took a couple of deep breaths and pressed on. My palms were moist and I almost slipped a couple of times, but each time I waited until the pounding in my chest subsided and resolved to be even more careful. Finally after what seemed like a very long climb, I reached my goal. I stretched my arm up and my eager hand wrapped itself around a real arrow! Wow!

For a suburban six-year-old raised on TV westerns, this was a thrilling discovery. Every kid in the neighborhood had a couple of toy guns, a Mattel Fanner Fifty or a Rifleman rifle, and many of us also owned a toy Indian bow and arrow set with those stupid suction cups on the arrows. But this was no toy. It was a genuine weapon, and I wasn't about to go home without it. So I gently, lovingly, set about to remove it from the tree.

It was tedious, difficult work. I needed all of the strength and balance my legs could muster just to keep from falling, while manipulating the shaft as it very gradually began to loosen. My thighs were aching, and my arms and shoulders were burning by the time I got it out. But it was worth it. The arrow had a mean looking pointed steel tip glistening with fresh sap, which I wiped on my shirt. It was white with red and blue bands and blue feathers. And it was long – much longer than my toy arrows. The words kept echoing in my head, "It's real . . . it's real!"

I now faced a serious dilemma – getting both myself and my precious arrow out of the tree. The complexity of the problem was staggering. My initial visions of a heroic descent with the arrow clenched between my teeth were immediately compromised. It was almost as long as I was tall, and every time I turned my head it slammed into a branch, rattling my jaw and whipping leaves into my eyes. I really needed both hands to climb down, plus an additional hand to hold the arrow. I knew enough to realize that I had to be careful, having seen plenty of "accidental" deaths in movies and TV shows. What would Maverick do, or Cheyenne, Bronco, Sugarfoot, Josh Randall,

Paladin, any of the Western stars that I watched every week? Finally it came to me – just drop the arrow and get on with it. Not as dramatic as I might have liked, but then again, no one was watching.

I dropped down from the last branch, picked up my arrow which had stuck point first into the ground, and cautiously headed for home. There was always the danger of being spotted by Big Boys or grownups, and having my prize confiscated, but my luck was holding, and I made it around the block and up the driveway, through the side door and into my room without incident. Closing the door as quietly as possible, I rummaged through my closet, among my toy guns and Tonka trucks, until I found the bow from my Authentic Indian Bow and Arrow Set. Fitting the arrow to the bow and testing the tension was intoxicating! I knew it would work; now I just needed a place to test it. With a stunning bit of insight, I recalled all the balls, darts, and other objects that my friends and I had lost in the ivy, tall grass, and bushes throughout the neighborhood. It was obvious that the best course of action was to conduct my test indoors, where the chances of losing my arrow were slim indeed.

Feeling confident that I had made an extraordinarily intelligent decision, I began to consider where and when the grand event should take place. It wasn't merely a question of selecting a room, because despite my confidence, I realized that neither of my parents would share my enthusiasm for such an experiment. I had means and motive, but I needed opportunity. My dad's car was gone, although there was no telling when he might return. My mom was taking a nap in the master bedroom at the far end of the house. It wasn't an ideal situation, but it would have to do. I grabbed the bow and arrow and stalked into the kitchen. Our kitchen was long and narrow, and initially appeared to be an excellent testing site. But I was struck by another possibility. I could launch my arrow from the kitchen, through the window of the wet bar, and out across our spacious living room. Perfect! Of course, I wasn't tall enough to see over the bar and into the living room, so I double checked to see that my mom had not emerged, and that the cat was not in danger.

Everything looked good, the house was quiet, all systems go, so I positioned myself for the shot, notched up my arrow, and really pulled on the Authentic Indian Bow string. It felt good, solid, tight – in fact, everything felt right. The earth ceased to rotate and the sun froze in the sky. The mighty elements of the universe dropped everything in order to concentrate on creating this incredible, fantastic moment just for . . . ME! I let go and the arrow flew.

Man, it really flew – higher and faster, much higher and faster, than I had anticipated; it shot out over the bar and disappeared from my view. There was a strangely loud thump as it struck something and my exuberance immediately transformed itself into dread. I ran out of the kitchen and into the family room, hoping that whatever had happened, I would be able to salvage the situation before my parents noticed anything amiss.

Nothing appeared to be broken. Both lamps were still standing. The chairs and sofa were unwounded. Hmmm . . . not too bad so far. Then I saw it. Above the sofa were three large paintings. My mom had done them as an art student and she referred to them as abstracts, which meant that they weren't really pictures of anything in particular. My beloved arrow was protruding from the northwestern quadrant of the middle painting. Many thoughts raced through my mind at that moment; realization that my test protocol was idiotic despite the impressive results, assessment of the damage as minimal, and most importantly, the strong possibility that I might retrieve my arrow and leave the crime scene without incident. After all, who would notice a tiny hole in that big, colorful painting?

I stood on the seat of the sofa but couldn't reach high enough, so I climbed up onto the back and slowly worked my way to a standing position while leaning against the wall. The cushioned surface beneath my feet felt spongy and precarious, but it was holding and I could now grab the arrow, which appeared to be firmly lodged in the wall behind the painting. Once again, as I had done in the tree, I began to work it out. This was tedious work of a different sort, for I had to stand on my tiptoes to grasp the shaft and my legs were getting tired. But I was making good progress. I could feel the arrow loosening, and it would only be a matter of seconds before . . .

"What are you doing?"

It was a tone of voice which clearly indicated that there was going to be Trouble. Even as I finally extracted the arrow from the painting and began to confront this new crisis, I felt hands around my waist. They quickly and aggressively lifted me off of the sofa back, and deposited me none too gently on terra firma. Mom!

"Answer me! What are you doing?"

I had nothing to say. It all seemed rather self-evident to me, and I wasn't about to make a formal confession. I watched her gaze alternate between the painting on the wall and the arrow in my hand. She began to inspect the painting more closely, and as she did so her eyes narrowed and her expression tightened. Kneeling on the seat of the sofa, she reached up and gently ran a finger over the canvas until she found the hole, then turned to face me.

"Give me that arrow," she commanded, as she wrenched it from my grasp. She studied it thoroughly, the expression on her face conveying anger and confusion. But instead of asking me the customary pointed questions about "what had gotten into me, etc," my mom was unusually quiet. The arrow continued to hold her attention for several long seconds – it seemed like an eternity. Then, with one swift and strangely graceful movement, she snapped it across her knee. With a resounding crack, my prize was instantly transformed into useless junk. Any feelings of guilt that I had harbored for damaging that big dumb painting immediately vaporized, and I was seized with a relentless seething fury of personal outrage, a fury so all consuming that it surged from my soul to my brain to my lips.

"You BASTARD!" I shrieked. I was beyond fear. This was horrible, a disaster, a time for black magic! I had now invoked the power of Gary's mighty word, and something big and terrifying was about to occur! But what?

"What did she do?" Gary was practically frothing at the mouth with excitement. "Called your mom a bastard, that is so cool, man." He was so agitated that he could barely stand still, let alone construct a coherent sentence. "What did she DO?"

I knew he wouldn't believe me so I hesitated. The story was incredible enough already and it had taken no small effort to convince Gary of my veracity. The fact that my parents had refused to let me out of the house for several days had finally persuaded him that I might be telling the truth, but . . .

"C'mon, man, what happened? What did she do?"

"She laughed."

"WHAT?"

"She laughed."

"That's crazy, man – why did she laugh?"

"I dunno." And I could see that Gary didn't know either. He was as confused as I was. The facts just didn't add up. I knew that grownups could be unpredictable, but this was unprecedented. The fundamental principles governing our childhood universe, principles as immutable as gravity and inertia, were being seriously challenged by my mom's behavior. What did it mean? It was frightening to consider the possibility that everything we believed might be wrong.

"Wow – what did your dad do?"

"He spanked me," I said.

"Yeah, I guess so. How bad was it? Did you cry?" he asked.

"No."

He paused for a moment, as if weighing all the information. I could see the wheels turning as he searched for a plausible theory. Then he smiled.

"Well, I think your mom is crazy. You know moms get crazy sometimes – my dad even says so!'

It was the only possible explanation, after all. Gary's logic was unassailable. Plus, it allowed our universe to reassemble itself with little discernable damage, aside from a couple of insignificant bruises.

"C'mon, let's go tell Butch," he said, as he started walking down the street. He turned around to see if I was following.

"C'mon," he called, "Hurry up! I want you to tell Butch about this."

"Wait up, I'm coming," I yelled, as I started jogging after him. He slowed down a bit so I could catch up, giving me a playful, but solid, punch on the arm.

"Butch is gonna love this," he smirked, "Maybe you should let me tell him. I can make it even better."

"OK," I replied. Why not? Gary could make it into an epic, and he would enjoy the rapt attention of Butch, his aloof and disdainful older brother. In fact, it would be better for me if he told it, so that I wouldn't run the risk of inadvertently adding certain details, because I hadn't told the whole story and I hadn't told the whole truth.

I had cried, a little bit, when my dad spanked me. However, no self-respecting six-year-old would admit to tears. It was that other bit of information so judiciously edited from my narrative that had me worried, for I had heard my parents talking that afternoon. My mom had looked at me and then turned to my dad, saying, "Let me tell you what your son did this morning." They left me standing in the corner and retired to the next room to confer in private. I couldn't make out what they were saying, but the low drone of two adult voices filtered through the wall. Then my dad started laughing, a full-throated booming that echoed through the house, and my mom joined in. Their conversation grew more animated and then gradually subsided. Finally they emerged. Instead of the stern expressions that I was accustomed to, I noticed flushed faces, watery eyes, and barely hidden smiles. My dad, regaining his composure, addressed me in an unusually reasonable manner.

"You know I have to spank you for this, don't you?"

Of course I did

That's right – my dad had laughed too. Did this mean that both my parents were crazy, or was the world just a little more complicated and unpredictable than I had thought? I suspected the latter, but only in a vague, inarticulate six-year-old way. I was also starting to wonder if Gary really did know everything. Maybe I should start thinking for myself a bit more. Maybe I should start looking for other sources of information.

I started spending more time with friends my own age, and Gary and I gradually drifted apart. The last time I saw him was on a rainy day at school. My classmates and I were standing outside the boy's bathroom talking about this movie, *Invaders from Mars*, which had been showing all week on a local TV station. Gary showed up with a couple of his friends, and pulled something out of his pocket. It was a ball-point pen with a picture of a woman in a bathing suit on it. He did something to the pen and her bathing suit disappeared, leaving her completely nude. He demonstrated it several times for us, laughing, and then entered the bathroom, leaving us, as usual, dazed and amazed. Later I learned from my parents that Gary's family had moved away. Now I was on my own.

# 3

# New Friends and Enemies

My neighborhood was full of kids. We generally interacted without many problems, and it was not uncommon to strike up an acquaintanceship with someone for a week, or even a day, without developing any lasting friendship. If I was digging a hole in a vacant lot, and someone wanted to join in, he could be my best friend for that day. If we were engaged in a hairy boy fight, and a couple of new kids showed up to help us out, we would be temporary allies. An adversary in a skirmish on Saturday could turn out to be a collaborator in mischief on Sunday. It was a community of children, sharing all of the shifting dynamics, good and bad, common to any community.

At the same time, I was also surrounded by adults. Almost all of them were in a position to exert some degree of authority over me, and because of this, I never felt that any of them could qualify as real friends. But there were a few who came close. One of these was a waitress at Hody's, a nearby restaurant which we visited often. This woman, whose name I can't recall, would have little toys and smiles for me when we arrived for dinner, and I enjoyed her attention. She may have genuinely liked me, or perhaps she was making up for the time when she had (accidently, I'm sure) served me some lime sherbet with chips of glass in it. There was also a man who sometimes walked with me to the bus stop in the morning. He was always dressed in a suit, carrying his lunch in a brown paper bag, and we had pleasant conversations about dinosaurs and spacemen. He seemed like a nice guy, and never said or did anything inappropriate, but I suppose he could have had ulterior motives. However, despite these pleasant relationships and a couple of others, the possibility of true friendship with a grownup seemed remote, and I much preferred the company of children anyway.

One morning I headed down the street and around the block. My destination was the Jungle, a favorite location for many of the children in my area. The Jungle consisted of two empty lots, side by side, which were so overgrown with trees and brush that the interiors were completely hidden. We could vanish into the Jungle, away from the prying eyes of adults and other kids. There were different geographical areas within - a large patch of weird prickly weeds that we referred to as "poison ivy," a couple of open grassy fields, and groupings of trees which were perfect for climbing. The two lots were divided by an old wooden fence with a couple of boards missing, leaving a space just big enough for someone my size to pass through. I knew the Jungle well, having spent many hours exploring it from end to end.

As I paused on the street, debating which side to enter, I noticed Denny Slater approaching me. The Slater house bordered the Jungle on the west side, and he was hurrying down his driveway and heading in my direction. Denny was a grade or two ahead of me in school, but we had spent a few afternoons together, and he seemed like a good guy. When he got close enough, he slowed down and looked around.

"Joel's coming!" he said, looking extremely nervous. That was enough for me – Joel was Denny's older brother, a known bully and genuine bad kid, certainly the baddest on our block.

"What should we do?" I asked. I was starting to feel panicky.

"RUN!" Shouted Denny, as Joel suddenly emerged out of nowhere.

I immediately took off for the Jungle with Denny close behind. We entered together, but the terrain was difficult for running, especially for someone like Denny, who was obviously less familiar with it than I was. So I took the lead position on hidden paths through the bushes and around the trees, skirting the "poison ivy" and heading for the fence. We could hear Joel yelling at us from behind, as well as the sounds of thrashing branches. Suddenly the fence was in front of me, and the space where the boards were missing was within reach. I scrambled through, then turned and waited for Denny. It was going to be a bit tight for him, but suddenly his arms and head appeared, and it looked like he was going to make it. I was confident that Joel was much too big to squeeze between the boards, and that we were home free, but just as Denny was almost through, he started yelling. As I watched, he was slowly being pulled back. He grasped desperately at bushes and branches, but to no avail. Joel had his feet and was relentlessly dragging him back to the other side.

I didn't stick around to watch. Thoroughly intimidated, I ran to the back of the lot, where a cyclone fence topped with barbed wire was the only barrier to freedom. I climbed the fence, carefully made my way over the wire, and jumped to the ground. I was on a path which paralleled the drainage ditch that ran like an alley behind the houses. Quickly scrambling down the path, my heart still pounding, I climbed another similar fence and dropped into another lot several houses away from the Jungle. I cautiously walked to the street. Looking west, I could see the Slater house, but no sign of Denny or Joel. I still didn't feel safe, but I reluctantly stepped into the street, took one last glance at the spot where the misadventure had begun, then raced around the corner and up the hill to my house. As I slowly recovered, I wondered what had happened to poor Denny. I was sophisticated enough to know that if Joel really beat him up, he would be in serious trouble with his parents. But I was unsophisticated enough to consider the possibility that Joel could have killed Denny and buried him in the Jungle where no one would ever find him. I was somewhat reassured when I saw Denny later that week, but I didn't feel safe around him, and soon found myself going out of my way to avoid him.

Even though I never had much actual contact with Joel, his presence in the neighborhood was enough to make me very cautious. I was angry at having to worry about him, and afraid of what he might do to me. He was the first person that I ever really hated. I wasn't thinking about him all the time, but if he was on the school bus, which wasn't often, I sat as far away as possible. As soon as we hit our bus stop, I got out fast, because sometimes he would throw rocks at me on the way home.

Whenever other kids in the neighborhood got into serious trouble, the shadow of Joel always seemed to loom over the event. One time the older brother of a friend of mine was caught shooting streetlights with a BB gun. I watched as his father discussed the situation with a policeman in front of their house. The brother was red-faced and tear-streaked, and I thought I heard Joel's name mentioned. Any of the children on the block who cultivated an acquaintanceship with Joel seemed to become tainted. Their hair got longer and their clothes and posture seemed to alter in a sinister way. Even my parents and other adults were aware of him. When he was old enough to drive, he acquired a Ford Falcon, and would race it loudly and recklessly through our otherwise quiet streets. My brother's friends once witnessed Joel and his associates under a car in the parking lot of Lyon's Drag Strip, stealing a drive shaft that they needed to repair his conked out Falcon.

Even the house that Joel lived in had an aura about it that was, if not threatening, at least eccentric. It was a large, white domicile, with a subtly eclectic architectural style, nestled in a slight cul-de-sac, and it seemed to be a magnet for unusual inhabitants. I recall being among a crowd of people who had congregated in front of the house to watch Joel's mother try to calm a donkey that she had purchased and tied to a post or something. It was an unprecedented event, and no one could figure out what the hell was going on. A few days later, the donkey was gone. A few years later, the mother ran for some local political position, and again, no one could figure out what the hell was going on. I would hear my parents talking about her at dinner, and they appeared to be alternately amused and baffled. I don't think she won the election. Once in a while someone would hear a loud explosion from the general vicinity of the house, and later, of course, Joel would come blasting out of their driveway in his Falcon, disturbing the general tranquility of Park Estates. After the family moved out, the house seemed to be vacant for some time before Captain Sticky moved in. He was some kind of "consumer advocate" complete with superhero costume and a custom built Stickymobile with guns that allegedly squirted peanut butter and jelly, and to my mind he seemed an appropriate and, thankfully, less malignant resident.

My brief digression on the subject of Joel ends on an ironic note. When I was nineteen I made my first and only attempt to buy some liquor illegally. My girlfriend and I walked into the neighborhood liquor store and picked out a bottle with as much nonchalance as we could project. We took it to the cashier, who actually knew me by name, and I attempted to make my purchase. He just laughed at me. But then a voice behind me said, "Oh hell, I'll buy it for him." I turned around, and saw Joel standing there. It was an interesting moment. I hadn't seen him, or even thought about him, for years, and even though he didn't scare me at all, his posture and general demeanor still spelled BAD BOY. My girlfriend and I walked out of the store with our bottle, and I was left to speculate – was he actually doing me a favor, or hoping that somehow that bottle would prove my undoing? Probably the latter.

My best friend on our block was Bruce. We spent a lot of time together during the second and third grades. His house was just around the corner from mine, and it was only a quick walk or bike ride down the hill and into his driveway. An empty lot bordered the west side of the house, and we spent many pleasant days there, digging fox holes and climbing trees. Bruce's house had a large back yard and a bomb shelter full of canned food and bottled water which was fascinating to me. I knew about radiation and bombs from movies like *Rocketship XM* and *Godzilla*, as well as the air raid "duck and cover" drills we endured at school. Bruce and I would sometimes have conversations about how much room there was in the shelter, and whether my family and I could squeeze in. We would also go for long walks to some of the distant regions of Park Estates, and explore other lots and construction sites. The construction sites were terrific places to play, even though we had been warned to stay away. They were deserted on the weekends, and the temptation to trespass was too tantalizing to ignore. During the week we would watch *Felix the Cat* cartoons or play ball after school.

Bruce was my age and he also attended Minnie Gant Elementary School, but we were never in the same class. He was a big, well behaved kid, and I don't recall getting into any real mischief with him. His parents, especially his mom, were very nice to me, and his dad once took the two of us to Catalina Island for Bruce's birthday. Bruce had two brothers, Mac, who was a few years younger, and Doug, who was a few years older. Doug was starting to get into trouble, and I attributed this to the influence of the Bad Kids in the neighborhood. Doug was the one who shot the streetlights out with a BB gun, among other things. But he was never mean to me as far as I can recall, even though he scared me with horrible stories of Nazi torture, and explained to me what "castration" meant in graphic detail. It was Doug who inadvertently destroyed my relationship with Bruce.

One afternoon, Bruce and I were bouncing a ball around in his driveway. I had ridden my bike over and parked against a fence that bordered the driveway. We noticed a big kid approaching on foot. I had never seen him before, but Bruce identified him as a friend of Doug's. We were naturally apprehensive because some of the big kids would harass us on principle, so we tried to ignore him and hoped that he would leave us alone. I felt that we were reasonably safe because we were on Bruce's property, and his parents were home, but with big kids there were no guarantees. He walked up the driveway and passed us with a disdainful look, heading for the entrance to the house. It appeared that we were not going to have any trouble, and I breathed a sigh of relief. But then he walked over to my bike. For a moment he was standing in front of the bike with his back to me. He appeared to bend over the seat of bike, as if looking for something, then turned to us and smiled. I didn't like the look of that smile, and trotted over to see if anything was amiss. It was! There was a big pool of syrupy saliva in the middle of the seat!

I was stunned by the discovery, and then I was furious! Even though there was a little voice in my head reminding me that this was a big kid, there was a much louder voice telling me that I wasn't going to stand for such an insult! "You son of a bitch, you bastard!" I was screaming at him. He grabbed a long pole that was used to dislodge the basketball when it got caught behind the backstop, and started poking me in the chest with it, gradually backing me into the garage door and laughing. He was clearly enjoying himself, but I was so angry and frustrated that tears were running down my cheeks, and I continued to call him every bad word that I could remember. Suddenly Bruce's mother came out of the house, and everything came to a dead stop. The kid, whose name turned out to be Hollis, told her a lame story about how I had suddenly attacked him for no reason, and I shouted that he had " hawked a loogie" on my bicycle seat. She inspected the seat, and then turned to us.

"That wasn't a very nice thing to do," she said to Hollis, "but there's no reason for you to get this upset," she said to me.

I started to disagree with her, "But he . . ."

"No, I think you better go home now, Billy," she said.

I felt tired and defeated. I had been sure that she would see that I was right to fight back. What the hell? Bruce stood by quietly as I got my bike and began to walk it to the street. I sure wasn't going to ride until the seat was restored to its normal condition. I was disappointed that he hadn't said a word on my behalf, but maybe he would defend me later. It was all very depressing.

A few days later, I called Bruce to see if he wanted to mess around, but he told me that he was busy doing chores. I called him several times after that and his response was always the same. It wasn't too hard to figure out that he was avoiding me. As I considered the situation, I realized that his parents must have told him to stay away from me, but I couldn't quite believe it. It was true that I had used some bad words, actually a lot of bad words, but I still knew that I had stood up against oppression just like Errol Flynn, and I was proud of that. Besides, what were those bad words for? If there was ever an appropriate occasion for profanity, that had been it. I had no remorse, felt no guilt - this was absolutely unfair. His parents were idiots and Bruce was a coward. We still could have gotten together if he really wanted to. I wrote them all off, and I never spoke to Bruce again. It was another lesson, a big one, and it taught me what real friendship might mean.

Minnie Gant Elementary School was probably typical for its place and time. When I attended, the student body, as well as the administration and faculty, was almost entirely white and middle class. The school was safe and well organized, and the teachers that I encountered were kind, patient and extremely good at leading classes of up to thirty-five energetic youngsters. Finding myself in a new environment with a bunch of kids that I didn't know was always an interesting experience for me. It was different from meeting new children who lived nearby because my parents frequently vetted them before introductions were made. It took a little time to sort out names, faces, and personalities, but I always found it exciting to begin the school year. Friendships could materialize quickly over a common interest.

"Do you like lizards?"

"Yeah!"

"I have three alligator lizards. Wanna come over and see 'em?"

"Yeah! Let me ask my mom."

As I entered the first grade, I started spending more time with kids who did not live in my immediate area. I was now wandering beyond our block, gradually extending the boundaries of my empire to the outermost limits of our entire tract, which was known as Park Estates. The school was about a mile from my home, and the bus picked up all the children from Park Estates at several different stops along Anaheim Street, so I had a sense of the size and general population of my domain.

But most of my fellow students were living in the homes which surrounded the school, in an area known as Los Altos. Initially this was all new to me, but I soon started developing friendships with some of the Los Altos kids. We would usually go to their homes after school, and my mom would pick me up at around five thirty, giving us a couple of hours to "mess around." Being in a new environment without much adult supervision was an invitation to adventure that I couldn't resist.

I met Mike in the second semester of first grade, and he was the first of the Los Altos kids that I befriended. For some reason, I had been shifted from Miss Powder's class in a bungalow to Miss Sieta's class in a regular classroom. The big difference was that the new class consisted of first and second graders together. As I consider it now, this was probably a challenging situation for Miss Sieta, a calm, self assured, Japanese woman, but for me it was simply a new social experience. The older kids were initially intimidating, and there was some bullying. In particular, there was a hapless individual named Carl who was the primary target of some of the bigger boys. Carl seemed custom designed for bullying. He was frail and withdrawn, and his personality, or lack of personality, seemed to invite harassment. The most egregious event that I witnessed was when the older boys took his pants and threw them over the playground fence, where they hung out of Carl's reach. The sight of this poor kid in his underwear struggling to climb up and retrieve them was hilarious and horrible at the same time. This incident, and other similar episodes, seemed to cause the first graders to bond with each other, perhaps out of a sense of self preservation, and at some point Mike and I struck up what would become a lasting friendship.

Most of the friendships I had at that time were based on common interests, and frequently did not extend far beyond those interests. With Greg it was science fiction stories, with

Jerry it was Civil War trading cards and later, monster magazines and Edgar Rice Burroughs, with Bill Neuhauser it was a board game called Stratego, a ball game called Bombardier, and lighting fires (more about that later.) But with Mike it was different. We had common interests of course, but more than that, we seemed to share a common attitude. As I look back on the things we did, it appears that the cornerstone of that attitude may have been an obsession with sabotage. And that obsession was specifically directed toward the authority of adults. We took the keenest pleasure in causing trouble in such a way as to avoid confrontation and apprehension - "getting away with it" was at least half the fun.

I can't recall exactly what we did the first few times that we got together, but it seems that we spent more time at his house than mine. It was a post-war tract house with three little bedrooms and one bathroom, surprisingly small compared to what I was accustomed to in Park Estates, but I really felt comfortable there. Mike's mom was my favorite of all of my friends' parents. She was always warm and encouraging, and she always made me feel welcome. She was one of the few working mothers that I knew, and must have been tired much of the time, between her job, keeping the house in order, and dealing with three kids, but I never saw any evidence of pessimism or disharmony in her personality. Mike's dad was an altogether different experience. He looked like one of the gunfighters on the TV westerns that I watched, and he was always engaged in some kind of domestic chore or repair job. His general demeanor suggested that he was resigned to an endless list of such chores, and would brook no interference. As I got to know him, I learned that he was actually a very kind and compassionate man, but initially I found him to be quite intimidating.

One of the great things about Mike's house was its proximity to the Los Altos Mall. All we had to do was exit the backyard gate and walk across the alley and the parking lot, and we were able to check out the latest toys at Brownies Toy Store and buy candy at Sav-on where they gave us three five cent items for a dime. We could drink as many soft drinks as our budgets would allow (RC cola was the best deal at sixteen ounces for fifteen cents) and then go over to Thriftymart, and get rubber lizards and insects, called Scare-ems, which came in little clear plastic capsules from a gumball machine for ten cents. The mall, which Mike's family referred to as "the Stores," was a great place to hang out on a Saturday afternoon

We also began to develop an arsenal of mischief. We started with simple things like smashing rolls of caps with a hammer, which created a satisfyingly loud explosion. We then initiated a spider extermination program at Mike's house. We were always finding large garden spiders in his front and back yard bushes, and they were creepy. Besides, we had seen movies with horrible giant spiders like *Missile to the Moon*, *World Without End*, and, of course, *The Spider*, so it didn't take much to convince ourselves that we were doing the world a favor by getting rid of them. We found a bug spray and a white powder repellant in Mike's kitchen closet, and started systematically assassinating the spiders. First we would apply a liberal coat of the spray, and then an even more liberal coat of the powder. The end result was a large white blob bearing a vague resemblance to the original arachnid, which we referred to as a "White Mama."

Soon we graduated to roasting bugs with magnifying glasses. We first tried it with a large glass which belonged to Mike's dad, and the results were spectacular. We found that different bugs cooked in different ways, each with its own distinct but similar odor. Then we got the bright idea of melting plastic soldiers. We figured that we could make the soldiers look authentically wounded by melting off arms and legs. Since we were both interested in blood and mayhem, particularly in the Italian muscleman flicks like *Son of Samson* and *The Slave*, it was perfectly logical to try to achieve an even higher level of authenticity by melting bits of red crayon to the severed limbs. The results were quite satisfying to us, but not so much for our parents, who clearly felt that our creative talents could be put to better use. The culmination of our activities was Mike's "Man of Many Arms and Legs," which was a soldier to which he welded all of the orphaned limbs from our previous efforts. It was a masterpiece!

Mike and I never got into lighting fires with the glasses. That activity was shared with another kid from my neighborhood, Bill Neuhauser. Bill and I would burn some dry grass in the lot next to his house, and then, once we had a good little blaze going, dump a pile of long fresh green grass on top. The result was a large amount of steamy white smoke, which would have been perfect for smoke signals if there had been anyone to signal. I am still amazed that nobody in any of the houses that surrounded the lot noticed what we were doing, and doubly amazed that we never started a serious fire. It seems a bit surprising that Mike and I refrained from this activity, based on our later infatuation with pyrotechnics, but it may be that merely lighting up the tinder in a vacant lot was too obvious. We needed a more subtle and elegant form of self expression.

One day after school, we walked to Mike's house. It was a sunny afternoon, so after a brief "tour "of the house, we verified that no grownups were around and went out to the back yard. The three storey Broadway store was directly across the lot from Mike's yard. For some reason, we decided to climb up onto the wooden structure that housed the family trash cans. Standing on the structure we could see over the fence and across the lot. The Broadway had an outdoor deck on the second storey, and something interesting was going on there. It was far away, and hard to see, but we felt like army guys spying on the enemy, which was totally cool, and finally determined that a magician was performing for a large group of women seated on the deck. Watching the show was mildly interesting, but the possibility of interfering with it was intoxicating. I don't know how we arrived at that intention, but it was immediately understood by both of us. Could we mess up this show, and of course, not get caught?

We determined that the only way to intervene would be to use a trick we had seen on TV. Mike went back into the house and got his mother's hand mirror from the bathroom. Fortunately for us, it was late afternoon and we were facing west. I held the mirror up, caught the sunlight and tried to direct the reflection into the magician's eyes. It was difficult to tell how effective our strategy was, although the magician seemed to falter a bit. We needed a higher level of accuracy. Mike went back into the house and came back with his dad's binoculars. Now he could direct my efforts with greater precision.

"A little higher!"

"Left, go left!"

"Just a little higher!"

"Yeah, cool, that's it!"

Again, the magician seemed to be losing his poise. Of course we were too far away to hear anything, but our imaginations supplied the dialog. We could see the white spot of the mirror's reflection on the guy's face, consistently around the eyes, and, within a few seconds the performance was over. I think that we were hoping for a more dramatic conclusion, with people yelling and milling about, but nothing like that happened. The magician started packing up his things, and the ladies slowly left the deck. We were a little disappointed that we hadn't wreaked more obvious havoc, but after talking it over, we were pretty certain that our little trick had stopped the show, certain enough to be delighted with ourselves, alternately laughing and recounting the details of our exploit to each other. It was like the movies when the army men fired mortar rounds - hard to be sure if the target had been hit, but satisfying to know that we had at least harassed the enemy and caused some damage. We were concerned that somehow "the enemy" would figure out what had happened and march across the parking lot to catch us, so we retreated into the house feeling triumphant, sharing the camaraderie of soldiers who have won a decisive battle together. It was my first real incursion against the adult world, and it felt great. Mike and I would be co-conspirators for many years to come.

# 4

# Nature and Nurture

Suburban life in the Fifties and early Sixties was characterized by conformity. Men went to work in the morning and came home at dinnertime. Wives stayed home and did the cleaning and shopping. Kids joined the Cub Scouts and Indian Guides. And everyone went to church. My situation, however, was a bit different. My father was a college professor and was frequently at home during the week, either reading or snoozing on the couch. My mom did prepare breakfasts and dinners, but we often went out to restaurants. We also had a housekeeper, Mrs. Marshall, who came in three times a week to do the cleaning. I never joined the Cub Scouts or Indian Guides, because my father was a self-avowed iconoclast, and wasn't interested in "organizations." We didn't attend church because my father was an atheist, and was strongly opposed to religion in any form.

None of this was problematic for me. I occasionally hung out with my Cub Scout buddies and participated in their activities, even though I didn't have a uniform. I even attended Sunday school a couple of times with friends, but didn't find it very interesting. I didn't feel handicapped by the lack of these experiences, but every once in a while something would come up. I recall learning to sing "Silent Night" at Christmas in Kindergarten. The lyrics "Holy infant so tender and mild" conjured up an image of a dinner table with some kind of tasty but mysterious meal, as I had only heard the terms "tender and mild" applied to food in TV commercials. So I sometimes asked questions that may have seemed strange to my friends and teachers, but no one seemed to mind.

My dad would take me along with him when he wanted to see or do something that my mom wasn't interested in. We went to hydroplane races at the Marine stadium, jalopy races at the local track, bookstores, and movies. These were all things that I enjoyed, but sometimes being with him wasn't much fun. He would take me to Long Beach State College where he was employed as a professor in the Education Department. We would run into his colleagues, and there would be interminable conversations about things that I couldn't comprehend. When I got bored and fidgety, I would be told not to interrupt, and to be patient. Instead of calming down, I would get a peculiar feeling of urgency to escape that was hard to ignore. Eventually, I began to dread these trips, and would decline his invitations to accompany him. He never insisted, so it wasn't a big issue, but I decided to try to avoid similar situations. It seemed to me that when the grownups outnumbered the kids, things could get pretty dull.

My dad would also tell me stories of his army days, or his childhood, or sometimes even make up tales about an alligator named Harvey. Most of his stories involved situations where he had to stand his ground against authority or a bully, and it was impressed upon me that courage and defiance were important qualities in a man. This lesson was consistently reinforced by comic books, movies, and TV shows, and I subscribed to it wholeheartedly. TV was relatively new, and although the major networks offered many original programs like *Gunsmoke* and *The Untouchables*, most local stations ran old movies. I was immediately taken by *Captain Blood* and

*The Adventures of Robin Hood* with Errol Flynn, *The Mark of Zorro* with Tyrone Power, and *The Last Command* with Sterling Hayden as Jim Bowie at the Alamo. The cultural standard was abundantly clear. Courage and defiance – absolutely!

I was also very excited about dinosaurs. I think my fascination began with *King Kong*, which was frequently shown on Channel 9. I was mesmerized by the beautiful stop-motion animation that brought Kong and the dinosaurs of Skull Island to life, and tried to catch the film every time it was shown. Another movie, *Lost Continent*, featuring stop-motion dinosaurs, was often broadcast on Channel 5, and although not quite up to the magnificent technical standards of *Kong*, it was still a favorite. I started getting dinosaur books from the school library, and my parents, noticing my interest, began buying me more books and toy dinosaurs. Soon I was knowledgeable enough to realize that the big lizards used as dinosaur stand-ins in the original *One Million BC* and *King Dinosaur* were totally fake. My dad encouraged me, partly because he liked my enthusiasm, but also, I suspect, because he liked having a kid with a huge vocabulary of complicated dinosaur names. He would prompt me to name my favorite dinosaur and I would weigh the relative merits of a long list of herbivores and carnivores for any adult unfortunate enough to be in our presence. When I told him that I wanted to be a paleontologist, he suggested that I be a paleozoologist instead. That way I could focus exclusively on dinosaurs and ignore the boring prehistoric plants and insects. I promptly adopted the term, and would solemnly correct anyone who commented on my destiny as a paleontologist. I became so pretentious on the subject that, with the help of my parents, I even sent a letter to DC Comics about the numerous inaccuracies in their depictions of dinosaurs in *Star-Spangled War Stories*. I expected a grateful reply and a promise to be more careful in the future, but all I received was a generic "thank you" card. They were probably fielding similar missives from hundreds of kids all over the country.

My excitement about dinosaurs naturally led to an interest in reptiles. My earliest exposure to the indigenous lizard population took place when a friend and I were meandering along the dirt path that paralleled the drainage ditch which formed the northern border of Park Estates. We noticed some older kids in the ditch who appeared to be searching for something in the bushes and puddles. I yelled down to them to ask what they were doing and they yelled back that they were hunting for frogs.

"Did you find any?"

"Heck yeah!" One of the boys held up a large burlap sack that seemed to be squirming a bit.

"Can I have one?" It didn't hurt to ask.

"No, we're keeping the frogs." He paused for a moment. " Ya wanna alligator lizard?"

Wow – that would be even better! "Yes!" He glanced up at me and reached carefully into the sack, then pulled out the lizard and casually tossed it in my direction. I was alarmed at his handling of the transaction, but the lizard landed right in front of me, and I grabbed him before he could recover from what must have been a traumatic experience. He was about ten inches long and snakey looking, with short legs and cool brown and black markings. Unfortunately, I wasn't very skilled as a lizard wrangler, and he managed to get a good grip on one of my fingers with surprisingly strong jaws. I yelled, flailing my hand around until he let go and was launched into the weeds and freedom. Although I was disappointed, I had learned that the lizards were out there, and I knew that I would be more careful in the future.

In fact, alligator lizards were quite common, and now that I knew what to look for, I found them fairly often. Sometimes

I would catch them and put them in jars, and later my dad got a small terrarium for them which I kept on the porch in the side yard. They came in a variety of colors, predominantly brown, black, or yellow with speckled backs. Sometimes our cat, Rover, would catch them, and, if I didn't manage to intervene, it was usually curtains for the lizard. Several of my friends and I found one of Rover's victims in the grass one afternoon. We were trying to figure out what to do with the corpse, because it seemed like a great opportunity for expanding our horizons. Finally we decided that the most interesting option would be to put it through my mom's meat grinder. I went into the kitchen and came back with the grinder, a simple instrument with a hand crank and a funnel-like element for inserting whatever required grinding. Now that the moment was at hand, no one seemed particularly enthusiastic about completing the task, but finally we selected a volunteer. The lizard was stiff and dry, so although we had visions of reptilian hamburger, the actual result was simply a flatter, yet lumpier version of the original. Our collective curiosity having been satisfied, I replaced the grinder in a kitchen drawer. I don't remember if I washed it or not.

It turned out that my dad also had an affinity for reptiles, particularly snakes, and an unholy alliance was born. He went down to King's Pet Shop and purchased a four foot long gopher snake and a terrarium. My mother was not happy when he got home with these items, and after some protracted, and heated, negotiations, finally allowed us to keep the snake on the workbench in the garage. She was even less happy with the weekly ritual of feeding the snake, now known as Fast Jackson, a live mouse. As I mentioned previously, the snake and the mice created a big stir among the neighborhood kids. I was already fairly popular, but this gave me a bit of local celebrity. I was sometimes asked to bring Jackson over to friends' houses, but this didn't sit too well with their mothers. There seemed to be something about the sight of a six year old kid wrapped in snake that could chill the heart of any mom. They were afraid, and rightly so it turned out, because on one of my jaunts I had just started walking down the driveway with Jackson when he bit me on the lip. My screaming brought dad out of the house, and he quickly took control of the situation. There was a little blood, a trip to the doctor, a shot of some kind, and a slightly swollen lip. My dad told me that he was proud of me for not letting go of Jackson, who was now safely back in his terrarium, and I felt like a glorious wounded hero.

At this point, my mom was even less enthusiastic about Jackson, so I was very surprised when my dad bought another snake. We had gone to King's to get Jackson his weekly mouse, and as we walked up to the door, we met a woman with a huge black snake wrapped around her neck and upper body. My dad started talking to her and found out that she was a professional snake-charmer in a carnival, and was planning to sell this one to the pet store if she could. It was an extremely docile, nine foot long indigo snake with no teeth, and we stroked it and scratched its head while a deal was struck. My dad gave her twenty bucks, and "Blacky" was ours.

When we arrived home, my dad parked in the garage, and asked me to stay in the car for a minute. He soon returned and proceeded to carefully drape Blacky around my neck and upper body. There was so much of him that I had to hold him with both hands, and his tail almost hit the ground. I was then directed to exit the garage through the door that led to the pool deck. I followed these instructions as my dad opened the door for me, and was surprised to see my mom, who had apparently decided to take a swim, standing waist deep in the shallow end of the pool. She turned to look at me with the sound of the opening door, and immediately let out a horrified shriek and submerged herself with a splash. As my dad came out of the garage laughing, she resurfaced and demanded that he "remove that snake" from her son. I was an extremely interested witness to my mom's anger and my dad's amusement as he explained that the snake was harmless. She didn't see the humor in the situation, and it took some time for things to return to normal. Meanwhile, Blacky was deposited in the terrarium with Jackson. A few days later, when I went out to the garage to visit the snakes, Jackson was gone and Blacky did not have a lean and hungry look. Later, after we had moved Blacky to a larger wooden box in the back yard, he escaped through a small hole in the screened top. Mothers in the neighborhood were extremely concerned, and kids around the block were reporting Blacky sightings for weeks, frequently making up goofy stories about seeing him with another, bigger, white snake. He was never apprehended, much to my dismay, but I had learned something extremely important.

It had been obvious to me for some time that most women did not like snakes, but after seeing my mom's reaction to Blacky, I realized that it was not mere dislike. I had also noted my dad's behavior. My conclusion was that reptiles could be a useful weapon in the ongoing battle between boys and girls. Both of my snakes were gone, but I still had several lizards in a small terrarium on the side yard porch. These were little brown swifts with detachable tails, and they were accustomed to being picked up and carried around. I wasn't sure if a small lizard would have the same impact as a large snake, but I knew that my mom wasn't fond of the lizards either, so it seemed worthwhile to investigate.

I had a test subject in mind, a girl who was particularly obnoxious – my next door neighbor, Mary. There was a low concrete wall which separated our parallel driveways, and we frequently engaged each other in a debate as to whose property it was. Property lines were significant to us because there were unwritten rules about them that could be important in a crisis.

For example, Gary's brother, Butch, had found out that my dad had shared a simple secret code with us, and he wanted it. The whole situation was idiotic because we had no top secret info to disguise, and I barely knew how to write anyway, but it didn't matter - Butch wanted that code! I noticed him furiously pedaling his bike toward me one morning as I was walking up the hill to my house, so I ran as fast as I could and just beat him to my driveway. As I was now standing on MY PROPERTY, he could not cross the line, beat me up, and steal the code, while I could spit at him and call him names. These protocols were accepted throughout the neighborhood, so it was crucial to establish clear boundaries, hence the importance of the debate with Mary. I felt that I had the winning argument because the wall had been built with the rest of our house before Mary's family arrived. Their house had been built after ours, so the conclusion seemed obvious, but she was a year older and felt that her seniority leant her some authority. So, the next time I saw her playing in her driveway, I went to the side yard and grabbed my best lizard. Keeping him hidden behind my back, I put one foot on the wall and allowed her to start the debate, which, admittedly, was not very sophisticated.

"It's our property!"

"No, it's ours!"

"Is not!"

"Is so!"

I allowed this to last for a couple of rounds to get her warmed up, and then quickly swung a handful of lizard from behind my back to a point a few scant inches from her stupid freckly face. The results were spectacular! She turned red, gulped for air, and without saying a word, turned and ran. I was ecstatic! Not only had I proven the merit of my theory, but I had won the argument, even if it was by default. From that point on, Mary went out of her way to avoid me, and I felt confident in my newfound ability to handle troublesome women. I was hesitant to tell my dad about it, and apprehensive about the possibility that Mary's dad might come over to complain. But when nothing happened, I told him the story and he got a big kick out of it. It made me feel smart and grown up – I was learning how to solve problems.

Because I had learned about women and reptiles from my dad, I kept an eye out for other important life lessons that he might offer. Although he was not the kind of guy who would take his son outside to play catch, he did sometimes engage me to participate in mischief. When he bought one of the new Polaroid cameras, he would often take "mugshots" of me with a penciled in moustache, a dangling cigarette, and a pair of his dark glasses. He also liked to dress me up as devil for Halloween, in a red leotard complete with horns, pitchfork, and tail. He definitely had a subversive sense of humor.

When I was six or seven, we had a problem with our next door neighbor. Mary and I were silently avoiding each other, and there were evidently some hard feelings toward our family. This was demonstrated by the frequent deposits of dog crap left on our lawn by their poodle. The incidents always occurred at night. My dad would go out in the morning to get the paper, and would come back in a rage, muttering and cursing, and vowing revenge. I believe that he stayed up for a few nights on stakeout, and actually saw Mary's older brother, Lamont, allow the dog to trespass and evacuate, because he was absolutely certain that they were the culprits. The fact that the dog was a large caramel colored poodle named Garcon merely doubled his fury. He grumbled about the situation for several days and then devised a plan.

I walked into the kitchen one day to find him at the stove stirring a large steaming pot. I had rarely seen him cooking before, so naturally I was curious. He lifted me up so I could see into the pot, but instead of soup or stew, it was full of a bright green liquid. I could tell that he was really excited about whatever he was doing, because he began to explain it to me in very precise detail. Earlier that day, he had gone out and bought a bunch of rat traps. These looked like mousetraps on steroids, and presumably were much more dangerous. Then he got some green food coloring and some breakfast steaks. He was now in the process of dying the rat traps green, and was then going to bait them with the cooked breakfast steaks and set them out on our front lawn shortly after dark. I thought it was a terrific idea. My mom, when she learned about it, was less receptive.

"I really think you should just talk to them again," she said.

"I've already done that, and Lamont swears he's not letting the dog out."

"Well, I just don't think it's a good idea –we don't need more trouble with them."

They went back and forth for a few more minutes, but my dad was determined to proceed, and despite my mom's reservations, he seemed to be in a very good mood. That mood carried him through the afternoon and dinner. As dusk approached, even I could tell that he couldn't wait to get out there and set his traps. As soon it was full dark, he went out, deliberately leaving the porch light off, and very carefully placed them, at strategically calibrated intervals, all around our lawn. It reminded me of the war movies I'd seen on TV when the soldiers dealt with mine fields, and I had a brief moment of compassion for Garcon – very brief. Then the anticipation of actually seeing that idiot dog get his nose snapped got the best of me, and I could barely contain my excitement.

Unfortunately for me, I had to go to bed before anything

happened. And evidently, nothing did happen that night. My dad was very disappointed. He stayed on watch for the next two evenings with no luck, but finally on the fourth night his vigilance was rewarded. Of course I didn't get to see the event, but it was gleefully recounted the next morning. Lamont had let Garcon out at around 10:30, and the dog had confidently ambled onto our lawn. He noticed the traps right away, but was tentative, cautiously sniffing several before taking the bait. My dad said there was a loud snap and a louder yelp as Garcon raced back to a very surprised Lamont, and both retreated into the house. My dad was too cagey to go out immediately, and waited until morning to investigate. The snapped trap was still there, so at least Garcon was not looking forward to rhinoplasty. I think my dad was slightly disappointed. He felt that he had Lamont in a classic Catch 22 situation, and was just waiting to be confronted. However, there were no repercussions, and the depredations ceased. Both Lamont and Garcon made themselves scarce, but my dad continued to set those traps for quite a while. I was extremely impressed by the entire affair, and hoped that I could be as resourceful in dealing with my problems.

My mom had a good sense of humor, but she declined to participate in things like the rat trap caper. I had the impression that she sometimes regarded my dad as big kid who was out of control. She was not an active participant in many of my activities, but was willing to lend me a scarf if I wanted to be a pirate, or to make me a cape out of a towel and safety pin if I was going to be Superman, and she would let me make forts out of the furniture as long as I was careful. She was also fairly tolerant of some of my carelessness. We had white wall-to-wall carpeting which was a magnet for grime and mud, and my friends and I would sometimes forget to take our dirty shoes off before entering the house. Other bad habits included leaving toys underfoot, and wiping my mouth on my shirt sleeve after drinking grape juice.

She could be clever at utilizing my natural proclivities to her advantage. My friends and I would sometimes discover an interesting bug and capture it in a jar. We would usually leave the jars in the kitchen. My mom was as fond of bugs as she was of reptiles, so discovering these jars in her domain was not a pleasant experience for her. But when our front lawn became infested with cut worms, she had a brilliant idea. She hired me and a couple of my buddies, gave each of us an empty Yuban coffee jar, and sent us out to collect them at one penny per worm. We were thrilled at the high rate of pay, and collected so many worms that she ended up giving each of us a dollar. We did this for several weekends until my mom determined that the crisis was at an end, and we buried ourselves in candy and comic books from our profits.

Although she did not share activities with me very often, my mom was the one who sometimes made unilateral decisions about what those activities might be. She enrolled me in play school and nursery school, and once, when I was very young, determined that I should play softball on a team. I didn't want to play because I didn't know anything about the skills required or the rules, but she insisted that it would be fun. It wasn't. I felt embarrassed and humiliated at my lack of ability, and refused to go back. I was also angry with her for putting me in such an untenable position. When she decided that I should go to a local day camp in the summer between the first and second grades, I was not happy. I wanted to stay home and play with my friends. My first few days at camp were spent sulking, but soon I was having a great time with a bunch of great kids, so I had to admit that sometimes she got it right. My mom also tossed me into art classes at the local recreation center, and several other similar programs. Some of these experiences were fun, some just OK, and some, like the softball debacle, were horrible, but my real complaint was that I was never consulted on any of her decisions even though they sometimes worked out well. It seemed unfair.

My mom had studied art in college and was inclined to be tasteful and reserved, although she did have an interest in stories about crime and murder, and frequently bought movie magazines to look at the pictures and read about the scandals. Any story that involved crime, murder, and movie stars would get her attention immediately. Our house had many built-in bookshelves, and they were full. My dad was a voracious and indiscriminate reader, but my mom was more selective. She often bought large, colorful books on art and esoterica, and at some point I started looking at them. The Jansen *Picture History of Painting* was particularly fascinating because it had a lot of nudity and violence. This was evidently OK because the paintings were all by geniuses who were allowed to do anything they wanted to. Also many of the images were religious which made it double OK. My mom was pleased and impressed with my interest in art, but I don't think she understood what I was really looking for when I perused that book. There were also many magazines in the house. Naturally, my mom's fashion and movie magazines didn't hold much appeal for me. I didn't find *Scientific American* or *Popular Mechanics* very stimulating either. But I did manage to sneak a look at *Playboy* once in a while, and I found that very stimulating.

My little brother, Gordon, had been keeping my parents, especially my mom, occupied as he gradually metamorphosed from an infant to a toddler. I found myself alternately fascinated and repulsed with his presence, but I was largely indifferent to him until he was mobile enough to follow me around. Sometimes I found this extremely annoying, and then the trouble would start. My dad hated it when Gordon and I did not get along. His reprimands, usually directed to me, were always to stop "squabbling" or "bickering," and I soon came to despise those words. I think that it was really just the noise that bothered him, the shrill raised voices and the crying, because he never tried to act as an arbitrator or to determine the source of our conflicts. Gordon and I would get into another silly disagreement, I would push him out of the way or yell at him, and he would cry. My dad would intervene, and I would sometimes get a spanking. I understood that I was usually at fault for being impatient with my brother, and that I deserved the punishment because I was older and supposedly more responsible, but Gordon sometimes drove me crazy. In the wake of one such incident, I had resolved to be more tolerant, and the two of us were horsing around in the back bedroom. He tripped and fell on the hard linoleum floor, and started howling. I had done nothing, and was in no way responsible for his accident, but my dad came running in and immediate blamed me, yelling and swatting my backside. I tried to explain, but he wouldn't listen, and Gordon was not yet articulate enough to say anything in my defense. I was simply assumed to be guilty. There had been occasions in the past when I had not fully understood parental justice, but this was the first time that I knew that my dad was being absolutely unfair. I was shocked and confused, but above all, I was angry. This was injustice, abuse of power, tyranny, exactly the kind of oppression that Robin Hood, Captain Blood, and even Tom Sawyer, fought against so valiantly. Vague thoughts of rebellion and heroism were swirling around in my head. My perception of parental authority had been irrevocably altered. The seeds of defiance had been sown.

# 5

## He Ain't Heavy...

Having a younger brother was a mixed blessing. Because there was a four and a half year age gap between us, he always seemed like a little kid to me, and little kids are often annoying to slightly bigger kids. It's not that Gordon was a particularly obnoxious individual. In fact, he was actually a sweet and well behaved child, but he seemed to be unduly interested in hanging around and getting underfoot when I had things to do. I have distinct memories of getting into stupid altercations with him as we grew up together. Once he was annoying me by repeating some insulting nonsense over and over again, and I told him to knock it off or I would stick my chewing gum in his hair. He did not knock it off, and I applied the gum. Gordon was shocked and extremely dismayed by my willingness to follow through on my threat, and so was my mom, who was forced to cut a nice chunk of hair out of his scalp while he sobbed and shrieked.

My dad continued to admonish me to be patient with him, reminding me that, "he is your brother, after all." The admonishing was frequently done in a less than patient manner, with a raised voice and threatening scowl. When, as an adult, I asked my mom about my dad's relationship with his siblings, and she replied, "Oh, they all hate each other," I recalled his words with cynical amusement. But despite the hypocrisy, it was good advice. Gordon was just trying to figure it all out, and probably couldn't understand why I wasn't always happy to have him involved in my activities.

On the plus side of the ledger, especially when he was very young, he occupied my parents enough to divert their attention from whatever I might be up to. I suddenly had much less supervision, which was fine with me. Sometimes, if I was very lucky, I could blame Gordon for a minor indiscretion like spilled juice or a broken bottle. And sometimes he was inadvertently amusing. When he was around two years old, he developed an obsession with popsicles. Popsicles were regarded as a healthy snack, especially the ones which were made with "real fruit juice," so my parents made sure that there was always an ample supply on hand. After every meal, Gordon would request his favorite dessert, using the word "begus" to describe it. We could never figure out why he referred to popsicles as begus, or begi, or whatever the plural might be, but he did and it stuck. He would grab one out of the freezer, which he could barely reach, and scamper off to enjoy it at his leisure.

When he was a little older, Gordon became a Beatle fan. My mom bought him the first Beatle album, which he played over and over on our little red and white portable turntable. Much to my aggravation, he consistently referred to the song *Twist and Shout* as *Twist and Chow*. I tried to correct him, but he wasn't buying it until I showed him the words on the record label. He was just old enough to read them, but still not entirely convinced. At about the same time, my mom was picking up the laundry from the local cleaner with Gordon in tow. She was engaged in a discussion with the other customers, and after some undoubtedly piquant anecdote, one of the women said, "Of course, you know the moral of that story," at which point Gordon blurted out, "If you're gonna fool around then you better pull the shade!" It was a lyric from *The New Frankie and Johnny Song* which was a favorite at home, but the ladies at the cleaners evidently were not familiar with it, and were somewhat taken aback to hear such words of wisdom from a six year old. My mom thought it was the cutest thing ever.

Sometimes it was difficult for me to figure out how to integrate Gordon into my world. I couldn't avoid him the way I could avoid other little kids in the neighborhood, because he was permanently installed in my home. He seemed to have a knack for making my life more difficult without even trying, so when I discovered that he was extremely ticklish, it was a revelation. I suddenly found that I could instantly neutralize him, even though it was only temporary. Because I was so much bigger than he was, it was easy to grab him and hold him down on the sofa or the floor, and then begin to methodically and vigorously tickle him on his belly. He would laugh hysterically while I did it, but as soon as I stopped, he would cry and scream at me in frustration. Then I would start again and he would be back to the uncontrollable laughter. I took advantage of his vulnerability for a while, feeling that I had finally regained some control of my domestic situation, but when my dad finally realized that Gordon was not enjoying my brand of behavior modification therapy, he put a stop to it. It was a brief but intoxicating glimpse of total domination.

Much of my dissatisfaction stemmed from the fact that Gordon seemed to enjoy a special, protected status, which I found extremely unfair. One time, again when he was very young, he took my penny collection, a special binder which displayed each rare coin in chronological order, tore it apart, and hid all of the pennies under a sofa cushion. I doubt that he understood what he was doing, because he seemed quite proud of himself when he finally showed me where he had stashed them. It had probably seemed like a brilliant idea in his little toddler brain, but I was outraged, and demanded that my parents punish him appropriately. I lobbied for a good spanking. Instead, my dad explained to me that even though my collection was ruined, it wasn't entirely Gordon's fault because he was too young to understand what he was doing. It was not a satisfying explanation, probably because I was too young to understand what my dad was trying to explain.

I got a much clearer impression of how protective parents could be a few weeks later. A friend of mine and I were returning to my house after a morning of playing in the vacant lots. There was a fire engine parked at the curb, which was exciting and unusual, and the front door was wide open. We walked up the path to the door, and were standing on the porch, when a fireman strode heroically out of the house carrying my mom in his arms. She had a little blood on her face, but otherwise didn't seem damaged, and when she saw me, she gave me a sheepish smile, as if she felt silly at being caught in such a situation. It turned out that she had been drinking coffee in the kitchen, and had seen Gordon outside through our sliding glass doors. Some real or imagined threat to him had propelled her out of her chair and through one of the glass doors. Amazingly, she had sustained only a few minor cuts, and Gordon had emerged completely unscathed. After she returned from the hospital later that day, I had all kinds of questions about the event. Most of them remained unanswered, and I was confused as to how such a crazy thing could happen. My mom seemed sort of confused as well, but she assured me that she would have done the same for me if necessary.

There were other, less dramatic accidents around the house, and Gordon seemed to be involved in many of them. Perhaps that was not really the case, but it appeared to me that he was injured much more often than I was. When we were very young, I accidently smashed one of his fingers while we were playing with the kitchen pots and pans. He ended up with a sprain and a splint, and I ended up with a spanking. Later, when he was around two or three years old, he tried to help my dad chlorinate the pool. The chlorine came in glass gallon bottles which were too heavy for him to handle, and he somehow dropped one and slashed another finger quite severely, requiring a trip to the hospital. For a while we had a large wooden bin which we kept in the back yard to house snakes and lizards. The top consisted of a standard screen door on hinges. Gordon managed to fall through the screen and into the cage. This time, fortunately, neither he nor the reptiles were injured. When he was a little older, he received a skateboard for Christmas. Skateboards were originally designed for surfers to use when they couldn't get to the beach, but younger kids would often use them like sleds. Gordon was inclined to ride on his belly around the pool deck, where he collided with a heavy piece of patio furniture, knocking out a top front tooth. For some time after that, he had a cool gold-framed incisor, bringing some early "bling" to the neighborhood. When he got to elementary school, he became adept at doing various stunts on the playground bars, but as fate would have it, he broke his arm doing "the baby arm-breaker," and wound up with a cast, sympathy, and a funny but painful anecdote.

One of the biggest issues that I had with Gordon was "sharing." I had some very cool toys, and the notion that he should be allowed to play with them was anathema to me. There were many reasons for this attitude. Number one was, of course, that they were MY TOYS! He had his own toys. Even though sharing went both ways, and I could have had access to his stuff, it seemed like a rotten deal to me because he only had a bunch of infantile Playschool items that I wouldn't touch with a ten foot pole. My main concern was that he would break something. The Tonka trucks, metal cars, and Mattel guns were sturdy, but there were many plastic toys, like my Fighter Jet Cockpit, that were elaborate and fragile. Gordon did destroy a couple of my prized possessions, and again despite my righteous indignation, I was told to cool off and be tolerant. I had noticed that my dad was not so tolerant when his "toys" suffered a similar fate at my hands, but decided not to comment. When I got a little older I actually bought Gordon some cool gifts like the Ideal Reading Crusader 101, a large electric model car. I had to pay it off in weekly one dollar installments at Thriftimart for three months, but I felt like a genuine big brother when he opened it up on Christmas morning, and realized that maybe I wasn't such a bad guy after all. I like to believe that my initial ambivalence about him metamorphosed into real affection over the years, and it did, but I think my beneficence was also a way of atoning for my indiscretions.

By the time Gordon was in elementary school, he was finding his own friends and activities and becoming less of a problem for me. When he was around seven or eight, he adopted the "mod" look, complete with wide wale corduroy pants with a wide belt to hold them up, paisley shirts, a reversible Sonny Bono vest, and black Beatle boots. This was quite a fashion statement for such a young kid in a conservative suburban milieu. My mom thought it was pretty cool, and would buy the gear for him without hesitation, but I think that my dad was unenthusiastic, because he disliked the Beatles and pop culture in general. Some of Gordon's friends also adopted the style, and they would cruise around the neighborhood on their Schwinn Stingray bikes looking, well, fashionable. My friends and I thought that they looked ridiculous, and we would constantly tease them. We nicknamed Gordon "Boots," which he hated, and never passed up an opportunity to make disparaging comments about his appearance. When he switched back to more conventional attire, I never knew if it was because of our harassment, or because the fad had simply run its course, but I was glad to have a less outrageous looking kid brother. Gordon's lack of coolness was something to be considered as a subtle but tangible liability for me. Although I was not going to lose any friends because of his wardrobe, it was still somehow less than desirable to have my peers regard him as a goofball. When he began to develop an avid interest in bikes and motor vehicles, an area in which I was sorely deficient, and gradually became known as something of a prodigy, I was much happier.

As far as I can recall, Gordon was always interested in cars. My dad subscribed to various automotive magazines like *Road and Track* and *Car and Driver*, and was always looking for, and buying, cool and exotic vehicles, so his influence may have stimulated my brother. Gordon went from building plastic models of custom cars, to racing slot cars, in short order. The slot cars were little racers with engines that were powered by electrical contacts in the race track. The bottom of each car had a tab which fitted into a slot in the track, keeping the car in its own lane and enabling it to execute tight turns. The "driver" had a hand held device to control the car's speed. The cars and engines could be customized and raced, and the tracks could be purchased and assembled at home. I liked the cars, and would sometimes race with Gordon and his friends when they set everything up on the floor of the living room, a large, well furnished area that was never used except on formal occasions. My interests led more to crashes and accidents, and I would sometimes place a plastic model car in the path of one of the racers just for the sake of some mayhem. Gordon was more focused on legitimate racing, and finally started competing at a place called Model Raceways with big professional looking multi-lane tracks. I believe that he was regarded by the other slot car kids as a good racer, but he was always modest about his accomplishments.

At around the same time, when he was still in elementary school, he somehow got a job assembling ten speed bikes at the local bike shop. This was extremely impressive to me, and I remember dropping by the place once or twice to watch him in action. Yes, he was still a little kid, but now he was actually respectable, and even useful. From that point on we were hardly ever in conflict, and sometimes he would assist me when I needed mechanical expertise. He designed and built a custom motorized tricycle, rode mini bikes, and when I was in high school he worked on my friend's dune buggy. When I was fourteen I bought him a cheap electric guitar at a pawn shop. I don't know why I did this – it was an impulse. Maybe I was merely hoping that the noise would drive my dad crazy, but the gift was well received and my mom arranged for Gordon to take lessons. As he learned to play, he started customizing speakers and lights to go with the guitar. I was always amazed at his patience in executing these projects. He took his time and did a good job in a very adult-like way. My dad was quite supportive, and, I believe, quite proud of his younger son. I felt that he favored Gordon, but I didn't mind. Their shared interest in cars and mechanical devices seemed like an appropriate bond, and I had no interest in competing for my dad's attention. It seemed to me that I had a better chance of avoiding trouble if I stayed off of his radar.

My relationship with Gordon was very similar to the relationships that my friends had with their younger siblings. At best, they were treated with benign neglect, and at worst, they were bullied and tormented. One of my best friends had a younger sister, and he would tease her relentlessly. It was often funny, but sometimes brutal, ending in tears. When she developed a childish crush on me simply because I didn't engage in the harassment, I had no idea how to respond. It was weird to have a little girl following me around, and I finally had to be a little surly with her in order to cool her affection. Most of the time we tried to ignore or escape from the younger kids, and go on about our business. With the older brothers and sisters it was another story.

As I've mentioned, some of the kids that I knew had older brothers who were real bullies, like Butch and Joel. I sometimes received reports about their activities, and often what I learned made me glad that I didn't have an older brother. I don't recall any of my friends bragging about the accomplishments of elder siblings, or calling on them to help in a playground crisis. Under the best of circumstances, they were sometimes sources of interesting information, but the quality of that information was variable. When I learned about an elementary school teacher named Miss Lynch from the older brother of a friend, I was shocked and skeptical. He told us that she had earned the name by lynching uncooperative students, and I was young enough to give that scenario serious consideration before dismissing it as being highly unlikely. Obviously, the older boys had a good time with this type of nonsense, but we could usually see through it. Once in a while though, something truly interesting would be divulged, usually about the mysterious subject of sex. The data was usually garbled and inaccurate, but tantalizing nonetheless.

My new friend, Mike, had an older sister named Jan, who was several years ahead of us in school and in life. During our elementary and junior high years, she frequently and inadvertently gave us some fascinating insights into what we might expect to encounter in the near future. Jan was always up to date on popular music, and although I heard many top forty songs on the car radio, it was interesting and informative to hear the records that she played when I was at Mike's house. I wasn't impressed with the soundtrack to *Beach Party*, a dumb but influential film that catered specifically to the teenage drive-in market, but I was intrigued by the complex and energetic dancing that went with it. She would boogie unselfconsciously in the living room while Mike and I watched and wondered – would we ever be called upon to participate in such insanity? When Beatlemania struck the airwaves, Jan was right at the forefront, and when the lyrics to *Louie Louie* by the Kingsmen were reported to be obscene, she cheerfully sang them to us while she danced. Once in a while, we could talk her into taking us along when she went to the beach, and her transistor radio was only one of many that blasted the new tunes across the sand.

Jan had boyfriends too, so we sometimes got a glimpse of the elaborate social structure that we would soon encounter. We once managed to talk her and her friend, Susie, into taking us to the drive-in to see several horror films, and were surprised and unnerved when the car became a way station for an endless parade of teenage guys and gals who seemed to have no interest whatsoever in the images on the screen. She and Susie were both cute and amusing, and were, as far as I could tell, completely dedicated to being cute and amusing, but they were always very nice to me. Susie would even flirt with me a bit, and my total discomfort cracked them both up. The only time that Jan was clearly annoyed with us was when we showed up at the Tastee-Freeze where she worked, and both ordered a ten cent coke with no ice, and a large cup with ice, which was free. We poured the cokes into the large cups, giving each of us the equivalent of a fifteen cent coke for ten cents. We thought it was clever, but it made her look bad in front of her boss, so we reluctantly gave up the ploy. Sometimes I would accidently see her traipsing around Mike's house in her bra. I would cover my eyes and apologize, but she would just laugh and say, "Don't be silly - it's OK." I was dazzled by her worldliness.

Although I don't know how Mike and Jan got along when I wasn't around, my experience with her was always positive, and I don't recall any complaints about her from Mike. This led me, in a very slow and roundabout way, to reevaluate my attitude about siblings in general. I finally realized that, even though some of us were younger and some of us were older, we were all still kids, and we had much more in common with each other than we did with the grownups. I think that my treatment of Gordon improved as a result of this realization. I gradually learned to tolerate him, and ultimately even grew to like him. Once in a while I would take him to the movies with me or spend some time hanging out with him, but usually he was involved with his pursuits and I was involved with mine. It was not uncommon for each of us to leave the house in the morning and not see each other until dinner. In the evenings we would usually be occupied with homework, TV programs, or our own individual projects. The days when I could barely resist the impulse to smash his fuzzy little head passed, and I was glad that he was no longer a constant source of resentment and annoyance, but he was rarely included in my activities, especially the subversive ones. Looking back at his childhood, it seems likely that he really was a "good kid," whereas my status as such might be considered questionable. When, as an adult I asked him if he remembered any of the instances when I was mean to him, he said that he didn't. So maybe I wasn't as bad in those early years as I thought I was. Or maybe he truly didn't remember. Or maybe he was just too nice to remind me.

# 6

## The Power and the Fury

At the same time that I was expanding territorial horizons and relationships, my domestic situation was changing. My parents were still running the show, of course, but the show itself was becoming more complicated. I was diagnosed with asthma at around the age of seven. It never bothered me much. The coughing and sniffles were like a cold without a sore throat or headache, and the wheezing was weird, but it produced a slight tickling sensation in my chest which I sometimes found rather pleasant. It kicked in periodically, and sometimes my parents would keep me away from school for a couple of days, but that was perfectly fine because there were plenty of cartoons on TV, and my mom would usually come home from shopping with comic books for me. But even though I didn't consider the asthma a big deal, my parents did.

I was taken to a specialist, Dr. Spears, and given a series of tests to determine what was triggering my "attacks." The first two rounds of tests were easy. On both occasions, Dr. Spears applied a bunch of different allergens to my back. I couldn't see what was going on, but the process was not very painful at all. After a few days he would check and note the results. Soon he had a list of things that needed another, more comprehensive tryout, so back I went for round three. I wasn't expecting anything substantially different from what I had already experienced, so I was shocked when he administered the first of about twenty incredibly painful injections into my back. I did not want to cry, but even though I made no sound after the first shot, a couple of tears leaked from my eyes. I felt betrayed, and Dr. Spears' comment, "I know this hurts a little bit," just made me angry. The treatment was much worse than the asthma.

It was determined that I would need a series of shots to create immunities to what seemed like a huge list of "triggers." There was cat dander (I didn't even know what that was) and house dust, feather pillows, mustard, horses, and a bunch of other things that didn't make sense to me. The asthma was never specifically triggered by anything as far as I could tell. It wasn't as though I started sneezing when our cat was nearby. But what could I do? My parents thought that they were doing the right thing regardless of how I felt about it. So, for two years, I would walk home from school every Tuesday and stop at the Medical Center, which was on the way, for my shot. The shots never bothered me, although I knew other kids who would cry or faint at the sight of a needle, and I would pick up some candy, usually a Berry Pop, from the Pharmacy in the building. Along with the shots, Dr. Spears gave me prescriptions for a white pill, a red pill, and cough syrup. The white pill, actually half of one, was for wheezing, the red pill for sneezing, and the cough syrup for guess what.

Even though, to me, the asthma wasn't severe enough to warrant so much attention, I went along with everything without any fuss. I was getting credit for being brave and responsible, which was great, even though I was not convinced that I deserved such accolades. I didn't know any other kids with asthma, but a few of my friends had hay fever, which seemed suspiciously similar and sometimes much worse. I never needed an inhaler, and wasn't even aware that they existed until I was much older. And except for the wheezing once in a while, there was no evidence that the typical activities for kids my age were inappropriate for me. I usually felt fine, and even when I had some symptoms, they never slowed me down. But my parents insisted that I take the pills, so I complied.

The problem was the cough syrup. Because the asthma did cause me to cough at times, the syrup looked like a good bet. The first time my mom gave me a spoonful, I was optimistic because it was supposed to be cherry flavored, and I liked cherry candy. But as soon as I tasted it, I was horrified. It was absolutely the foulest taste that I had ever experienced, and I had a lot of trouble choking it down. My mom observed my reaction and said, "Oh come on – it wasn't that bad, was it?" I assured her that it was, but she seemed amused and unconcerned as I washed my mouth out with water, trying to get rid of every trace. Despite my anguish, I was willing to give it the benefit of the doubt. I figured that something that bad had to work, and waited for the cough to disappear - and waited, and waited. After thirty minutes, I was still coughing, and the only difference was a vague metallic taste that I couldn't shake. The cough syrup was obviously a dismal failure.

But the next time I started coughing, my mom got it out again. I told her that it didn't work, but her response was, "Oh, you're just saying that because you don't like the flavor." I kept trying to persuade her, but she wouldn't budge, so I was forced to take it. It was still horrible, and I was mad. This became a routine with us, the frustration and hostility escalating with each new episode. Finally, my mom got fed up, and my dad took over. When I protested that the syrup never worked, he would tell me, "Look, this is for your own good, and I don't want any backtalk!" I couldn't understand why my parents wouldn't listen to me, and that was the most upsetting element of the whole situation. I asked each of my parents to try the syrup, but they declined. I felt like they, and especially my dad, were just being mean, and I decided that I was not going to put up with it, no matter what the consequences. When the dreaded syrup came out again a few weeks later, I refused to open my mouth. My dad was really steaming by now. I'm sure that he felt that I was way out of line. He snarled, "If you don't take this, you're going to be punished!" I looked up at him with my best defiant Errol Flynn glare, and said, "Go ahead and punish me. I don't care!" There was a moment of silence, and his features started to soften. "Is it really that bad?" He asked.

"Yes, it really is. And besides, it doesn't work. It never works; I've been trying to tell you guys."

Another, longer pause, then, "Alright, I give up. You don't have to take it anymore."

It was a hard won victory for me, and even though I was glad that I had stood my ground, I still didn't understand why it had taken so long. If my mom had just listened to me the first time, and maybe tasted the stuff, we could have avoided the whole thing. It made me apprehensive about the future.

I should have anticipated the cough syrup debacle, because a similar scenario had been playing out for years at the dinner table. I had never been a picky eater. Even as a toddler, I could handle vegetables without much fuss, and as I got a little older I grew to enjoy them. When I was around five or six, my mom started giving me more exotic items, like black olives, mushrooms, and artichokes. I liked them all. I was also a huge dill pickle fan, and sometimes my mom would include one when she packed my lunch for school. I ate halibut, and I didn't know any other kid who would. Sometimes when we had halibut in the school cafeteria, the other kids would pass their portions to me under the table because we wouldn't be allowed to leave without a clean plate. There were, however, three food items that I could not tolerate: lima beans, Oscar Meyer hot dogs, and zucchini slippers.

When any one of the terrible three was served, I would be required to eat it, or at least a portion of it. It was my dad who issued the command to, "Finish that! You're not leaving this table until you do!" The lima beans had a nauseating taste and texture, but at some point I figured out that I could swallow them whole with a little milk. Fortunately, they were always a part of a mixed vegetable medley, so I never had more than two or three to deal with at one time. If I was really lucky, I could quickly pick out my lima beans and shift them to my parents' plates while they were rounding up my brother for dinner. I watched my parents carefully when the lima beans showed up, and never saw any evidence that either my mom or dad liked them. Why couldn't we all just pick them out and toss 'em down the garbage disposal? That question was never answered.

The Oscar Meyer hot dogs and the zucchini slippers were a different matter. I couldn't swallow them whole and I couldn't shift them elsewhere. Plus, they were even more toxic to me than the lima beans. I would actually gag on these items, and my dad would get mad at me, and accuse me of faking. The situation was resolved for me when my mom finally threw in the towel, and decided to rotate those items off the menu. My brother wasn't so lucky. He was very picky about his food, and rejected most of the things I liked. I recall him glaring at the single mushroom that my mom had put on his plate, when told that he had to eat it. I was glad that he had to suffer the same torture that I had endured, but I felt that he was being bullied too. It seemed like a very mean- spirited application of authority.

To be fair, my parents were generally nice people, but they sometimes seemed reluctant or unable to see things from my point of view. They spoiled me with toys when I was very young, but after a while I realized that the toys themselves had a very limited appeal. I had a lot more fun when I was running around the neighborhood with my friends, or drawing, or reading. My dad would buy me any book or comic book that interested me, but sometimes he would insist that I read something that he felt was important, and if I didn't, or if I found it dull, he would get annoyed with me. He would take me to movies, which was great, but when I wanted to make a picture of something, and would ask him what I should draw, he would frequently say, "A deep breath," and go back to his reading. My mom was less involved in my day-to-day affairs, but she would deliver me and pick me up when I visited friends who were outside of my bicycle range, and organize birthday and swimming parties for me. She usually let my dad deal with me when there was a problem, but there was at least one occasion when we went head to head.

Perhaps as a result of the asthma, my mom would often ask me if I was feeling alright. I'm sure that she was just trying to be a good parent, but it began to bother me. I usually did feel alright, and I would tell her, but then she had to investigate. "Let me see if you have a fever," she would say.

"But mom, I don't have a fever. I feel fine."

"Well, just let me check."

"Mom – come on! I DON' T have a fever!"

Now she would start to get annoyed, "Just stand still and let me check."

At this point, she would put her hand on my forehead. "Well, I don't know. I guess you're OK." And she would finally let me go. This became a regular routine, almost a ritual, which, in itself, was harmless. But I resented the fact that she didn't believe me when I told her that I was alright. After all, why would I lie? It didn't make sense, and I was insulted that she didn't trust me. Finally there came a day when I felt that familiar surge of anger, and I slapped her hand as she reached for my forehead. She was shocked, and I could tell that I had hurt her feelings, but I figured that she had been hurting my feelings for months, and that she deserved it. I can't recall the consequences, if any, for my outburst, but I'm sure that my mom did not understand why I had rebelled, and merely thought that I was an ungrateful brat.

My dad had very specific tastes in music, which ultimately led to another series of battles. He was a big fan of Gilbert and Sullivan, particularly *H.M.S. Pinafore*. In fact, I think the only reason that he purchased a Chrysler in 1961 was that it came with a record player. As far as I know, it was the first opportunity for a driver to choose his own music instead of just listening to the car radio. The player would only accept seven inch records, so he took the *Pinafore* album to Garrison's studios in downtown Long Beach, and had them transfer the album to a stack of five or six appropriately sized discs. He would play them over and over while we were driving, and explain the lyrics, and the humor, to me. Thanks to him, I learned to love *Pinafore* and *The Mikado*. He was also deeply enamored with bagpipes. He took several of his bagpipe records to Garrison's and gave them the same treatment, and he seemed to get a huge kick out of turning up the volume and rolling down the windows as we rode around town.

I thought all of this was pretty cool, but I wasn't quite as enthusiastic as he was. At eight years old, my taste leaned toward *Ahab the Arab* by Ray Stevens, and instrumentals like *Swingin' Safari* and *Outer Limits*. But when my dad told me that I was going to take bagpipe lessons, I wasn't opposed to the idea. Most of my friends were being forced to take piano or violin and I liked the idea of learning something less commonplace. Soon after his announcement, we were at the home of Robert Burns, who was going to teach me how to play. It was more complicated than I had anticipated. He gave me an instrument called a practice chanter on which I was to start by learning the scale. The chanter was a bit like a flute or recorder, enabling the student to play the songs without the added difficulty of working the airbag. Learning how to handle an actual bagpipe would come later.

I took lessons from Mr. Burns for a while, working on several "exercises." It wasn't exactly fun, but it wasn't bad either. Mr. Burns was patient and encouraging, and even though my fingers were small, I was doing well. But at some point, it was decided that I should switch to a new teacher. I was not involved in making the decision; my dad simply announced that we would be meeting with James MacColl on Saturday to see if he would accept me as a student. Mr. MacColl turned out to be a great guy with a wonderful Scottish accent. He was a highly acclaimed piper, and I was extremely lucky to be taught by him. I played the things that I had already learned, and his response was, "Well, that's pretty good, but you should be playing some tunes by now." With that, he picked up a sheet of staff paper and wrote out a song for me.

It was decided that I should practice for at least thirty minutes every day. That was tolerable at first, because I was still learning fairly simple tunes. I would go to my dad's den and shut the door, listening to tape recordings of Mr. MacColl playing whatever song I was supposed to learn, and reading the music he had written out for me. As the songs became more difficult, I had to deal with various combinations of quickly executed notes, one of the distinctive elements of bagpipe music. I was reasonably patient with the process, but after attempting to play some passage ten or eleven times without success, that sudden wave of frustration would possess me, and

I would slam the insidious chanter on the sofa repeatedly, as hard as I could. The result would be a cloud of dust which didn't seem to affect my asthma, and the sudden entrance of my dad, angrily admonishing me to behave. I would sullenly go back to work, but again, I felt that there was something unfair about this arrangement. Maybe my dad would be a little more sympathetic if he tried to play the tune. After all, he was the bagpipe fan! Why wasn't he learning to play instead of me? After a while, my frustration would subside, and I would feel some pride in my progress, but I never was passionate about the pipes, and they would continue to be a source of conflict.

There were other instances when I felt that unseen forces were tampering with my right to a happy, well adjusted existence. For example, my dad had never shown any interest in sports; so as a consequence, I wasn't familiar with the rules or skills required for football, baseball, or basketball. When we started playing kickball at school I was woefully unprepared. Fortunately for me, not only were there a few other kids in similar straits, but my classmates were very patient and encouraging. Nonetheless, it was embarrassing to miss a catch, or kick some feeble little dribbler, and not even make it to first base. I determined to improve my game, and by the end of third grade, I was actually a good player. I remember kicking some solid high fly balls out to right field, far enough so that kids would have to run for them. I was pretty smug about my achievements, and the world was wonderful, until one day, without explanation, kickball was out and softball was in. I didn't know how to hit or catch a softball, and I was suddenly back at square one. Why? How? Who had orchestrated this debacle? I took it extremely personally, but I had no specific target for my indignation. The teacher, Mrs. Asher, was simply following the curriculum guidelines. Someone in an office somewhere had simply decided that it was time for softball, and there was nothing that I could do about it. The only benefit I received from this event was a feeling of compassion for other kids in similar situations. The students in the "slow" reading group in our class certainly must have felt wretched when they were required to stumble through some passage in a text book. I couldn't take any pleasure in jeering at their mistakes or in bullying anyone who looked or acted strange. It's true that I sometimes couldn't help laughing when other kids did the bullying, but I always felt a little guilty afterwards.

I was on the playground one overcast morning, when an older kid began to pick on a little guy who was part of our group. One of my classmates, Dan, intervened. Dan wasn't so big himself, but he was an excellent athlete and a good guy, and he quietly made it clear that he was ready to fight the big kid if he didn't back off. I don't know what the outcome would have been if they had actually duked it out, but the big kid did back off, and I was impressed. After witnessing so many heroic acts in movies and TV shows, it was inspiring to see someone step up. There weren't any guns or swords involved, no pirate ships or battlegrounds, but even among kids on an elementary school playground, it qualified as an act of courage as far as I was concerned. Witnessing Dan's behavior reinforced my willingness to hold the line against such aggressiveness. When a couple of big kids tried to extort my lunch money from me, I boldly yelled, "Forget it," and they were so surprised that they didn't pursue the matter. I felt vindicated.

But most of the time I couldn't be like Dan. It didn't come naturally to me to calmly assess the situation and then address it with finesse. I would simply explode, and this usually caused trouble for me, even though I felt that I had simply reacted appropriately to an unjust or extremely frustrating state of affairs. I was consistently baffled when my parents didn't, or wouldn't, understand my feelings, and this increased my disdain for authority. I wasn't walking around in a constant state of rebellion, and in fact, most of the time I was a happy, good natured young man. But when I felt provoked, I would react. Some of my responses were probably pretty outrageous to my parents. I remember kicking doors a couple of times, and leaving splintered holes in the veneer. I would also sometimes break things when under duress. These "outbursts" didn't happen often, but they did happen, and they would enrage my dad, which just added fuel to the fire. If anyone had taken the time to ask, I might have been able to convey something of what was going on in my mind. I could respect authority when it was obviously sensible, but when it was arbitrary, or idiotic, I drew the line. All of the books and comics that I was reading, and the movies and TV shows that I watched, presented characters that were clearly heroic when oppressed. I couldn't imagine a young Zorro or Robin Hood putting up with the same nonsense that I was supposed to accept.

There were a couple of other kids at school who had explosive tempers, but I didn't relate to them at all. They would become extremely aggressive about winning at baseball or football, which seemed crazy to me. Sometimes we would organize football games in the park, and one of these hotheads always assumed the role of quarterback for his team. We would tackle each other, and be fairly rough for a bunch of elementary school boys. I obviously didn't know anything about the game, so one day my teammates told me to concentrate on taking down this kid, and to ignore everything else. I did exactly that, and every time I nailed him, he got more and more angry. I thought it was fun – I was actually playing football, and doing a good job of it. Finally, after six or seven clean smashes, he flipped out. I was still on the ground, and he jumped up and kicked me in the stomach. It was shocking and painful, and everyone seemed taken aback by what he had done. When I finally caught my breath, I got a half-assed apology from him, which averted an all out fight, but I still believed that his conduct had been inexcusable. In my mind, his outrageous example of bad sportsmanship had nothing in common with my behavior under duress. I had learned that aggressive response was clearly appropriate when one was in the right, but absolutely inappropriate when one was in the wrong. Of course, none of this rationalizing really mattered - right or wrong, there was nothing that I could do to stop that impulse when it emerged. It almost seemed like some little devil inside my head would flip a switch, and then I couldn't control myself. Sometimes it frightened me a bit, but I secretly thought it was kind of cool. And so far, I had been lucky.

# 7

# Love and War and the Whole Damn Thing

Cupid hit me hard and fast. I was only three when I developed a crush on my cousin, Betta. She was my mom's sister's kid, one year older than I was, cute, charming, and infinitely sophisticated. Her family lived in Berkeley, so I didn't get to see her very often, but for the next two years she was my main squeeze. My mom would take me with her, and we'd fly out of Long Beach Airport on a big silver plane, and arrive in San Francisco in about an hour. My aunt would pick us up and drive to the house in El Cerrito, a large, modern structure surrounded by shady trees, where deer would sometimes stroll through the yard. Most of my memories of Betta are fragments of the times when we visited. We would watch cartoons together in the morning on the new black and white TV. The cartoons and the hosts of these shows were different from what I was watching at home. They seemed more exotic and refined, but I'm sure that it was because I was watching them with my cousin. We went to a theme park in Oakland called Fairyland on one visit, and I was delighted to wander around the attractions with such a cool chick. Betta and her mom came to visit us once or twice, and we had delightful afternoons catching hermit crabs in the tidal pools at Point Fermin in San Pedro. I attempted to convey my feelings to her with lessons on how to burp at will in the back seat of her mom's car, and by sending her one of several treasured skins that my snake, Jackson, had shed. Fortunately for me, I was not so smitten as to suffer in her absence, but I was always thrilled to see her.

I also liked another cousin, Victoria, who was the daughter of my dad's older brother. Victoria was a year younger than I was, and looked a lot like the dolls in the TV commercials. I saw Victoria more often than Betta because her father was an Air Force officer stationed in Southern California. She and her parents would visit us fairly often at the new house, and sometimes we would take what seemed like a long drive to visit them in San Bernardino. Once we left Long Beach, we would cruise through fragrant orange groves and winding uphill roads to their little secluded house. I don't have specific recollections of our activities, but I always enjoyed her company. I also enjoyed the company of the girls next door. There were three of them, all older, and we had fun swimming, and drawing with colored chalk on their driveway. Even when I wasn't necessarily smitten, there was some mysterious quality about these young ladies that sometimes made them more interesting than my male friends.

When I was in Kindergarten I fell for two girls. The first was Terry, who taught me how to tie my shoes at recess. Terry was taller than I was, and so I ultimately determined that it - whatever "it" might be - would never work out. But the second girl, Perri, was just about perfect. She had exquisite dimples and a big pile of curly hair. We both had hand puppets, and on at least one occasion gave an impromptu puppet show for our fellow students. Sometimes after school we would get off of the bus together at her stop, and go to her house for lime popsicles. I was fascinated by her room, which seemed to be filled with dolls, stuffed animals, and all kinds of girly items and décor. I felt like I was getting a glimpse of a world entirely different from my own. When she came to my house to see my snake eat a mouse, and didn't even scream or gag, I was sure that we were made for each other. My infatuation with Perri extended into the first grade, when we began the formal process of learning to read. One of the exercises was to draw illustrations to simple sentences with crayons on newsprint paper. We were both good at this, but Perri had a way of drawing people that I admired, so I copied her style, which further enhanced my affection. After the first semester, when I was transferred to Mrs. Sieta's class, I didn't see as much of Perri, but she still lingered in my heart.

My friend Ricky Sherwood and I invested a fair amount of our playground time in chasing the girls that we liked, and even some that we didn't like. We had an informal alliance with a couple of other kids, and called ourselves the "Screeches" for no particular reason. Our gimmick was to flip our jackets up over our heads and hold them out like bat wings while we ran. The girls obliged us by running away at our approach, laughing and shrieking. We were very careful not to catch any of them, in order to avoid cooties. We didn't know what cooties were, but we were convinced that the girls had 'em and that we didn't want 'em. The truth was that none of us had any idea what to do with a captive female. It was all just harmless fun.

Evidently, there were other kids who were having their own crushes, so at least I wasn't alone. One little girl, Sandy, somehow got permission from her teacher to hand deliver an invitation for her birthday party to me in front of my entire class. I was flattered and embarrassed at the same time, but I did go to the party, and Sandy was very sweet to me. On Valentine's Day we were expected to provide cards for every classmate of the opposite sex. These were usually cheap and simple, but in some cases passion trumped discretion and a couple of boys and girls would receive elaborate cards with candy, sometimes unsigned. It wasn't very difficult to determine who they were from, and there was sometimes a bit of childish teasing as a result. The only kid that I recall admitting to being stuck on a girl was Dan, the boy who had stood up to the bully. My mom had picked us up at school, and had asked about "that pretty little blond girl in the front row." Dan told her that the girl's name was Cindy, and that he liked her. None of the rest of us was as forthcoming about our affections as Dan.

Despite my crushes, there were still times when girls could be a problem. If one of them chose to be mean or rude, on the playground or in the classroom, retaliation options were extremely limited. It was not acceptable to push or strike a girl, and it was humiliating to be teased by one in front of the other kids. The only viable option was to say something rude and walk away, which was not entirely satisfying. My secret weapon – the lizards – had to stay at home, and I sometimes felt as disabled as an unarmed gunfighter when I was being annoyed by some young vixen. Fortunately, most of the gals at Minnie Gant were not inclined to be difficult. But even the nicest young ladies with the best of intentions could chill the blood of a young boy. I was once invited to a birthday party by one of the girls on my block, and when I arrived it was immediately apparent that there were no other males on the premises. Even her father was nowhere to be found. I was surrounded by giggling, party-dressed females and coerced into participating in all sorts of horrific games. It was one of the most agonizing afternoons that I ever spent, and yet I never could figure out why. I liked all of the girls individually, but as a group they were too much for me to handle. Perhaps it was simply the amplified estrogen level.

In the second grade I was seated next to Donna. This classroom was equipped with tandem tables, so it was a much more intimate arrangement than I had previously experienced. Donna and I sat side by side at our double desk in extremely close proximity. My most vivid memory of our "relationship" involves a note that she wrote, folded up, and handed to me. When I opened it, it said, "Go lay an egg." It seemed cute and funny to me, and started a chain of "Go lay an egg" notes that passed back and forth. "Go lay an egg" wasn't exactly a declaration of undying love, but it seemed to signal some degree of mutual affection, and that was good enough for me. When the seating chart was shuffled around, I lost Donna, but quickly replaced her with another girl. We would sometimes stay after school together and play in the sandbox. I derived quite a bit of pleasure from these affairs, but by third grade it was somehow understood that liking a girl was not cool. There were only a couple of girls who were acceptable to my classmates, and this was usually due to their athletic abilities. Nancy could play ball and run as well as most of the guys. She was funny and attractive, not inclined to cry over a skinned knee, and seemed very comfortable joking around and bantering with a fairly rowdy group of young males. My guess is that most of the boys in our class had a collective crush on Nancy even though they would never admit it, and that it was tacitly sanctioned because she wasn't a "girly girl." I thought that she was terrific, but there were other girls who were equally terrific without Nancy's qualifications for acceptability. This mysterious shift in the social order meant that my friends and I had to avoid any behavior that could possibly be construed as an indication of affection, or even interest, in any female. After all, being teased about having a "girlfriend" was considered a fate worse than death by my classmates. I continued to have crushes, but because they now had to remain secret, I had no way to find out if they were reciprocated. However, now and then there was a tantalizing hint of possibility.

For reasons unknown to me, our teachers would shift our seats around during the year, and after one such shift, I found that there was a girl sitting behind me who was everything that I was looking for. Of course, I had made no indication of this to her or anyone else, and in fact had gone out of my way to avoid even the merest hint of my adoration. Next to her was one of my oldest friends, Conn. We had known each other since our days at Peter Pan Nursery School. Conn was smart, funny, and an extremely precocious provocateur. On this particular day, we had our crayons out, and the good Manila paper rather than the crappy newsprint, so we were taking our drawings pretty seriously. I'm almost certain that we were supposed to be drawing birds, because Conn worked out a composition involving a tree full of them in various stages of dissolution. They were all dangling from the branches, drinking booze, smoking cigarettes, and looking stupefied. It was a masterpiece, and while I was admiring it, the girl, who was obviously disgusted, said to Conn, "Why can't you be a nice boy, like Billy?" He turned to her, acting surprised by her remark, and replied with a knowing smile and suggestive drawl, "Oh . . . you just don't know Billy . . ." She seemed to be alarmed at this response, and I knew that whatever positive feelings she might have felt for me had been completely eradicated by Conn's comment, which was exactly his intention. It was getting more and more difficult to reconcile my affection for girls like her with the appropriate social conventions of my peers, and finally, I decided to just let it go. There were other, more important issues to deal with, and I didn't have much time for dames.

Once again, I had been tossed into a class with a new group of kids. There were still some students from my previous classes, including Mike, and another friend named Greg, but there was also a group of boys that I didn't know, and they weren't very friendly. Tom, Tommy, and Phillip were the most determined to give us trouble, perhaps because they felt that we were encroaching on their turf. Initially it was just the usual teasing and sniping. Phillip was an expert in this area. He sat close enough to me to keep a running commentary going without attracting Mrs. Kelley's attention. I can't remember the specific things that he said. Some of it I recall as being genuinely funny, but all of it was calculated to provoke me, and it did. Soon we evolved into two little gangs. Tom, Tommy and Phillip would harass, and be harassed by, Mike and Greg and myself. This mutual harassment usually took place on the playground, and involved such outrages as chasing and pushing. If one of the gangs was involved in a game of four-square, or dodge ball, the other would attempt to interfere by stealing the ball or creating a distraction. My two friends and I were not usually the aggressors, but after a couple of weeks, we were starting to get feisty. Things came to a head one day during recess, when I was trying to concentrate on some game, and my adversaries were pushing and tagging me as they ran by. I was already extremely annoyed when Phillip gave me another nudge as he flew past. That nudge lit my fuse, and I was suddenly ready to do battle with whichever of the three I could catch.

At that moment, Tom was fast approaching. I stood and waited until he was within reach, and then grabbed him. He seemed surprised at this turn of events, and tried to struggle out of my grasp, but I wouldn't let go. It soon became a crude grappling match. We were both still on our feet, stumbling around on the asphalt, and a crowd of kids was gathering around us. Some began calling for the playground monitor, Nina. Usually, according to ritual, the call was, "One, two, three, four, five, six, seven, eight, Nina," but this situation seemed more serious than usual to some of the girls, who ignored the count. I was still feeling very aggressive, and having read too many comics and seen too many cheap Italian Hercules films, decided to lift Tom over my head and throw him across the playground. Since he was almost exactly my size, and didn't appear willing to co-operate, it probably wasn't a very good plan. I did manage, with a great deal of difficulty, to pick him up, hold him at chest level for a second, and then drop him, just as Nina arrived. Tom slowly got up, displaying scraped and bloody elbows, and we were escorted from the playground. As we walked, Nina calmly asked us what had happened. I admitted that I had started things, but neither of us could give her a coherent account of the details. It was a sunny day, and she parked us about fifteen feet apart in the shade of our classroom, and then left us to sit and cool off while she reported to the office. I was now feeling bad about picking on Tom, because Phillip had been the one to trigger my temper, so I got up and walked over to where he was sitting.

"Sorry, Tom. Are you OK?"

He looked up at me for a few seconds before speaking, and then replied, "Yeah . . . scraped my elbow." He didn't seem very angry.

"Sorry."

We paused for a moment, then I said," This is really stupid. I was mad at Phillip, not you."

"Yeah," said Tom, "Sometimes he's a butt."

"Well, can we shake hands?"

Tom appeared to be considering my proposal. Finally he said, "Um . . . yeah, OK."

I stuck out my hand, and he shook it, and suddenly we weren't enemies anymore. We sat together and started talking, and by the time our teacher, Mrs. Kelley arrived, everything was alright. We explained that we had shaken hands, and that we wouldn't fight any more, and again I admitted that it was mostly my fault. Mrs. Kelley seemed pleased that we had resolved our differences, and took us into the classroom without further comment. When the rest of the students showed up a few minutes later, they were surprised that Tom and I appeared to be friendly. Our little gang war was over, but we weren't yet one big happy family. Phillip continued to taunt me a bit, but with more caution, and Tommy was standoffish. The ice was finally broken when Phillip noticed a book that I had brought to school. It was the Ace paperback edition of *At the Earth's Core* by Edgar Rice Burroughs. The Ace editions of Burroughs' science fiction classics were terrific. The covers were beautifully designed, with great typography and fantastic illustrations by Roy Krenkel, and later, Frank Frazetta. I was enthralled by the look and content of these novels, which were full of outlandish heroism and romance. I noticed that Phillip was checking out my book, and that he had lost his usual squinty-eyed aggressiveness. I decided that if he was interested in Burroughs, we might be able to reach an accord.

"Do you want to see it?" I asked.

Pause. "Yeah, I guess."

"OK, just don't lose my place."

I handed him the book and he took a long look at the cover, and then read the blurb on the back.

"Can I borrow it?"

"Well," I had to think about this. "When I'm done, you can borrow it, but you have to give it back."

"OK, "he said. There was a long pause. Then, "Thanks."

"OK."

When I actually gave him the book several days later, he seemed taken aback. I don't think he believed that I would come through. But he took it, read it, and returned it, and then we were buddies. Soon after that we were all friends, and in the strange way that kids have of shifting alliances, I started hanging out with Tommy and Phillip, and going home with them after school sometimes. Greg and I saw each other less frequently. Tom and I were cordial, but never became real friends. Mike, however, remained my best friend.

Playground fights were not a frequent occurrence at

Minnie Gant, at least not when I attended. There were probably only two or three each year, and most of them were little scuffles like mine. I did get into another one at about the same time with an older boy, and the circumstances were similar to the "bicycle seat incident." It was a tradition for the big kids to run through our games and kick the ball to the far end of the playground when they were called in from recess. This was grudgingly accepted as a rite of passage, but someone still had to run after the ball, and that someone was often yours truly. On this particular day, I snapped, and instead of chasing the ball, I chased the kid who had kicked it, and leaped onto his back. He was big enough to shake me off with ease, and I hit the asphalt on my butt, cursing and fuming. This all took place in a matter of seconds. He was more confused than angry, and didn't seem inclined to press the issue, but Nina was there in a flash, and again I was taken away. This time I had to go directly to the office, and confront one of the vice principals. I told her my story, and she was very sympathetic, but firm.

"I know that it's not fair for the bigger kids to take your ball, but there are other ways to handle the situation. I would be mad too, but it's against the rules to fight, and besides, somebody might be badly hurt. I'm going to talk to them, and they probably won't do it again, but if they do, you come and talk to me, OK? No more fights. I know you're a good boy, but you've been getting into some trouble lately, and I don't want to call your mom and dad. You don't want me to have to call them, do you?"

"No."

"OK, Billy, I won't this time. But please behave. We don't want anyone to get hurt!"

I understood her position, and felt that she was being very considerate. In fact, I can't recall a single incident when I felt mistreated by any of the teachers or administrators at Minnie Gant. They were a fabulous crew, and handled us with a perfect balance of support and discipline. I always believed that I would get a fair hearing, and that every effort would be made to fully understand why there had been a problem and how to solve it. Because I could usually offer compelling reasons for my actions, I was still regarded as a good kid, even though I had a tendency get into a little trouble now and then.

I was shifted back and forth between different groups of students for the remainder of my elementary school years. I never understood why this happened, but it wasn't necessarily a bad thing. I ended up with a lot of friends, and learned to adapt to new social situations. The fact that I could burp at will was an asset. The only kid who could outburp me was John Moralda, but he was a prodigy. I could also spit well, meaning that I could launch a condensed globule with reasonable accuracy over a distance of approximately six feet. This was known as "hawking a loogie." My drawing skills in some way compensated a bit for my lack of ability in team sports, although I was good at dodgeball. In general I got along well with almost everyone without any more physical altercations, aside from a shove now and then. In fact, everyone seemed to get along with everyone most of the time. As I mentioned, fights were not common, and when they did occur it was unnerving. I only witnessed a couple of real slugfests, with two kids standing toe to toe and punching each other in the face. One time, probably around the fifth or sixth grade, two friends of mine, Tim and Johnny, got into it. I don't know what set them off – they were both good guys, and neither was a bully. Tim was much taller and heavier than Johnny, and when they started swinging, we all thought it would be over very quickly. But Johnny stood his ground, giving as good as he got, until Tim hit him squarely on the nose and blood started to flow. Johnny backed up a bit, and wiped off some of the blood. Nina was fast approaching. Nothing happened for several seconds, and then Johnny spat a mouthful of blood all over Tim's shirt. He showed no fear or remorse – it was total defiance all the way! Of course they were both taken to the office, and I can't recall whether or not they patched things up, but I was extremely impressed with Johnny's courage, and also very aware that my little dust-ups didn't amount to much. What would have happened if they had fought somewhere else, and no one had intervened? Of course it was just a couple of kids, but I had heard the dull smack of a fist hitting a face, and I had seen real blood flow. It wasn't like the movies, and it didn't look like fun.

# 8

# The File on Mom and Dad

As I was growing up, I was gradually and inadvertently assembling little bits and pieces of information about my parents. It was probably instinctive, because they seemed to exercise complete control over every aspect of my life, and I was simply trying to understand the forces that governed this brave new world of mine. I wanted to do whatever suited my fancy with as little interference as possible, and I desperately needed good parent management skills to achieve this. I couldn't develop these skills without some understanding of what made them tick, so data collection was essential. Unfortunately for me, the acquisition of information usually generated questions which required the acquisition of more information. As I got older, my parents became more and more of a mystery to me, but as a kid in elementary school, I thought I knew them fairly well. Here, then, are the contents of my file at eight years old.

My mom's name was Nell. She thought it was a stupid name. She was born in Tampico, Mexico in 1924. Her father was working in one of the many oil refineries there in some engineering capacity. I have the impression that he was well educated and possibly involved in the financial side of the business as well. The family moved to Southern California when my mom was very young, and around this time, her sister was born. She did not talk much about her past, but when she mentioned her early childhood it sounded like a good one. They were evidently well off, and she spoke of her mother with great affection. Then everything fell apart within a very short period of time. Her father died in an accident. I'm not absolutely certain, but I believe that it was an auto collision, and then her mother, who had been ill, passed away. The disease was scloderma, which gradually hardens the skin, and evidently my mom witnessed the gradual transformation of a vital, energetic woman into a living corpse. She was only around six years old, and her world had been completely destroyed. She and her sister were now orphans, and were taken in by her aunt and uncle, who lived in San Pedro.

My mom was diplomatic when talking about growing up in San Pedro, but it was clear that she did not enjoy the experience. She had lost her parents, which must have been devastating, and was living with a family that was caring for her out of obligation rather than affection. In particular, it was her Aunt Leah who made the situation unpleasant. She had two children of her own, a boy and a girl, and the unexpected addition of two more made her life more difficult. My mom was the most popular of the three girls, which created tension and jealousy in the household. She rarely went into details about her day to day life in San Pedro, but I easily gathered that she did not like Aunt Leah. When I was very young, we would sometimes visit Aunt Leah or "Granny" as we called her. She lived in the same house that my mom had grown up in, and would assemble the aunts, uncles, and cousins for Thanksgiving dinners. I remember eating in her big old kitchen with the other kids while the adults ate in the dining room. I found her to be cold and off-putting. I couldn't figure out why I felt that way, because she never said or did anything to warrant such an attitude on my part, but I never warmed up to her. On the other hand, my mom really liked her uncle, Bertie, a jolly bloke with an easygoing attitude who died before I was born.

My parents first met in church when they were in high school. My dad was two years older, and kind of a wise guy. The story of their initial courtship, according to my mom, starts with my dad sitting behind her in the pews. I'm guessing that both families were in attendance as well. My dad somehow attached a handwritten note to his shoe, and then slid his foot far enough under my mom's seat so that she could read it. The note was an invitation to get together, and it cracked my mom up. I believe that it was my dad's intelligence and sense of humor that interested her. She always laughed when she recounted the event. She also told me that he would sometimes arrive to pick her up with a snake coiled around the steering wheel of the car, which she didn't find as amusing. They apparently dated for a while before the War intervened, and then went their separate ways.

During the War, she worked as an Occupational Therapist for a military hospital. What I didn't know was that at this time she had serious affair with a soldier who was recovering from an arm wound. After my mom died in 2014, I was contacted by a woman who told me that her father had been searching for Nell Fogg for years. His name was Stan, and he was still, at age ninety, harboring a profound regret that he had "let her go." I talked to Stan, and he told me that my mom had been instrumental in saving his arm from amputation, and that he had always been in love with her. He gave me a sense of how attractive and charming my mom had been as a young woman. It was an unexpected glimpse into her past. When I saw a photo of Stan as a young man, I was startled by his resemblance to my dad.

After the war, she attended college at Berkeley. She studied art there, and maybe music and dance, because she was a good piano player, and had some impressive photos of herself doing ballet poses. It was sheer coincidence that my dad was at Berkeley at the same time, studying on the GI Bill. They reconnected, graduated, got married, and moved back to Los Angeles so that my dad could do graduate work at USC. He was in the military reserve when the Korean "conflict" started, and the army sent him, with my mom, to Japan, where he had some kind of position as a therapist or psychological counselor. They stayed there for at least a year, and returned to Southern California when my mom became pregnant with me.

When I was very young, my mom would tuck me into bed and kiss me goodnight, but aside from that, there was very little display of physical affection in our family. I remember seeing a copy of Dr. Spock's book on baby and child care around the house, but perhaps my parents didn't read it. In fact, I rarely saw my mom or dad engage in extreme behavior of any kind. They would indulge in a martini or gin and tonic before dinner, but that was about it as far as alcohol was concerned. They were both moderate smokers, but didn't have too much trouble quitting when it was determined that the cigarettes might exacerbate my asthma. Although my dad had no compunctions about yelling at me, I rarely heard him raise his voice to my mom. I don't remember any exchange between them that could legitimately be characterized as an argument, although once I saw my mom, who was not easily moved to tears, quietly sobbing after a "discussion" with my dad. Most of the time, however, they maintained the appearance of a relationship that looked very much like what I saw on *Leave It to Beaver* or *The Donna Reed Show*. Most of my friends seemed to be living under similar circumstances, so I had no reason to believe that my situation was unusual.

On a day to day basis, my mom was easy to get along with. She prepared breakfasts, and would drive me to visit my friends in her Cadillac. Sometimes she would take me to get clothes or shoes, and she was always the one to accompany me to the doctor or dentist. She was also the one to organize swimming lessons for the kids on our block, pool parties, dinner parties, or any other social event in and around our house. My dad was never involved in such things. My mom had an edge of formality most of the time, and was very private, as if it were important to maintain appearances, but when she relaxed she was funny and playful. She was also well-read, and extremely interested in art, film, culture, and good clothes. The family room table was stacked with magazines including *Glamour*, *Mademoiselle*, *Town and Country*, *Art in America*, *Art Forum*, and other similar publications. She was an excellent bridge player, eventually becoming a Life Master, and she often participated in jury duty. Although she was a rule follower and good citizen, she sometimes revealed a bit of whatever case she was hearing, and it was clear to me that she enjoyed being involved in the legal process as much as she enjoyed courtroom dramas on TV. She also belonged to a number of social organizations, but didn't seem to have many close friends. She started painting again when my brother and I were old enough to require less supervision, and continued to produce portraits and still life pieces for many years. By most standards, she would probably be regarded as a good mother, but she always seemed somewhat distant. My biggest problem with her was that I felt that she didn't understand me or trust me at times. She often seemed to regard me with skepticism, and she could be very stubborn when making decisions that I didn't feel were in my best interest.

My dad's name was William, and he named me after himself. But his middle name was Edwin, and mine was Martin (my mom's maiden name) to spare me the indignity, he said, of being referred to as "Junior." His family was from the Boston area. There is a long genealogy of Foggs there, and some of it is a little crazy, but as a child I didn't know anything about that. Both of his parents were still living and could have been models for a Norman Rockwell painting. In just about every way, they were quintessential grandparents and I really liked them. When I was very young, my dad would take me to visit them in his latest sports car. He had, at various times, an MG, Austin Healy, Corvette, and Jag XKE, all convertible, so we would zoom over with the top down to see "the Folks," as he called them. They lived a few miles away in a perfect little grandparent bungalow with a neatly trimmed lawn and garden. The neighbors had a Siamese cat named Sammy, who would always greet me when we arrived. To me, my grandfather was a sweet old man, but he had led a very interesting life.

The story that I was told involved his father taking him down to the waterfront at the age of fourteen, handing him a quarter, and signing him into the US Navy. I know that he did his initial training on the Monongahela, the last of the commissioned clippers, and that he was required to climb the rigging to the highest spar and furl the sail. As a boy, I thought that this was fantastic, and I envied his experience, but as an adult it seems frightening, and I wonder what life was really like for him in the Navy of the early twentieth century. He served in World War One, and was offered an opportunity to test for officer training, which he did. When the Japanese bombed Pearl Harbor, he was attached to the USS Arizona, but was ashore when the bombs struck. For much of the war he was in charge of Shore Patrol for the Los Angeles area, and, according to my dad, faced down an angry mob during the Sleepy Lagoon Riots. He retired from the Navy as a Commander, and when I knew him he was comfortably retired. He was missing half of the ring finger on his left hand, which fascinated me, and he had a cool sword which had been presented to him by one of his crews. Sometimes he would take it down from the wall and let me hold it, or tell me about something exotic that he had seen or done during his travels.

I never learned much about my grandmother. She was about ten years younger than her husband, and came from the Boston area as well. Because my grandfather was away at sea for long periods, she had the unenviable job of supervising their five children, who evidently didn't get along with each other, and keeping the house in order. She was active with church activities, as well as various military and social groups. After my grandfather's retirement, they did a lot of travelling, driving around the country, and sometimes going abroad. One time my grandmother told me a story about some road hog who was giving her a bad time. "I finally passed him by, and watched him eat my dust," she said, laughing. She and my grandfather always seemed to be in a good mood, and treated me with great affection. I looked forward to seeing them pull up in their pink and white DeSoto when they came to visit.

When my dad spoke to me about his childhood, he was very selective. He never had stories about his brother and sisters or about the family in general. I have the impression that he admired his father, because he sometimes talked about his military career, but there was never anything about activities shared or wisdom dispensed. It was always about exploring the woods, or taking a stand against some bully. He told me that he had done some boxing, but he was not athletic at all, so I wasn't entirely convinced. He also told me some war stories. He had been a medic in Europe, and had seen combat. One of the stories that I remember involved an armadillo stealing chocolate from his tent. That must have been stateside, because I don't believe that they have armadillos in Germany. He also said that he had been blown off of his feet by an explosion once, and that he and some other GIs had forced some captured Germans to walk through a mine field.

My dad was Dr. Fogg to the public at large, and was referred to as such by neighbors and colleagues. I didn't realize it then, but he was very proud of his title, and took great pains to make sure that everyone was aware of it. I wasn't sure what kind of doctor he was, and when I finally learned that he had a doctorate in education, I was even more confused. He explained that he taught classes for people who wanted to become teachers. My guess is that he was probably a very good instructor, because when he would help me with homework, particularly math, he was patient and easy to understand. He had an incredible range of general knowledge, and could speak with authority on almost any subject, which he frequently did, sometimes to the TV when he disagreed with whatever was being broadcast. He could be particularly disparaging about certain public figures, and seemed to harbor a personal grudge against Walt Disney for no discernable reason. Even as a child I was sometimes baffled by his obsessive criticism. For example, he would turn on the car radio while we were driving, and listen to the new rock and roll tunes, but then he would complain about every one of them. He particularly hated a song called *"Sherry"* by the Four Seasons, and would denigrate Frankie Valli's shrill, whining voice at great length. I would innocently ask him why he didn't change the station, but that would irritate him. He obviously enjoyed the opportunity to impose his assessment of popular culture upon a captive audience. He often claimed to have had a scholarship offer from MIT when he was very young, and after he died I found the letter to verify it. I never learned why he didn't take the offer. He had attended medical classes, dental classes, and law classes before settling on education, and sometimes told me how hard it had been to work and study, and not get enough sleep.

My dad was extremely committed to sleeping. I never knew anyone who slept as much as he did. As I've mentioned, he was often stretched out on the family room couch. When my friends would come over, he would sit up and chat with them, and then return to slumberland. I suspect that he was also lazy. He rarely did any chores around the house, and was certainly not a handyman. He seemed to have a knack for avoiding certain civic responsibilities such as voting and jury duty, even though he had plenty of time for them. His work schedule involved teaching a few classes, and only kept him occupied for a few hours, two or three days a week. Once in a while he would briefly get fired up about something, but it would never last long, and whatever equipment he had purchased for this new endeavor would find its way to one of the many closets in the hall, or the garage. Once he bought a set of weights, and I briefly entertained the hope that he might end up looking like Steve Reeves in *Hercules Unchained* , but after a week or two the weights were disassembled, and relocated to their final resting place under the bed. Despite his love of the hot cars that he drove, he never worked on them, or even washed them, preferring to take them to the Los Altos Car Wash while we breakfasted at Hof's Hut. He had made some fairly extravagant promises to me when I was little, about building go-karts and similar projects, but none of them materialized. I wanted him to take me lizard hunting, which we had discussed at length, but he kept putting it off. Finally my mom intervened on my behalf.

"You've been promising him for weeks," she said.

He gave her a grouchy look.

"Oh for heaven's sake, Bill," She was annoyed with him, and she had a good point. It was one of the rare occasions when my dad was pinned to the mat, and he didn't like it.

"All right, all right," he groused, getting up from the sofa. It was still early enough for several hours of bagging big game, so we took a coffee jar with holes punched in the lid, and set out on foot. I was only five or six years old, following Bwana, and trusting him to lead me to a place where lizards roamed. It was an easy ten minute walk to get out of Park Estates and into the large fields that lay across Clark Avenue. My dad set a fast pace, and I found it a little difficult to keep up with him but I was very excited and didn't mind jogging a bit.

"Keep your eyes peeled," he mumbled, as we began to traverse the field. The grass was high and yellow, interspersed with rocks and weeds, and there were a few trees casting dark shadows in the bright sunlight. I thought we should slow down. Those lizards were good at hiding, and we were moving too rapidly to spot them. Soon we were halfway across the field. I hadn't seen a single lizard, and my dad didn't appear to be scouring the terrain. We were now almost through the field and approaching a little group of stores and restaurants. My dad strode out of the field and across the street to the Thrifty Drug Store. He stepped up to the pay phone outside the store, inserted a dime, and told my mom to come and pick us up. I was bewildered and disappointed. We hadn't seen a single lizard! My dad took me inside the store, and told me that I could pick out a toy. I don't recall what toy I selected, but I felt a little better. When my mom arrived and saw the toy, she didn't say anything. Our safari had lasted all of thirty minutes. It was a very frosty ride home.

I must admit, however, that my dad did arrange some great excursions for the two of us. Once he took me with him for a helicopter flight, and another time he managed to get us a ride on the Goodyear Blimp. Not too long after the lizard hunt he arranged a spectacular trip to Dinosaur National Monument in Utah for us. It was during the summer, and he chartered a private plane out of Long Beach Airport for the round trip. The plane was a four seater, so he and the pilot sat in front while I stretched out in the back with my dinosaur books and comics. We had a brief stop in Las Vegas, where I won a dollar and ten cents in a slot machine, A few of hours later, we landed at the airport in Vernal, Utah, where we spent the night at a nice motel. We had breakfast at the motel café, where they had pictures of dinosaurs on the paper napkins. The Monument was a big excavation site enclosed by an expansive structure with exhibits and murals. I thought it was pretty neat, and I got some toy metal dinosaurs to add to my collection.

Like my mom, my dad did not seem to have close friends. No old army buddies or childhood pals ever dropped by. He did spend time with some of his campus colleagues, but not on any regular basis. He was actively involved with the college, and would recount his trials and tribulations with the administration and the academic senate during dinner. He didn't talk about his students or classroom activities, but instead painted a picture of epic battles with unjust policymakers and incompetent fools. Most of this went over my head. I figured that it was all grownup stuff, and therefore I could safely ignore it.

My parents never talked about money. I didn't realize that there was a huge discrepancy between what my dad earned as a college professor and our actual standard of living. I never really thought about it. Sometimes my friends from school would comment on our built in pool, or the size of our house, but not often. I remember the first time I visited my friend Mike after school. He lived in a different area of Long Beach, and I was surprised at how small his house was, but too young to wonder why. When my friends and I would walk to the store for candy or comics, I often "loaned" them nickels and dimes so that we all could buy something and rarely thought about asking them to pay me back, probably because there was no evident concern about such things in my household. My parents did encourage me to save money, and helped me open a savings account when I was very young. I would get five dollar bills in cards for Christmas and my birthday, and most of that would go into the account at four percent interest. This was the standard "fiscal responsibility "lesson that many kids were being taught at the time. The idea that most people were very anxious about money matters never entered my mind.

Not too long after we moved to Park Estates, I was made aware of the fact that my dad suffered from migraine headaches. According to him, they were extremely painful, and there was at least one instance when I could tell that his sinus area was red and swollen. He was not reluctant to talk about how horrible the headaches were. "Like a red- hot spike being driven through my forehead" was a refrain my brother and I heard repeated numerous times. Sometimes he'd change it up - a white-hot spike, or nail being hammered - but he was determined to make sure that we understood what he was going through. He was obsessed with the idea of pain, and when I had a cut or scrape that required the application of a stinging substance like merthiolate, he would tell me that the sting was caused by the dying germs. He explained that his headaches were so bad that he had to take a drug called belladonna, so powerful that it could only be used in extreme cases. I would sometimes see him giving himself injections, and once or twice he had me "help him" by pushing the plunger on the syringe. I didn't like doing this, and later, when he asked for my assistance, I refused. On the positive side, my dad seemed very concerned that I be well informed about the dangers of drugs. He had me watch an early TV program about heroin addiction that showed some poor junkie going through an agonizing withdrawal. He also explained, in great detail, what happened to the body during the addiction process. I was vaguely troubled by these things, along with the fact that he was always going to see doctors. He had a black appointment book that was kept scrupulously up to date. He would have everything written down, including his weekly haircuts and doctor appointments. All of this made a lasting impression on me, but I didn't put the pieces together until much later.

There was one other member of our household who must be mentioned here. This was Mrs. Marshall, our housekeeper. She was much more than that, of course, and an important part of our family for many years. She worked for us on Mondays, Wednesdays, and Fridays, and sometimes would babysit on nights when my parents were out. There were a few instances when my mom and dad took a short vacation together and left Mrs. Marshall in charge while they were gone. She was absolutely reliable and loyal, and there was great affection between us. Some of the comments that my mom made later in life suggest that Mrs. Marshall was one of the few people she truly trusted and genuinely liked. Even though she was about the same age as my parents, she seemed more grandmotherly to me. I think it was because she was always sweet and kind. I can't remember her ever being angry or judgmental, and once I saw tears in her eyes when my dad had some medical problems later in life.

Mrs. Marshall was a Native American from Oklahoma. Her husband, Charlie, also Native American, was a TV repairman. He was an alcoholic, but I don't believe that he was mean or abusive. He was always very friendly, and had even caught some lizards for me. They had two children, Tiny, and Sonny, who were much older than I was. Sonny was married, and I rarely saw him, but Tiny, the younger brother, would sometimes come over and swim with us. He was a cool guy, sharing comics, fried pork rinds and RC cola with me. My general impression of their situation was indistinct, although I remember visiting their small apartment once or twice. I think Mrs. Marshall's life was difficult, but she never complained about anything, and she was very generous within her means. She didn't talk much about her past, but she would answer any questions that I asked. One thing that she said made a lasting impression on me – that sharing was very important within her culture. I think that was one of the reasons why she would always be happy to prepare lunches for me and my friends, or just be willing to listen to me and see my side of things. When she was babysitting, we would play games like Yahtzee or Monopoly, and watch monster movies on TV. In conversations, she often used words and phrases that were unique to her, like "over yonder," and "us and them." When I would come barging into the house, she would let out a little "Eek," and say "You scared me!" But this was always said with a smile, and it became one of our little rituals. I can still see her in the family room, with the ironing board set up in front of our black and white Magnavox TV, watching *As the World Turns* while she worked. She was terrific.

# 9

# Kulture with a Kapital K

It was simply pure blind luck that gave me an upper-middle class childhood in Southern California during the post-war years. Even without the warm glow of nostalgia, it was a terrific time and place to be a kid. There was a pervasive sense of "newness" about almost everything. The houses, streets, and stores in my area had all been recently constructed, the toys and appliances kept getting better and more elaborate, and every year the cars became bigger and more stylish. I frequently felt a joyous optimism about the possibilities that a new day might bring. It was not uncommon for me to walk into a store like Sav-on and encounter amazing toys, comic books, candies and soft drinks that I had never seen before. Between what was genuinely new, and what was simply new to me, I felt that I was living in a world where cool discoveries were always right around the corner.

In our Park Estates neighborhood, virtually every house had at least one television set, if not more. These were the days of black and white broadcasting, and limited channel selection. We considered ourselves blessed to have a grand total of seven channels to choose from, some national and some local. When I was very young there were many cartoon shows with hosts like Sheriff John and Engineer Bill. I was fortunate enough to see original animated classics that were being packaged by the film studios for local broadcasters. My favorites among these were the Betty Boop and Popeye cartoons which were loaded with crazy violence, hot jazz, and a peculiar kind of depression era surrealism. Popeye solved every problem with his spinach-propelled fists, which was probably not the best model of behavior for young children. Betty Boop was a strange but sexy little vamp who seemed to overcome adversity through flirtatiousness. Of course these and the other old theatrical cartoons had originally been made for adults, but there were new animated features designed specifically for young TV viewers, including *Crusader Rabbit*, *Ruff and Reddy*, and *Colonel Bleep*. I watched them, but I always preferred the old cartoons. There were some shows which attempted to create a child-friendly fantasy world, like *Captain Kangaroo*, but for me they were kind of weird and a little scary. The Captain didn't act like any adult that I knew, and he reminded me of some of the villains in the comics that I read, who would lure young kids to horrible fates with promises of games and candy. He personally endorsed Tootsie Rolls.

I was more interested in monster films than anything else on TV. There were several local stations which presented a different horror or science fiction film every week. These were all broadcast during different timeslots on Friday and Saturday evening, and I caught every one of them. My parents would go out at least once on the weekend and sometimes would be gone on both Friday and Saturday nights. Mrs. Marshall would babysit me and my brother, and watch the movies with us. I have lovely memories of viewing dreck like *Fire Maidens of Outer Space* and happily chowing down on Granny Goose Fiesta chips and Dad's Old Fashioned Root Beer. Actually some of the memories aren't so lovely – once I was watching *Missile to the Moon* and eating barbeque potato chips, when a rock monster scared an astronaut into direct sunlight. He was immediately engulfed in flames and burned to a skeleton – barbequed! I had to switch to regular chips. The worst was when my mom served me tomato soup while I was watching *Mark of the Vampire*. It took me a long time to get over that.

There were all kinds of toys, foods, candies, beverages, movies, comics, and books being designed especially for an emerging target market, the "Baby Boomers," and TV commercials could now show us these wonderful new products in action. I liked the ads for toys like Great Garloo and Mr. Machine, as well as all the guns from the different western shows. Western programs were on every major network, and I watched many of them. Boys my age sported toy pistols, rifles, hats and other accoutrements in keeping with their favorite cowboy heroes. We also had toy swords, which were always broken within minutes of engaging in a duel, as well as machine guns and army helmets. My favorite activity for a time was playing night fighter with Gary Scott, the delinquent. We would scuttle around in the bushes at dusk, blowing away snipers and commandos with our Tommy guns. During the day we would stock up on Pixie Sticks, Red Vines, and candy bars, and have battles in the vacant lots. If the battle got too heated we would sometimes dispose of the toy guns in favor of dirt clods and hairy boys. The commercials were very persuasive, but I was beginning to realize that they sometimes made items look much more interesting than they really were. Watching a Slinky "walk" down a flight of stairs was not my idea of a good time, and crap like Play-Doh and wood burning sets was downright insulting.

My favorite commercials were the movie previews. I saw the trailers for *Return of the Fly* and *The Alligator People* in a theatre when I was around five years old, and they made a huge impression on me. I actually believed that it was a single film with the Fly and his good friends, the Alligator People, rampaging together against mankind. The hyperbolic sales pitch was enthralling, and from that moment on, I loved the previews as much as I loved the movies. Saturation TV advertising for films such as *Goliath and the Barbarians*, *Hercules Unchained*, *Gigantis the Fire Monster*, and *Gorgo* gave me glimpses of major cinematic thrills all week, and sometimes I had to work hard to get my dad to take me to the matinee on Saturday. Later, when I was old enough to go to the movies without an adult in tow, I would comb the evening paper for science fiction, horror, and adventure films that Mike and I could see on the weekend. The newspaper ads were as lurid and sensational as the previews, and the posters displayed at the theatres were even better. Long Beach had great old movie theatres, many of them with ornate Art Deco styling inside and out, and the matinees were full of boisterous kids and few adults. There was a distinct odor of stale popcorn, and usually the floors were sticky with spilled soda and gummy candies. The snack bar had items that we could not find anywhere else – giant candy bars and boxes of Dots for fifteen cents, and Carnation malts which were frozen solid. We would load up on junk food and spend four or five hours in the dark, watching attentively if the film was good, or jeering and laughing if it wasn't. We were particularly interested in cool monsters or copious bloodshed. Sometimes the movie delivered the goods, and sometimes it didn't, but the possibility of seeing something spectacular kept me coming back week after week.

As I rode my bike home from school on a sunny afternoon in June, 1962, I was gleefully contemplating the various weekend offerings of *Shock Theatre*, *Strange Tales of Science Fiction*, and *Chiller* on TV, as well as the strong possibility of a monster movie matinee. I cruised up the driveway and through the side yard gate, parking my bike on the porch, and entering the kitchen through the sliding glass doors. It took several seconds for my eyes to adjust to change of light from the brightness outside, but I was operating on instinct. I was heading for the refrigerator to forage for the traditional after school snack, when something caught my attention. It was a magazine with a bright red cover that had been very conspicuously placed on the kitchen table. As I approached it, I realized that I was looking at the ghoulishly hysterical face of Renfield, Bela Lugosi's loony sidekick from *Dracula*. The word "Monsters" floated above his head in drippy monsterish lettering. I picked it up and began to turn the pages - monsters everywhere! There were photographs and articles on horror and science fiction films that I had seen, and, better still, films that I'd never even heard of. I sat down at the table, oblivious to everything else, my snack forgotten, totally engrossed. I have no idea how I was sitting there, but eventually I realized that my mom was trying to communicate with me.

"Well, I guess it's a hit," she said, "I saw that at Thriftimart and thought you might like it. But you'll have to move now because I need to set the table."

She was right - it was a hit, and probably the coolest thing that my mom ever did for me. I was fortunate that both of my parents were open minded. Other kids were sometimes discouraged or even forbidden to read comics and monster magazines. This particular publication, *Famous Monsters of Filmland*, was sometimes cited as being a bad influence on kids, usually by people who had never taken the time to read it. I loved it. It was the first actual magazine that I owned, and the editor, Forrest J Ackerman, presented the information a way that was warm and uncondescending, with a goofy sense of humor that I found amusing. The photos and articles inspired me to try to draw things like mad scientist laboratories, severed and/ or shrunken heads, and, of course, monsters. I immediately began collecting monster magazines, and there were quite a few of them. Aside from *Famous Monsters*, there were *Fantastic Monsters, Horror Monsters, Mad Monsters, Castle of Frankenstein*, and several others. I learned about special effects and film techniques from these magazines, and was inspired to experiment with creepy make- ups. Mike and I even made some eight millimeter films using the same stop-motion animation techniques that had brought *King Kong* to life, after I persuaded my dad to buy a used movie camera for sixteen dollars at Winstead's Camera Store. We used silly putty to create a blob monster attacking a toy car, and later animated a GI Joe doll with a messed up face, running amok and killing people. We always got parental support for our cinematic efforts, even though the content may have been questionable. The drawings that I did were another matter. Usually I was complimented on my abilities, but sometimes the subjects that I chose made adults a little nervous. The severed/shrunken heads, especially the ones with dripping blood, did not sit well with some of my teachers, but I never got into any real trouble over them.

Although *Famous Monsters* had a profound impact upon my cultural development, there were many other significant, and equally questionable, contributors as well. Comic books were available almost everywhere. There were all kinds, ranging from genuine cartoons like *Donald Duck*, which I hated, to war stories, westerns, superheroes, and even *Classics Illustrated*. The only ones that really interested me initially featured dinosaurs. In fact, the first comic I ever owned was a DC title, *House of Secrets*, which depicted a tyrannosaurus threatening New York. I had talked my dad into buying it for me, and from then on I would try to get any comic with dinosaurs. My favorite for a while was a Dell publication, *Turok, Son of Stone*, about two Indians trapped in Lost Valley. They had to fight dinosaurs in every issue while they looked for a way to get back home. There were a few things that annoyed me about *Turok*, though. He and his buddy Andar always referred to the dinosaurs as "honkers," with no explanation as to why, and there was no reference to Stone except in the title. Who was Stone? Was he Turok's dad? Was Turok's full name Turok Stone? These kinds of unanswered questions frequently interfered with my ability to fully enjoy the stories. I wanted more details. Also, while the covers were great, full color paintings, the interior art was not impressive. I was already getting picky.

*Star Spangled War Stories* was another book that I purchased regularly. It always offered a cover story with soldiers fighting dinosaurs, usually on some uncharted island in the Pacific. I was starting to recognize the styles of the different illustrators, especially the great ones like Russ Heath, and would sometimes pass on an issue if the drawings weren't up to snuff. I was actually quite a snob about comics, and wouldn't bother with anything that didn't meet my exacting standards unless I was desperate. One day I was at Paul's Market with a quarter burning a hole in my pocket, looking through the comics on the news rack. There were no new issues of any of my favorites, so I picked up a Marvel book called *Strange Tales* out of sheer boredom. Most comics had bold, colorful covers, but the Marvel covers were always line drawings filled with weird, dull browns and grays. This cover, despite the usual dreary Marvel palette, did look kind of interesting. It had a big ugly monster, Pildorr, forcing a man to "walk the plank" off of his space ship. I bought it, went outside, and sat on the curb to check it out. This was another of those magic moments when I felt that I had discovered something fabulous. There were four stories filled with monsters and *Twilight Zone* plot twists. I fell in love immediately, and from then on, the Marvel monster comics were my favorites. I was especially enamored of Steve Ditko's art - it was unique and odd but fitted the stories perfectly. I was very disappointed a few years later, when Marvel dumped their monsters for superheroes. Ditko was now drawing something called *Spider-man*, which bored me to distraction.

Monsters seemed to be everywhere during my formative years. There was an "official" monster craze sweeping the nation, and the magazines were only part of it. Monster models, plastic figures of the classic Frankenstein, Dracula, the Wolf Man, and many others, were being glued together and painted by kids all over the country. I eagerly purchased every one, along with Weirdos and Rat Finks, which were cartoonish hotrod-driving fiends with bulging eyes and lots of sharp fangs. My friends and I would build them and they would sit on our bedroom shelves for a while. Then there would be a day when it was time to blow them up with firecrackers, or torch them with matches and airplane glue. All of our models seemed to suffer the same glorious fate, and we would sometimes record it for posterity with my movie camera. This activity did not receive the Good Housekeeping Seal of Approval.

Monster cards were also popular. These were just like baseball cards, but they had monsters and jokes instead of players and stats. The first set came out in 1959, and consisted of full color cartoon monsters painted by Jack Davis, with corny captions. I stumbled across them at Park's Toy Store, and it was love at first sight. For the next few years, I was constantly on the prowl for monster cards. For my eighth birthday, Mrs. Marshall bought me two boxes of *Horror Monster* cards with great photos of creatures from various movies and horrible jokes on the backs. I ripped through those boxes, trying to put together a complete collection. The kitchen table was littered with hundreds of cards, and I was in heaven. It was one of the best birthday presents I ever received.

One day at school, my friend Greg came running up to me on the playground. He was very excited. "Look at this," he said, "I got 'em at Lucky's." They were brightly colored cards with gruesome paintings of skull faced Martians and giant insects invading the earth. The Martians were relentlessly zapping, freezing, and burning anyone who stood in their way. The insects were chomping people and smashing buildings and military vehicles. There was a lot of blood and destruction. It was beautiful! Needless to say, as soon as school was out, Greg and I sped to Lucky's, a large supermarket near his house. We locked up our bikes and ran inside, clutching the lunch money that we had saved to buy cards. We had to exchange our dimes and quarters for nickels because these cards were not sold in the standard wax pack with a slab of stale bubble gum, but in vending machines which offered five for five cents. We managed to get a fair number of cards, but many were repeats, and the collecting mania was upon us. We returned on Saturday morning, armed with allowance money, and put it all into those machines, then took our piles of unsorted cards to Greg's house, where we had a wonderful time organizing them and reading the stories on the back of each card, which detailed the invasion and Earth's ultimate victory.

I later learned that these cards, referred to as *Mars Attacks*, were test marketed on the east coast, where they were met by outrage on the parts of parents and teachers. One card, depicting a dog being fried with a heat ray as boy recoils in terror, was deemed particularly offensive. The entire series of fifty five were subsequently withdrawn and "dumped" without fanfare, ending up in machines like the one at Lucky's. Ironically, the same company had produced an extremely bloody series of Civil War cards the year before, painted by the same artists, which were hailed as educational by the very folks who decried the Mars cards. Each Civil

War card depicted an event, usually a battle, from that period, with a "newspaper" report on the back. What the parents and educators did not realize was that many of the bloodiest events presented on those cards were completely fictional.

I was a voracious reader, devouring everything from classics to irredeemable trash. I would check out books on mythology and dinosaurs from the school library, but after school I would check out the paperbacks at the nearest Pharmacy or liquor store. There were several bookstores that carried a large selection of fantasy and science fiction, and because my dad was an equally voracious reader, it was easy for me to persuade him to go book shopping. My favorite store was Maxwell's Books on Fourth and Locust in downtown Long Beach. The downtown area was a little scruffy, and the store itself was dimly lit and funky, but that just made the whole experience more interesting. Maxwell's had unusual items, like imported Tarzan paperbacks from England, that I found exotic and cool. I bought all of the Edgar Rice Burroughs books that were being republished, science fiction novels if the cover art was good, and horror and fantasy anthologies like *Weird Tales*. Much of this material had originally appeared in the pulp magazines years before, and had not been considered to have any literary merit, but if I had known that, it would only have increased my ardor. I was hopelessly obsessed, and would stay up all night and read under the covers using a flashlight. This practice continued throughout elementary school, as I graduated from Burroughs to James Bond, and later to counterculture non-fiction like the *Hell's Angels* book by Hunter Thompson, and the autobiography of Lenny Bruce. Even though I didn't realize it at the time, I probably had insomnia, because I could never fall asleep quickly. This seemed normal to me because I didn't know any better - I never felt tired during the day, and I always had plenty of energy. When I was much older, I found out that my mom suffered from insomnia, so it is likely that I had a genetic predisposition for it. Although she hated her inability to sleep, it never seemed like a big issue to me. It may have taken a while for me to zone out, but I always had great dreams, many of them incorporating elements of whatever novel I was perusing at the time.

In the sixth grade we kept a list of the books that we had read throughout the year. My teacher, Mrs. Emerson, was impressed with the number of volumes that I had logged, but slightly alarmed by titles like *Goldfinger* and *Thunderball*. She handled the situation diplomatically, merely inquiring as to whether my parents were aware of my interest in such adult fare. I assured her that they were, and that was that. If she had read those books herself, she probably would have been less sanguine about them. I was finding that many people, including teachers, drew conclusions about various subjects without much investigation. I had become a skeptic after purchasing a paperback edition of *Famous Monsters*. A blurb on the cover asserted that it contained one hundred and fifty photos, so one day, just for the hell of it, I counted them. I can't recall the exact number, but it was significantly less than one hundred and fifty. It really bothered me that the folks at *Famous Monsters* had lied, and it taught me that the printed word was not sacred. Now I felt that I couldn't necessarily trust every bit of info that came my way, and I became even more skeptical about the voice of authority.

*Playboy* was a hot topic with all of the boys, and I was no exception. Most kids had to ferret out pop's hidden stash for a furtive glimpse of paradise, but my dad left his issues right on the family room table along with less provocative titles like *True*, *Argosy*, and *Esquire*. I would peek at

*Playboy* when no one was around, but finally I gathered the nerve to ask him if I could "read" it.

"Well . . . do you think you're old enough?"

"Um . . . yes?"

"Are you sure?"

"Yes!"

There was a brief hesitation. "Alright . . . I guess it won't hurt you."

And that's how I became the only kid at Minnie Gant Elementary School who was allowed to read *Playboy*. After a while I started keeping the issues as my dad discarded them, and pretty soon I had a collection. By the time sixth grade rolled around, I was becoming interested in the stories and the articles, as well as the girls. I can't say that I envisioned myself as a fashionable man about town with a sports car and penthouse, but I did have some tantalizing notions of the pleasures that the adult world might provide. My study of *Playboy* led me to read a paperback titled *The History of Sex in Cinema*, and when my dad picked up a copy of Kenneth Anger's notorious *Hollywood Babylon*, I pulled it out of the closet after he had finished it, and added it to my library. My biggest score was made when I was looking through his bedside table drawers. I don't remember what I was looking for, but what I found was the pot of gold at the end of the rainbow. There was a copy of *Fanny Hill*, a book that I had read about in *Playboy*. It was erotic, explicit, and had been banned as obscene. There was also a copy of the *Kama Sutra*. I couldn't believe it! I carefully placed them back in the drawer, but on nights when my parents were out, I would do some serious reading. I learned a lot from those books.

*Mad Magazine* was also a significant contributor to my cultural awareness. It had a clearly defined attitude of subversivness that was aimed directly at the social conventions of post war America. *Mad* attacked everything that I was familiar with in a humorous and intelligent fashion. The film and TV parodies were especially well written and illustrated, and the anti-smoking ads were brutal, relentless, and funny. Lyrics for popular songs and poems were altered, and clever word play abounded. The artwork was executed by some of the best in the business, and visual puns were everywhere. *Mad* had a direct influence on the way kids all over the country interpreted, and responded to, the world. We knew that the magazine was created by adults, but these adults seemed to share our "us vs. them "sensibility. It was interesting to consider the possibility that all of the grownups in the world might not be on the same page regarding rules and authority.

There were some parents who, when confronted with the need to throw a birthday party for the Kid, would resolutely transport a carful of boisterous youngsters to the Museum of Natural History, or the Griffith Park Observatory. These were educational, appropriate for elementary school children, cheap, and, theoretically, fun. They were OK to visit once, maybe, but I could never understand why anyone would waste time on those dreary venues when there were so many other fantastic places to go. The list of attractions in Southern California at that time is pretty amazing. Within easy driving distance we had Disneyland, Knott's Berry Farm, the Hollywood Wax Museum, Pacific Ocean Park, Marineland, the Alligator Farm, and the Nu-Pike. Disneyland was new and heavily promoted by Walt himself on his Sunday evening TV program. We all enjoyed the special occasions when someone's parents could be persuaded to take us there for the day. Everything was clean and colorful, and the rides and attractions were perfect for children. Knott's Berry Farm was not as exciting as Disneyland. There were only a few rides, but they did have a gold mine and western town which were fun to visit. The Hollywood Wax Museum had scenes from classic movies with wax replicas of the actors. The best ones for me were from the horror films of the Thirties and Forties. There was an opportunity to pose for a photo with the Frankenstein monster which my friends and I did several times. I never got to go to Pacific Ocean Park, and was always tortured by the commercials for it because they were spectacular. Marineland was my least favorite amusement park. I found the fish and dolphins boring, and it was the kind of place where we would go with distant aunts and uncles instead of friends. The Alligator Farm was right across the street from Knott's. It wasn't for everyone, but because of my affinity for reptiles, I found it very interesting. They actually had a trained alligator which would laboriously climb a ramp and then slide into the big pit with all the other gators. They would snap and lunge for a few seconds, and then settle into a pile of snouts and tails. I thought it was asking a lot for an alligator to perform at all, so I wasn't inclined to find fault with the ridiculousness of the performance.

My favorite amusement park was the Pike, or Nu-Pike, as it was known then. The Pike had been a major attraction in downtown Long Beach for years, starting as a bathing resort around 1900, and gradually becoming a huge labyrinth of rides, booths, arcades, shops, and food stands. My dad seemed to like the place, and I recall being taken there by him several times when I was very young. By then the Pike was pretty sleazy. There were stories about kids who stood up while riding the huge, rickety Cyclone Racer roller coaster and literally got their heads knocked off by low beams, and murders on the various "dark rides." Although these stories were almost certainly apocryphal, they gained credibility when the mummified body of a genuine train robber was accidently discovered dangling from the ceiling of the "Laff in the Dark" Funhouse. The general appearance of the place did nothing to diminish its reputation. Everything looked weathered and scuffed up, and there were food wrappers, cigarette butts, and splashes of sticky liquids everywhere. It was also very loud, with calliope music from various attractions, barkers competing for business, girls screaming on the rides, and the conversations of inebriated patrons. The little shops had strange, exotic items for sale, and their windows advertised "curios from around the world." There were bars, and tattoo parlors with faded black and white photos of heavily embellished men and women in the windows. The rides were obviously different from those at Disneyland – older, spookier; they had the same flavor as some of the classic cartoons and movies I had seen on TV. The Pike had a pervasive odor of greasy food and hot asphalt which was an excellent olfactory metaphor for the entire enterprise. Even when I persuaded my dad to take me on the Wild Mouse roller coaster (I was too scared to ride the Cyclone Racer) and found it way too intense to endure without tears, I still loved the Pike. My friends and I continued to go there through high school and it always evoked wistfulness in me for a time that I never knew. My most enduring specific memory of the place is from the age of five or six. My dad and I were heading toward the exit, and I turned around for one last glance. The sun was dazzling, and it seemed like it was all a continuously shifting pattern of shapes and colors, set to an idiosyncratic soundtrack. About twenty feet behind me, a skinny young sailor in his blue uniform and white hat wrapped his arm around a provocatively dressed not-so young woman, and casually spewed vomit all over the sidewalk. Those were the days!

# 10
## School Days

Although we usually groaned and complained about it, Minnie Gant Elementary School was a very pleasant experience for most of us. I would not have admitted this at the time, and there were some things about it that I did not enjoy, but I often found myself looking forward to getting there in the morning.

It was important to conform to the conventions of our social order in language and dress. There were certain colloquial terms that we applied to our conversations when conventional turns of phrase would not suffice. Spaz, ortho, and queer were obviously derogatory. A "chop" was an insult, as in "what a chop." Boss, wicked, and bitchen were accolades, although the latter was a dangerous word to throw around when adults were nearby. As far as clothing was concerned, it was advisable to wear a windbreaker or Pendleton shirt on cooler days. Anything other than a Pendleton would be derisively labeled a "flannelton," bringing shame and embarrassment to the wearer. A pair of Jack Purcell sneakers was recommended. Keds, Red Ball Jets, or P F Flyers were not cool. Billy the Kid jeans were absolutely out. Kids would not necessarily be ostracized if they failed to meet the standards, but there was a strong likelihood that they would be teased without mercy. We would arrive at school early, appropriately attired of course, and compare notes on TV shows, movies, homework, or whatever else we deemed worthy of discussion. There was always an informal kickball or softball game going on at the far corner of what seemed to be a huge playground, and it was there that we usually gathered. When the bell rang, we hustled across the asphalt to our classroom, took our assigned seats, and set about to look attentive as the official school day began.

As we progressed through the grade levels, the activities became more structured because someone, somewhere, had determined that we actually needed to learn a few things. We had at least thirty five students in my elementary school classes, and the teachers had to organize us into different groups for differing levels of ability in reading and math, along with the basic lessons in spelling, history, and science. We also managed to find time for drawing and music. I can't imagine how they managed to pull this off, but they did. They also sometimes supervised playground activities, maintaining a benign but incontestable control over our little academic world. Once in a while there would be problems or conflicts, but I can't recall any of us being overtly disrespectful to our teachers. Most of the time we liked them, but mischief was in our blood and couldn't be denied.

Singing in class was an activity that I absolutely despised. I have no idea who had selected the book of songs that we were forced to use, but it was obviously someone totally unfamiliar with the sensibilities of pre -adolescent boys. I have mercifully suppressed the memories of most of them, but I can still feel the humiliation of having to sing abominations like *White Coral Bells* and *Michie Banjo*. I was not alone in this – most of the other boys felt the same way. Our response, of course, was to alter the lyrics. One of the few examples that I can recall with any degree of accuracy went like this;

"Above the plain so clearly seen,

A young boy's head is turning green."

We would collaborate on these endeavors, and it wasn't too difficult to enlist five or six classmates to participate. There were brief moments when it was obvious that our teacher was hearing something other than the official lyric, but in a chorus of thirty five she couldn't possibly single anyone out for such irreverence. We, on the other hand, derived great amusement and a (possibly misplaced) sense of pride in our musical accomplishments. The best "adaptation" was authored by my buddy, Farley when we had to sing *Michael Row the Boat Ashore*. I can't remember the original verse, but Farley created this magnum opus;

"The river Jordan is deep and wide.

Tar and nicotine on the other side."

Hallelujah!

In the third grade, Mrs. Kelley allowed us to put on a talent show for our parents. We had some time to plan things and rehearse, but were left to our own devices as far as content was concerned. Mike and I, as well as our new friends Tom, Tommy, and Phillip, acted out a skit in which we were members of a club, having a meeting on how to undermine our parents. We got some laughs, but the true star of the show was my pal Conn, the kid who had drawn the drunken birds. Conn could be relied upon to come up with outrageous responses for any occasion. He once brought me a baby alligator in a plastic tub for my birthday, which did not please my mom. In this case, he outdid himself as a surgeon complete with costume, performing an operation on Tom, who was stretched out on an "operating table" with a sheet obscuring everything except his head and feet. Everyone was startled, and I think some of the parents were horrified, when he started picking up saws and hammers, and pulling slimy pieces of poultry and beef organs from behind the sheet, while gleefully explaining the nature of the procedure. We were in hysterics, and even the adults finally gave in and started laughing. It was great show, rivaled only by the unexpected performance of John Webb. John had been tagged as a "bad kid," but I never saw him do anything to warrant it. When his turn came, he sat down at the piano, with his back to the audience, and gave a wild and humorous impression of *Smoke, Smoke, Smoke that Cigarette* as the record played. He received a huge and well deserved round of applause for his efforts – not bad for an eight year old kid. It is a testament to the courage of Mrs. Kelley that we were allowed to do the show our way, without adult intervention, but I am sure that she was relieved when it was over.

When we were in the classroom under supervision, we were well behaved. There was a lot to do and we got it done. When the teacher wasn't lecturing or interacting with us, the room was quiet, enlivened only by the occasional inadvertent belch or fart. These were guaranteed to elicit a round of laughter and a patient mini-lecture on "normal functions of the human body." It was inevitable that at least once a year someone would barf in class, and that was not so amusing, although extremely noteworthy and possibly stigmatizing for the barfer. We did pass notes, whisper, and toss spitballs, all of the usual clandestine classroom stuff, but I think we liked our teachers too much to make things difficult for them.

The school cafeteria was another matter entirely. We had the option of bringing our own lunches and eating on the benches next to the playground, or paying twenty-five cents for a hot meal in the cafeteria. The price eventually went up to thirty cents, but it was still an amazing deal. We would pick up a tray and utensils and walk along the counter where the servers would assemble our meals. There would be an entrée of fish, pasta, ground beef, or pizza, with vegetables, potatoes, milk, and pudding, Jell-O, or fruit cocktail for dessert. We would joke about the odd and misleading titles given to some of these dishes like "Creole noodles," and "chopped steak (hamburger) on mashed potatoes", but it was actually pretty good food. The only problem was the cafeteria monitor, a tall, humorless woman who was empowered to determine whether we had eaten enough of the right foods to be allowed to leave. We had to raise our hands, holding our forks and spoons, and allow her to inspect our trays before heading out to the playground.

Naturally, there were some kids who were picky eaters, and they resented being forced to revisit some item that had been previously rejected. In such a case, the first course of action was to dump some of the food into our empty wax milk cartons. This worked for a while, but somehow the monitor found out about it and started checking the cartons. We suspected that her daughter, who was a student, might have tipped her off. The second course of action was to compress and scatter the food around the plate, making it look at least partially eaten. My buddy Albert was a master at this. He had a particular aversion to coleslaw, and when confronted with it would announce, "Time for the fake coleslaw bit." He would then arrange the offending item in such a convincing way that the monitor would allow him to leave the table. For less skillful kids this ruse was often unsuccessful. The third course of action was to find a kid with a good appetite and a taste for foods that others disdained. This only worked in specific cases. I liked halibut, but it was not a favorite with some of my friends, so they would pass their portions to me under the table, and I would eat enough out of each one to guarantee release, and then pass it back to be deposited on their plates. The fourth, and best course of action in my opinion, was to hide the unwanted food in the flower pots which were placed on the tables. We became quite proficient at this, but soon it was not enough to merely hide the food, and we graduated to draping noodles among the artificial leaves and blooms, and other decorative innovations. Someone must have noticed our work, but we never got into trouble for it. Sometimes kids would fling a bit of food, or use a spoon to catapult something to another table, but we knew that a genuine food fight was out of the question, so Mike and I came up with a subtle game which kept us thoroughly entertained. When the monitor wasn't looking, we would roll a couple of peas onto the floor, directly in her path, and then make bets as to how long it would take her to step on one. It was our brand of sabotage and we reveled in it. That monitor stepped on a lot of peas during our tenure, but she never caught on.

I would alternate between eating in the cafeteria, and bringing my lunch to school. At first I had a lunch box with an outer space theme. Lunch boxes were ubiquitous among the younger kids, and often provided insight into the interests and character of the carrier. They also provided a convenient container for transporting certain items back home. On a very hot day after lunch, I encountered a large black beetle on the playground. I watched him as he slowly ambled along, and decided that I had to bring him home with me. I carefully scooped him up and placed him in the box. There was a thermos inside which was held by a flimsy clip, but otherwise plenty of room for my captive. I felt particularly brilliant about smuggling him into class, but by the time I got home, the beetle was not uppermost in my mind. I left my lunch box in the kitchen, recalling its contents a few minutes later, as I heard my mom shriek. The beetle did not survive, and soon after, the lunch box was retired. Lunches were now to be packed in paper bags.

On rainy days, which were infrequent, those of us who had brought lunch would eat in the auditorium, and the cafeteria kids would join us when they were excused. It worked out fairly well, the only drawback being an auditorium full of noisy, active, albeit dry, boys and girls. When I got to the sixth grade there was apparently a change in policy. On the first real rainy day of the year, it was pouring outside at lunch time. Our teacher, Mrs. Emerson, announced that those of us who had brought lunches would eat in the classroom. Then she left us to have her own lunch.

At first we just sat at our desks, talking and eating. The level of conversation quickly became louder, and it wasn't too long before kids were shouting at each other across the room. I was engaged in conversation with the guy in front of me when half of a peanut butter and jelly sandwich flew past and struck another boy. He grabbed the sandwich and crushed it into a gooey fist sized wad, then hurled it in the general direction of its suspected point of origin. Within seconds, several more food items soared past me, and were returned. And from then on it was a food storm. I was hit with another sandwich, still in its wax paper bag and much the worse for wear. I picked it up off of the floor and fired it back. We all realized that apples and oranges could do some serious damage, so they were put aside. But snacks that were highly coveted under normal conditions were now airborne, demonstrating the commitment to engage even when there was no discernable enemy. I saw, and was pelted by, Oreos, Moon Pies, and Hostess Snowballs, as well as unopened bags of potato chips and Fritos. Everyone was laughing and screaming, and even some of the girls had begun to participate. I had pulled my jacket over my head for protection, firing back everything that I could lay my hands on. Some of the boys had left their desks to achieve tactical superiority, and others were hiding under their desks for self preservation.

It was absolute pandemonium until the door opened. Mrs. Emerson loomed in the doorway – all five feet of her! Everything stopped – we froze as the last sandwich thudded against the blackboard. The room was a mess. She did not enter, standing there quietly and taking in the disaster. Finally she spoke. "I'll be back in ten minutes. I hope this room will look presentable when I return." It did, and we were model students for the rest of the day. She made no comments regarding our betrayal of her trust, but evidently Mrs. Emerson thought that we had learned our collective lesson. In fact, quite the opposite was true. She had not learned her lesson. A few weeks later we had another rainy day, and once again, we of the packed lunches were left to our own devices in the classroom. We liked Mrs. Emerson, but the opportunity was impossible to resist, and once again the food flew. She seemed genuinely shocked and disappointed when she returned to the room, and we all felt that strange mixture of guilt and exhilaration about what we had done. The room was very quiet except for a barely suppressed giggle or two. We never had lunch in the classroom again, and it took a few days for Mrs. Emerson to regain her usual warmth and enthusiasm. Who could blame her?

Mrs. Emerson would take our class to the auditorium once a week for square dancing. This was another situation which bewildered and annoyed me. I couldn't imagine why anyone would believe that square dancing might appeal to middle class suburban kids. The girls seemed OK with it, but the boys felt embarrassed by it. I hated it. Passionately. Yet week after week, we trooped to the auditorium and practiced under Mrs. Emerson's supervision to the same dreadful music, doing do-si-dos and allemande lefts. Sometimes it could be amusing. My friend Craig was paired up with a girl he disliked, and he refused to let her touch him. He was wiry and athletic, and would execute amazing jumps and dodges to elude her, but Mrs. Emerson finally put a stop to that.

We had been working on the same routines for what seemed like an eternity, when it was announced that the class was going to dance for some kind of event at another location.

I can't recall the specifics, but I knew that I wasn't going to do it. I had already complained to my dad about the dancing, and he agreed with me that it was ridiculous, so when I came home that day, full of outrage, and explained the situation, it didn't take much persuasion to get him to write a note for me. I never saw the contents of that note, but I was officially excused from the event. Everyone else had to go. On that day, the rest of my class boarded a yellow bus to hell, while I retired to a comfortable seat in the office, and read *The Food of the Gods* by H. G. Wells. It felt great to know that I had bucked the system. Maybe it was possible to maintain one's personal integrity once in a while, even against overwhelming odds.

The strict ban on boy-girl relationships began to lift in the fifth grade, and by the next year some kids were actually "going steady." I had been shifted to another class again, and now my friends, Mike, Tommy, Phillip, and Conn were in a bungalow with Mrs. Seaman. I was in a classroom with the same group of kids that I had known in the first grade. There were also a few new faces, but that just meant a wider circle of potential friends for me. The class was still divided into different learning levels for some subjects, and I was now in the advanced group for mathematics. This was referred to as the "new math," and was a so-called innovation in education from a think tank known as the School Mathematics Study Group, or S.M.S.G. Some of us weren't impressed with it, substituting the words "some mad scientist goofed" as the true meaning of the acronym. I was not convinced that understanding points, lines, rays, and planes would be of much value in any of my future endeavors. One of the other kids in that group was Farley, the superb lyricist. He was extremely intelligent, and I think that he was serious about learning, but he also had a pleasantly caustic sense of humor. We became very good friends very quickly and spent a lot of time together in and out of school.

Although neither of us was yet prepared to acquire a girlfriend, we were both very interested and quite well informed about sex. We had an ambiguous relationship with three girls in the class, Laura, Cindy, and Nikki, which involved teasing and a bit of flirting. Some of the gals were developing a well-upholstered look which elicited comments and whispers among the guys. And then there was the sudden and mysterious gathering of all of the girls in our class for a presentation in the auditorium, from which the boys were summarily excluded. We were given no information about what the girls would be doing, and when they returned, they were extremely secretive. Farley and I had a good idea of what it was all about, but we wanted confirmation and details. At recess, we managed to corner Laura, Cindy, and Nikki on the playground. We cajoled them into admitting that they had seen a film about the reproductive cycle, and the specifics of "becoming a woman." Farley and I already knew what that meant, and were eager to find out which girls in our class had graduated to womanhood. A few were sporting nicely filled bras, and there was a need for information on this as well, specifically regarding authenticity. We were all having a good time with the subject, the girls gradually giving us bits of data and making us work for it, Farley and I feeling triumphant with each little admission. There was something particularly amusing about having such an illicit conference with young ladies in Girl Scout uniforms, but soon the bell rang and we had to return to class.

Evidently, the conversation was not over. The girls sent us a note asking if we would like to have another "discussion." We were thrilled with the idea and responded in the affirmative. We managed to arrange a get together after school, and ended up sitting on the low branches of a big walnut tree in one of the vacant lots in Park Estates. The "discussion" picked up right where we had left off, but aside from the few hints and teases that the girls provided, there was not much substance to our discourse. However, it was still exciting enough to keep us in the tree for quite a while. When I finally got home, I was a few minutes late for dinner, and my dad was angry. He kept grilling me about where I had been, and didn't seem to believe that Farley and I had merely been talking to some girls. Finally my mom intervened, "It's not important – let's just eat now. Everything's getting cold." Farley and I managed to have a few more discussions with our informants, but they degenerated into the typical "who likes who" speculations that were common with our other classmates. We never got all of the inside dope that we were after, but the fact that we had actually talked about matters sexual with girls our age was significant. Now we knew that they were thinking about the same things that we were thinking about.

Amid all of the shenanigans of my elementary school years there were some serious moments, and one in particular stands out as being especially significant. It was a very minor incident, and I'm sure that the other parties involved forgot about it within minutes, but it has always lingered in my memory and colored my perception of human relationships. We were playing softball, and it was my turn to bat. I hated softball because I was not good at it, but I managed to muddle through. My classmates were very tolerant of my lack of ability, and often would cheer me on without sarcasm or irony. There were several instances when my puny base hit turned into a home run because of missed throws and catches, and we all thought that was funny and cool. On this particular day, I struck the ball and ran. The short stop picked it up and threw to the kid at first base, who happened to be a very good friend of mine. The ball and I arrived at almost the same time. I thought that I had made it, but my friend screamed, "You're out!" I really didn't care all that much, but believing in fair play, I turned to him and calmly said, "I really think I was safe because . . ."

"You're out!" He was angry at being challenged, but I just wanted to be heard.

"But . . ."

He took a few steps toward me. "You're out! Get out!"

I had seen kids get into arguments like this many times, so it wasn't a complete surprise, but this wasn't just an argument. He seemed to actually hate me for questioning his judgment, and he had to win. I was so surprised at his fury that I couldn't respond. Had our previous relationship suddenly been eradicated by a stupid softball game? It was an extremely depressing possibility. My initial confusion quickly became dejection, and I turned away. As I walked back I heard him yell, "You weren't even close! What an ortho!" I went behind the backstop and sat down. A few tears leaked out of my eyes as I pondered the transitory nature of what passed for friendship among preadolescent boys. I certainly didn't feel like getting back into the game. I just needed some time to regain my composure, and to figure out what had happened. I was completely immersed in my misery when a girl sat down next to me. This was totally unexpected. I had been nursing a secret crush on her for some time, but we had never engaged in an actual conversation. Somehow she had known how I was feeling, and had taken it upon herself to alleviate my distress. We talked for a bit, and my spirits began to lift. She seemed to understand me, and was sympathetic to my sensitivity. After a while she stood up and went back to the game. I felt much better, and could think more clearly. I realized that, once again, I would need to adjust to some harsh realities, but I also knew that there were at least a few people in the world with compassion and insight. I learned a lot that day, and now I hated softball more than ever.

# 11

## On Our Own Recognizance

By the fourth grade we were no longer little kids. We had graduated, at least in our own minds, to simply "kids." We were now riding bikes, so we had mobility, and we were unsupervised, so we had autonomy. Daylight hours after school and on weekends were ours as long as we didn't get into trouble, which really meant "as long as we didn't get caught." We had enough pocket change to stop at Tastee-freeze or Bob's Big Boy to have a burger, fries, and a coke for lunch, which made us feel quite urbane. Although we engaged in the outdoor activities common to children our age, Mike and I often collaborated on projects which catered to our thirst for sedition. These projects usually began with a perfectly innocent interest in something, like my dad's tape recorder. I had noticed it in the study, where both he and my mom had their desks. The study was the most overtly adult room in the house, and the tape recorder was obviously no toy. It was a large, impressive looking, reel to reel Wollensak, which we rechristened as the "Swollen Sack." I asked my dad about it, and he somewhat reluctantly gave me a tutorial. I immediately began recording monster movies. When I showed Mike the recorder and played some of what I had recorded, we both agreed that monster movie soundtracks were not very interesting. But the recorder had possibilities, and sooner or later we would figure out how to exploit them.

One morning we were meticulously organizing our plans for the day.

"What do you wanna do?"

"I dunno. What do YOU wanna do?"

"I dunno. Wanna mess with the tape recorder?"

"Mmm . . . yeah, I guess."

We had noticed that there were two speeds on the recorder, and started to experiment with speeding up and slowing down our voices. Then we realized that we could use a record player, which had three speeds, and the Wollensak together, to slow songs down or speed them up. But that wasn't good enough. Mike's dad also had a similar tape recorder, so one day we got the two of them together, and recorded a burp, then by slowing it down, re-recording, and slowing that down, over and over again, we had about two minutes of something that sounded like throbbing African drums. Next we took a Beatle record and sped it up until it lasted for a few incoherent seconds. We were proud of our results, and started dialing random phone numbers, and when someone answered, we would play one of the recordings. Crank calls were a favorite pastime, so this was nothing new, but the combination of the tape recorders and the phone looked promising. We were just getting started.

The Beatles were hugely popular, so we decided to create fake Beatle interviews. We would make up stupid questions which could be answered by specific lyrics from their songs. We played these for our parents, who thought that the results were clever, but looking for a wider audience, we again picked up the phone. Some people would listen for awhile, but most were annoyed, so we decided to try a different angle. The biggest problem for us was that we couldn't hear the other person on the line very well, because the earpiece had to be held next to the Wollensak speaker. Mike was great with electronics, and he figured out how to take the phone apart and wire a large speaker to the earpiece. Now we had a speaker phone. Not only could we have an audience for the entire conversation, we could also record it. Armed with this new technology, we scoured the phonebook for people with unfortunate last names, and proceeded to harass them. Our favorite was a gentleman named Clifford Sexy, who must have been plagued by idiots like us.

"Hello,"

"Is this Mr. Sexy?"

"Yes,"

"How sexy are you?"

"Why don't you kids get your minds out of the gutter?!" He would snarl, and then hang up. We would make other calls and come back to Clifford ten or fifteen minutes later with the recording, and, of course, he would hang up again. I began to feel a bit of sympathy for Mr. Sexy, but finally concluded that he should have exercised some common sense and changed his name.

Sometimes our ambitions exceeded our abilities. This was the case when we tried to bug the room of Mike's older sister. We worked on it all day, with a hidden microphone and sneaky wires going out of the window, but we couldn't quite pull it off. I doubt that we had any real reason for doing this, except for the technical challenge, and the clandestine nature of the enterprise. We continued to experiment off and on, and once bought a pair of inexpensive walkie-talkies. This was another of those items that initially seemed incredibly exciting. We would walk around the neighborhood reporting to each other, but after a while it became painfully obvious that there was not much to report. The range for these devices was not great, so we decided to see if we could extend it. Mike managed to hook up his walkie-talkie to the TV antenna on the top of his house, and we set a contact time for early evening. At the appointed hour I was sitting on my front porch, about a mile away. Sure enough, I could hear him very faintly through the static. The experiment was a success, but so what? The walkie-talkies ended up gathering dust in our closets.

We enjoyed doing things like climbing over fences and barriers to get down into the drainage ditch behind Park Estates. We would take gunny sacks with us, and catch toads and the occasional lizard. These would be turned loose in the garden upon our victorious return. As far as I was concerned, anything involving reptiles or amphibians was worthwhile. Kites also engaged our interest for a while. We could buy cheap paper kites and string at Woolworths. Getting the kite aloft was easy, and we wanted to see how high it could go. We ran it out to the end of an entire spool of string, but it wasn't enough, so we dispatched Mike's younger brother to Woolworths for more string. Three spools took it very high, but now we wanted it so high that we couldn't see it. We sent for more string, and after a couple of additional spools, we finally achieved our goal – we could no longer see the kite. Again, the experiment was a success, but ultimately not as satisfying as we had hoped. Maybe someone in a passing plane would see it, but that was all. We craved better opportunities for genuine sabotage.

We weren't actively looking for these opportunities every day, but there were moments of inspiration which we simply couldn't ignore. One of these involved a product called "Fizzies." Fizzies were tablets like Alka-Seltzer, which would fizz when dropped in water. They came in various fruit flavors and colors, and were meant as a cheap substitute for soft drinks. We had tried them, and found the resulting beverage rather revolting, but the fizzing process itself was neat. One day we were at Woolworths looking at the aquariums full of goldfish, when the idea of popping Fizzies into the fish tank presented itself. It was simply too good to resist. We went to another store and bought a couple of packages of lime Fizzies. We took out all of the tablets, and casually re-entered the Woolworths, heading toward the fish tank, and watching for adults. When the coast was clear, we dropped all of tablets into the tank, watched the water start to turn bubbly and green, and then quickly made our escape through the mall, laughing all the way. We never saw the fruit of our labors, but scenarios that we imagined kept us entertained all afternoon.

The mall behind Mike's house was always beckoning. We stumbled across some photos that had been torn out of magazines in the parking lot one morning. They were startling black and white images of completely naked women, totally unlike the carefully posed, color babes in *Playboy*. We traced them back to a dumpster behind the Tire Center, and found some issues of the nudist magazine, *Sunshine and Health*. We had never seen full frontal nudity before and it was very provocative. We stood there flipping through the pages for some time, tearing out a few particularly erotic pictures for future reference. We were well hidden from prying eyes back there, but there was a huge parking lot full of cars right around the corner of the building. Suddenly our mission was obvious. We had been selected by fate to present these glorious nudes to the public. We cautiously started meandering through the rows of automobiles, ripping out choice pics, and placing them in the side mirrors or on the windshields behind the wipers. It was a big job, and no doubt some of our handiwork was being discovered even as we were finishing up. This was another situation where we reveled in the anticipated reactions of our victims. I could picture Dad and family approaching the car after some serious shopping, and the outrage and embarrassment when Sonny pulled the photo off the windshield and said, "Dad, what is this?" It was good, clean fun.

Many stores sold inexpensive items for kids, such as soap bubble kits, balloons, and pea shooters. The pea shooter was a classic – a colorful plastic tube about eight inches long which came with a small bag of Wonder Target Peas for a grand total of ten cents. The package advocated a safe approach to pea shooting, such as utilizing the enclosed paper target, but no All-American boy was going to be taken in by such nonsense. Mike and I had tried pea shooters, and had been less than satisfied with the results. The peas were a tight fit within the tube, and it was hard to shoot more than one at a time. We looked around for a better bullet, and finally came up with dried white beans, which worked much better than peas. A large bag of beans kept us stocked with ammo for a long time, despite the fact that we had become quite adept at "machine-gunning" huge mouthfuls of them at one go. The beans went farther and much faster than peas, creating a satisfying scattergun effect which was the bane of some of the neighborhood animals. We became so committed to shooting beans that we walked over to Horace Green and Sons hardware store, and searched out chrome tubes to replace our plastic shooters. I have no idea what these tubes were originally designed to do, but they were absolutely perfect for our needs. Having that chrome shooter made me feel the same pride that a professional pool player must feel when he steps up to the table with a custom cue.

Now we were well equipped, but for what? We couldn't just walk around shooting beans at people – that would be too risky. But . . . we might be able to ride around shooting beans at people. That was it! We could blitz in on our bikes, blast away, and blitz out! We were fast and skillful riders on streets, sidewalks, grass, you name it. Mobile tactical assault – take no prisoners! We got on our bikes, equipped with our shooters and plenty of beans, heading for the gigantic Lakewood Mall several miles away. The mall was a labyrinth of walkways and parking areas, providing excellent opportunities for ambush and escape. We cruised along Lakewood Boulevard, which led directly to our destination, at a very close proximity to the moving cars on our left. The traffic slowed down for a red light, and a car ahead of me swerved a bit to the right, crowding my passage. I took a mouthful of beans, aimed at his right side windows, and blasted him as I passed, creating a loud and satisfying racket as the projectiles bounced off of the glass. We were ahead of him when the light turned green, but he would soon catch up. We rode through the intersection on the crosswalk, and hopped the curb to the sidewalk. As the car caught up to us, we simply made a u-turn on the pavement, and zipped around the corner, out of reach. After that it was easy to find an alternate route through the neighborhood that would eventually get us to the mall.

Once we arrived, we began looking for potential targets. We were handicapped by limited range, as the beans would only cover about fifteen feet with any velocity, and, fortunately for all involved, their impact was not great enough to do any physical damage. We were limited to harassment, which was exactly what we wanted, so an unsuspecting victim was best. Mike spotted a man on a bench who was reading a newspaper. The paper was held high enough to obscure his head and upper body, but the pants and shoes looked expensive. He never saw us coming, and Mike machine gunned about twenty beans into the newspaper, which rattled and bounced all over the place. He immediately jumped to his feet, but we were already out of reach. We glanced back to see him picking up a bean. He didn't appear to understand what had happened, but we were confident that he would eventually figure it out, and that our window of opportunity was limited. We spent about an hour selecting and spraying cars and people, then decided it was time to go. Sooner or later someone would notify security or the police, and we didn't want to take that chance. Arrested for assault with a pea shooter? No, thank you!

We also devised an excellent ambush technique on the quiet street in front of my house. My parents had purchased trash barrels made of some type of fiberboard. Instead of having an attached handle, there was a two by four inch piece cut out near the top of the barrel on each side, perfect for lifting and carrying. It was also perfect for shooting beans. The barrels were left on the curb every week, and after they had been emptied, we could each climb into one, slide the lid on, and be ready to do some serious sniping. Luckily for us, the barrels were usually pretty clean. We didn't have plastic trash bags then, but we did have a garbage disposal unit in the kitchen sink, so all of the food scraps were chopped up and washed away. The trash barrels were just big enough for us to be reasonably comfortable for a short time, and they didn't smell too bad. We would wait for a car to cruise by, and spray the metal hub caps with a shower of beans, creating a loud clatter which we hoped would startle the occupants. Sometimes a car would screech to a stop, and we would have to stifle our laughter until it was moving again. We never got caught, but the amusement value of the beans was diminishing.

Most of our fads seemed to last for a couple of weeks, and then we'd get bored and shift our attention elsewhere. Again, I hasten to point out that we weren't creating trouble all of the time. We would also spend hours at the beach, either body surfing or riding the waves with our Styrofoam belly boards. We swam in the pool at my parent's house, played games like Yahtzee and Stratego, tossed a Frisbee around, and even played tackle football with a bunch of other neighborhood kids. But the so-called misbehavior was our stock in trade.

Sometimes I would collaborate with other friends on mischief, but these ventures didn't always work out as planned. My pal Jerry lived nearby in the messiest house I ever saw. The outside wasn't bad, but inside it was chaos. There were piles of books, magazines, and newspapers, clothes strewn everywhere, dirty dishes in and around the sink, and all manner of disorganized clutter in every room. I recall being there once after their cat had given birth to several kittens. We could hear the kittens squeaking, but could not find them. I didn't necessarily mind the mess, but it was amazing to me that people could live this way. Jerry didn't seem to mind either. He certainly wasn't being forced to make his bed or clean up his room. He had a cool three level tree house in his back yard, which was as ramshackle as the rest of the place. The third level was very high, and precarious enough to make it exciting. We would sometimes get up there with water balloons, and toss them down at their collie, who dodged them with ease.

Jerry also had a pigeon coop, a big messy thing made of wood and chicken wire that housed an unknown number of birds. As Halloween approached, we decided to collect the pigeon eggs and use them for tricks when we didn't get treats.

When the big night arrived, we had around a dozen ready to go. They were small, about half the size of a chicken egg, so it was decided that I would carry them in the chest pocket of my black pull-over windbreaker. This pocket was big enough for the eggs, and it had a Velcro flap to seal them in. We put on our masks, grabbed our candy bags, and joined dozens of kids roaming the streets of Park Estates. We went to quite a few houses, and collected a substantial amount of candy without incident. It seemed that all of the adults had stayed home to hand out treats, and no one was giving us an excuse to use our eggs, which was what we really wanted to do. The porches were becoming more congested as kids jostled to get their goodies. We approached another house behind a group of four or five costumed trick- or- treaters, and stood behind them in a close knit group as one rang the doorbell. The door opened to darkness, and then a masked figure jumped at us shouting, "Boo!" As the kids in front of us recoiled in surprise, one of them backed into me and crushed the eggs. I could feel the cool dampness starting to soak through my shirt, as the owner of the house laughed, took off his mask, and started handing out candy. I tentatively opened the pocket, and felt around to see if any of the eggs were intact, because I desperately wanted revenge, but they were all smashed. When I told Jerry what had happened, he thought it was funny. I was so angry and uncomfortable that I wanted to punch him, but instead I went home. It was, objectively speaking, a perfect example of poetic justice, but the only lesson that I learned was not to carry eggs in a pocket.

I don't recall when we started having sleepovers, but by the time I was ten or eleven they had become a common practice. Sometimes Mike and I would buy a bunch of candy and RC Cola, and spend Friday or Saturday night under a tent in his back yard. We would stay up late and maybe sneak out of the yard and ramble around the streets a bit, finally conking out at around one or two o'clock. By the time we got to the sixth grade, we were having "slumber parties" with five or six friends. We rotated between several houses, including mine, Tom's, and that of a new friend named Steve Baker. On this particular night we were at Tom's. His mom made us a tasty dinner, and we ate outside, then as darkness fell, we roasted marshmallows in the fire pit and ate them with chocolate and graham crackers. We got the sleeping bags out at around nine or ten, spread them out in the living room, and started to settle in, waiting for the parents to retire. Once we were sure that they were out of the picture, it was time to get moving. We had already selected our target, and purchased our supplies, which were hidden outside. The lights went out, and we very quietly stepped into the cool night air, carefully closing the door and making sure that it was unlocked so we could get back in later. It was around one in the morning, and the neighborhood was peaceful and silent. The streetlights dimly illuminated houses and parked cars, leaving dark shadowy areas where they couldn't penetrate. Everything was perfect. We were ready.

Our mission, of course, was to "toilet paper" the house of one of the girls that we knew. This involved draping toilet paper all over the house and yard. It was both harassment and homage built into one decisive act. We would never waste our time on someone we had no interest in, but the nature of that interest was not clearly stated, leaving the victim flattered on the one hand, but annoyed at having to clean up on the other. And cleaning up streaming yards of toilet paper soaked with morning dew was not so easy. The quality of the job was important. We needed to get the streamers high into the trees and onto the roof. Creative touches were also employed, like wrapping the paper around posts and bushes. We had pride in our ability to create a masterpiece, as long as we were uninterrupted, and we had the manpower to get a lot done in a relatively short time. All of us had expertise, and we were unrivaled as a team.

We walked to the house, which was only a few blocks away, discussing our plans as quietly as possible, and feeling anxious whenever a backyard dog would bark. We had ten or twelve rolls of paper between us, enough for comprehensive coverage. Everyone spread out around the house and began working. The trickiest tasks were throwing the rolls into trees and onto the roof. Sometimes they would get caught in branches or rain gutters, and we would lose valuable ammunition. Sometimes they would thump against something, and we would be concerned that the noise might awaken the inhabitants. It was genuine espionage, with all the requisite thrills and chills.

We had been on the job for about twenty minutes and things were looking very good. The hallmark of excellence in toilet papering was density, and we were in the process of achieving excellent coverage, when there was a noise from behind the gate leading to the back yard. Everyone froze. A harsh voice called out,"Alright, you boys – git!"

It was every man for himself, as we dropped our remaining rolls and sprinted down the sidewalk, hearts pounding. We raced back the way we had come, only slowing down when we were close to home base. We were panting from our exertions, but it was beginning to sink in that we had escaped, and suddenly we were laughing and trying not to make too much noise at the same time. It had been an excellent little adventure, and as we re-entered Tom's house, we recounted it in great detail, perhaps embellishing it a bit, and generally enjoying the hell out of the whole thing. In the morning, my mom came over to pick me up, along with Steve and Conn, and our sleeping bags, etc. We passed the house that had been last night's target on the way out of Tom's neighborhood, and silently marveled at our handiwork. It had been a terrific night!

There was not really much overt maliciousness in our little stunts. Most of them were calculated to annoy, but not to cause any real harm to anyone, and in that sense they were all kind of stupidly innocent. We bought Wham-o boomerangs and learned that they could actually do some serious damage, but never threw them at other kids or animals. Other toys like the water rocket, which was filled with water, then pumped full of air and launched, were also potentially dangerous, but we would only pump them up to the breaking point and fire them into the air, not at each other. We had BB guns and pellet guns, and sometimes we would shoot at sparrows, but not often, and we never shot at human targets. We would ride our bikes a little too far and a little too fast, eat more candy than we should have, and try to stay out past dinner time, just to test boundaries. When my friends and I would leave Minnie Gant without permission at lunch time, to bike home for a grilled cheese sandwich, it was as much to find out if we could get away with it, as it was for the food itself.

On the last day of the sixth grade, I went home with Farley, and we got out our boomerangs and threw them around in the little park by his house. That night, I stayed over with Mike and we made a few crank calls to girls that we liked and to girls that we didn't like. We also stayed up late and ate a lot of candy, speculating as to what might be lurking ahead in junior high school. Feeling slightly older, a tad more grown up, as though some kind of subtle milestone had been reached, I had an indistinct impression that I was still regarded as a good kid by most of the adults in my world, and that I had gotten through elementary school relatively unscathed. Of course, the fact that I had never been caught doing anything outrageously inappropriate weighed heavily in my favor, but even if I had been apprehended, I doubt that I would have labeled a juvenile delinquent. There were a few truly bad kids in the neighborhood who had been caught stealing high ticket items, and committing serious vandalism, for whom that designation might have been appropriate, but I wasn't one of them. Yet.

# 12

## Matinee Madness

My obsession with horror and science fiction movies continued unabated. The monster magazines that I bought kept me well informed about films that featured mutants, vampires, space creatures, giant bugs, blobs, dragons, and other cinematic marvels. I wanted to see them all. I was diligent in checking the movie section of the paper, because the Saturday Matinees for kids often featured horror and science fiction films from the Fifties and early Sixties as well as current ones, and I wanted to catch up on everything that I had missed. We had a subscription to *TV Guide*, and I would go through the entire schedule for the week as soon as it arrived, looking for new thrillers and old favorites. I sometimes organized large groups of kids from school to meet at a theatre on the weekend for a particularly promising double feature like *The Time Travelers* and *The Crawling Hand*. Some of the films were absolute junk, but it really didn't matter. Even though the film itself was mind-numbingly stupid, we all were thoroughly entertained when *The Crawling Hand* met its grisly demise in an alley full of hungry cats.

My parents didn't know much about the content of these movies, but sometimes the title alone was enough to raise a red flag. *Blood Feast* looked very promising to me, judging from the ad in the paper. "Nothing so appalling in the annals of horror," it promised, "You'll recoil and shudder as you witness the slaughter and mutilation of nubile young girls."

"You're not going to witness any such thing", my dad declared, "and that's that!"

These kinds of low budget films were sold with great posters and sensational previews that promised much more than they could ever deliver, but even though I understood this, I still had to check them all out. Most of my friends weren't averse to seeing such features from time to time, but few were as committed as I was. There was one kid, however, who was always game for a horror flick, good or bad, and that was Steve Baker.

Steve lived directly behind me, and after we became friends, I would sometimes just climb over the fence to his back yard rather than walk all the way around the block to his front door. The family moved to Park Estates when we were both in the fifth grade, and although we weren't in the same class, we gradually fell into the habit of walking home together from the bus stop after school. I can't recall exactly how or when we became friends, but by the sixth grade we were spending a lot of time with each other. They had a pool and we had a pool, so there were many warm weekends of swimming and playing "Marco Polo," and climbing over the fence to switch pools or bomb each other with water balloons.

Steve was an interesting kid, and although I liked him, I sometimes found myself observing his behavior with the clinical detachment of a scientist watching a rat in a maze. He was small and frail, a perfect target for bullies, and was nicknamed "Peanut" and "Mouse." I'm sure that he hated the nicknames, but he put up with them. What was fascinating about Steve was his attitude. Despite being a skinny little guy, he was anything but meek. He had a talent for badgering and annoying people, and when picked on, he would launch a verbal retaliation that was sometimes very effective. A friend of mine told me a story that illustrated this perfectly. The two of them were being harassed by some tough kids after school, and Steve pointed out that they couldn't be very tough if they picked on the smallest kids in the class. The thugs were so embarrassed that they retreated.

He would sometimes single out a particular person for abuse, on some basis that I never understood. I can recall one instance when he selected a girl who was slightly overweight, and started referring to her as "Fat Girl." He would casually greet her by saying, "Hi, Fat Girl," in a ridiculously cheerful voice. She could easily have thrashed him, and frequently responded with caustic remarks of her own, but ultimately this ongoing harassment became a kind of routine that they both appeared to enjoy. They were never friends, but there seemed to be a perverse affection between them. There was another girl named Carla who also captured his attention. He started calling her "Bobo," and then coined the phrase, "Bobo needs sex," which he would utter every time he saw her. Sometimes he would say it in a friendly tone, sometimes questioningly, sometimes aggressively, but it was always the same phrase. He would also pass notes to her with the same three words and nothing else. Carla was obviously baffled by this, and would often ask what he was talking about. He might respond by saying, "Sex is what Bobo needs," but he never disclosed anything that would alleviate her bewilderment.

Steve was more circumspect in dealing with male classmates. He was seldom inclined to start anything, but he was regularly teased by bigger kids, and would not hesitate to respond in kind. Most of the time this didn't result in a physical altercation, but once in a while he would goad his opponent into taking a poke at him. One punch was enough to stop Steve in his tracks. I think that the majority of people who picked on him felt guilty about it, because he was so obviously unable to defend himself. I was sometimes surprised that he wasn't thoroughly beaten up, but as far as I know, he was only hit on one or two occasions. What frequently saved him was the fact that his remarks were often genuinely funny. Once in a while he would shout out something during class, in response to whatever the teacher was talking about. We would laugh, and he would be admonished, but it was usually evident that the teacher was amused as well. Even though we were good friends, he would sometimes lose his temper with me. It didn't happen often, but when it did, I could never figure out what had set him off. He would become caustic and insulting, and I couldn't reason with him, so I would just leave him alone. The next day he would call as if nothing had happened. I don't know why I never became angry with him, because I wouldn't have tolerated that kind of thing from anyone else. Maybe I admired his defiant attitude in the face of overwhelming odds.

Another thing that I liked about Steve was that he was almost always willing to engage in any ridiculous endeavor, regardless of difficulty or danger. Although we all climbed down into the drainage ditches to catch toads, he was the only one who would crawl with me through the tunnels that lead out to the curbside drains and other runoff channels. These were dark and creepy, and small enough in diameter so that it was almost impossible to turn around. Once we were in, we were obligated to go the distance, and we did. It was quite a triumph to return to our point of origin with only damp clothes and scraped knees, knowing that we had explored the deepest secret recesses below our streets and houses. This spirit of exploration and discovery extended to our habit of following strangers. If we spotted someone who looked significantly different from the kids or adults in our neighborhood, we would tail him, using all of the tricks and techniques that we had picked up from TV shows like *The Man from UNCLE*. We once tailed a guy who was dressed like a riverboat gambler for what seemed like miles. We called him the Dude, and despite our diligence, learned absolutely nothing about him. One of our other quarries was a gentleman with a turban. We codenamed him the Hindude, and had a great time shadowing his movements, but again came up short on vital intelligence concerning his ultimate destination or intentions. It didn't matter – we just enjoyed feeling like secret agents for an hour or two.

When we weren't crawling through drainpipes or following suspicious characters, we would walk to Paul's Market or the Rexall Pharmacy, foraging for monster magazines and comics. It was exciting to discover a cool new issue of *Fantastic Monsters* or *Castle of Frankenstein*, and find out about monster films that were in production, or read about how the effects were done in a movie that we had already seen. There were also monster cards and other related items to purchase. One day, we came across Ugly Stickers, which were beautifully rendered illustrations of cartoonishly grotesque creatures in full color. The gimmick was that you could peel off the paper backing and use the now exposed adhesive surface to "stick" them wherever they would cause the most trouble. It was an opportunity that we could not ignore, and soon they were in bathroom stalls in school, on bikes and cars, and any other appropriate target that we could find. The manufacturers of Ugly Stickers had done their job well – the adhesive did not surrender easily!

Steve had a way of carrying his obsessions to an extreme. If he was excited about something, he was all in. If he disliked something, he had to express himself. This was the case with the Monkees. Steve was a devoted fan of rock music, and was extremely knowledgeable on the subject. He bought magazines like *Tiger Beat* and *16*, which, although designed for young girls, offered articles on pop stars and musicians. We had watched *A*

*Hard Day's Night* several times at local theatres, and had loved it. When Steve found out that there was going to be a TV program of a similar nature, he was initially skeptical, but then Monkees tunes started hitting the charts as solid pop hits, and he became intrigued. We watched the first episode of their show on the new RCA color TV that Steve's dad had just purchased, and were instantly captivated. I believe that we watched the entire first season together. Steve bought every record, and played them constantly. He purchased any magazine that had a Monkees related item. He was starting to take guitar lessons in order to play their songs. So it was a crisis when he found out that the Monkees didn't play their own instruments on the recordings. He didn't know that this was a standard industry practice at the time, and that it was true for many other groups that we admired. Steve took it as a personal affront, feeling that he had been deliberately deceived by a gang of gutless, no-talent frauds. He destroyed all of the magazines with Monkees material that he had collected, and started to smash the records, but it wasn't enough. He needed something that would truly convey the intensity of his contempt. To this end, he hung a string from the ceiling light in his room, and attached one of the despised records to it. The record had been melted and warped into a badly rippled disk. Just below that dangled the album cover from the Monkees first album, which had a group shot of their faces. Attached to the bottom of the album cover was a long thin box that had once contained a roll of Reynolds Wrap. It looked like a goofy Monkees mobile, and it was, but as Steve explained, there was an interactive component as well.

"You wanna be first?" he asked.

"First to what?"

"To spit in their faces," he replied.

"I think you should be first!"

"I think you're right!" He launched a glob at Davy Jones,

and the project was officially christened. I now understood that the box below the album cover was intended to be a trough which would protect his carpet from dripping expectorate. He had really thought this through, and obviously expected a lot of spitting.

Over the next few weeks, it was mandatory for any kid entering Steve's room to spew something onto that photo. Soon we were chewing up things like Oreos and pizza in order to express ourselves more eloquently. The album cover looked disgusting, and the "trough" was worse. I don't know how his mom put up with it, but one day I arrived and it was gone. Steve didn't seem to mind – he had exorcised his demons and was ready to move on.

We were soon to begin the seventh grade. I was not as excited as I might have been, because half of my friends from Minnie Gant were going to Stanford Junior High, and I, along with all of the other Park Estates kids, was going to Hill. I wasn't sure what would happen, but it would be a drag if I lost contact with all of the friends that I had spent so much time with over the last few years. Nonetheless, the summer had started out promisingly enough. We had sleepovers, pool parties, and a couple of trips to Disneyland and the Pike. On a typically scorching mid-August afternoon, I came home from Steve's house to find my parents glued to the TV screen. They were watching shots of burning buildings and crowds of people smashing store windows and cars. It looked like chaos, and it certainly wasn't a movie. I asked what the program was, and my mom said, "Be quiet," without looking up. I was aware of a newscaster's voice talking about rioting, and how the police were trying to control the situation. He mentioned Watts, a place that I had never heard of. "Where is Watts?" I asked.

"Not very far from here," my dad said tersely.

"Be quiet – I want to hear this!" My mom was pretty tense.

I sat down and started watching what turned out to be a special broadcast about riots going on in Watts, which was about fifteen miles from our house. I wasn't sure what to make of it, and the fact that I was watching the action on TV made it more like a show than an actual event. My parents were taking it very seriously, however. Later that day, I saw my dad cleaning the pistol that he kept hidden most of the time. "Is it really that serious?" I asked.

"I don't know," he said. "Sometimes these things spread. Maybe the police will get it under control. You better stick around the house until this is over."

"OK," I replied, but I wasn't very frightened. It was like the day that President Kennedy had been shot, when we came in from recess, and our teacher, Mrs. Knowles, was crying. I felt guilty because it didn't seem to affect me much, but I wasn't going to tell anyone. When Steve came over the next morning, we talked my mom into letting us walk up to Paul's market. The streets seemed quieter than usual, and there was a hint of smoke in the air, diluting the sunshine with a very slight rusty tinge. Things went on like this for several days, and then the riots were over and everyone relaxed, but the summer had taken a strange turn.

About a week later, I was studying the movie section of the paper. There was a small ad for a Saturday matinee on the coming weekend. It was for a movie called *Monsters Crash the Pajama Party*, which sounded utterly ridiculous. The ad boasted that the film was not in 3D, and that the monsters actually came out of the screen and into the audience. I was absolutely certain that it wasn't true . . . but still . . . what if it was? What if there was some new technical innovation that could perform such a miracle? I knew that I would probably be disappointed. I had been burned before by ads with similarly unbelievable claims. When I ordered "Horrible Herman, the Frightening Asiatic Insect" from the back pages of *Famous Monsters*, I was admittedly younger and more gullible, but I really believed that I would be getting something fabulous – "a horrible looking type of insect with a fur body, scaly head, red eyes, and twin tendrils coming out of the head. You can make him lift his head and move around! Looks absolutely alive!" I waited for what seemed like months for it to arrive, checking the mail every day until I finally gave up.

I had almost forgotten about Herman when my mom came out to the pool and handed me a package. I tore it open and found a small lime green box with a printed label that said "Horrible Herman" on the top. When I opened the box, I dropped from the highest pinnacle of anticipation to the deepest disappointment in a heartbeat. Herman was the stupidest looking thing that I had ever seen. It was a vaguely bug-shaped piece of plaster with glitter and feathers glued on, and two little red objects for eyes. There was a flat piece of tin stuck at an angle on the underside that went through the bottom of the box, which could be jiggled with a finger to make Herman look "absolutely alive." I was so angry that I tore Herman out of his box and hurled him across the pool deck. I had learned a valuable lesson, sort of.

I called Steve and told him about the matinee, and while we were on the phone he found the ad in his paper, and agreed that *Monsters Crash the Pajama Party* looked pretty dumb. However, the promise of monsters emerging from the movie screen had to be investigated. We couldn't imagine how they were going to pull this off. Steve's cousin, a tough little guy named Richard, was visiting, and he decided to come along. Richard was a couple of years older than we were. He worked out with weights and rode motorcycles in the desert. We considered him a cool guy, and were glad to have him join us.

On Saturday, Steve's mom dropped us off at the Lakewood Theatre. The Lakewood was a medium sized venue, and did not have the elaborate Art Deco styling of the theatres on Ocean Boulevard or Atlantic Avenue. It didn't have a balcony either, so it wasn't a favored make-out spot for young couples, but the Lakewood was the most kid friendly theatre in town. They had "Kiddee Matinees" almost every week, and they left us alone unless someone threw a firecracker. The only adults in the house were either in the ticket booth or behind the snack bar, so once we were settled into our seats in the dark, we felt like we owned the place.

When we arrived, there was already a long line that wrapped around the side of the building. This was typical for a matinee, and didn't bother us a bit. We joked around, and got Richard to tell us about his motorcycle while we waited. A group of younger boys near us was having a conversation about monsters coming out of the screen. One said that his big brother had seen it before, and that it was "real scary." Another said that he didn't believe it. It was obvious that no one cared about the movie itself, we just wanted to see what was going to happen. The line began to move forward, and we slowly made our way to the ticket booth, bought our tickets for fifty cents apiece, and entered the theatre. The snack bar was crowded, but I didn't mind because the top shelf of the display case contained an elaborate diorama with prehistoric animals and cave men. I was in love with it. The dinosaurs were waxy plastic figures from the J.H. Miller Company, and I had been trying to find them for my collection since the first grade. Every time I went to the Lakewood, I would try to persuade whoever was behind the counter to sell them to me, but to no avail. I figured that it was just a matter of time, so when it was finally my turn to be served, I tried again. Again my offer was refused, so I paid for the candy, and waited for Richard and Steve. There weren't many seats left, but we finally found some good ones in the center section, about six rows from the screen near the right aisle. The lights went out, and we watched the cartoon, the previews, and the first movie. This was a double feature, which was typical for a matinee. I don't remember what that first film was, but it couldn't have been very impressive. There was a fair amount of conversation while it was on. The audience was restless. We were all waiting for the monsters.

The first film ended, the lights came up, and we went back to the lobby for intermission. I checked out the dinosaurs again, and we bought some more candy, and then headed back to our seats for the main attraction. Again the lights went down. This time the audience was quiet. We were ready for anything. Well . . . anything except this. It was terrible! Everything about the production was crude and amateurish. There were girls running around in short nightgowns, people wearing obvious monster masks, a mad scientist, a guy in a gorilla suit, and some teenage boys who seemed to be trying to rescue the girls. The "acting" was abysmal. Sometimes it appeared that the film was intended to be a comedy, but it was hard to tell. There were immediate "boos" and shouts from the seats around us. Flattened popcorn cartons flew. Gradually things calmed down as we waited for the moment when "Fantastic Horrorvision" would kick in and we would see the "actual, flesh and blood monsters" come out of the movie screen. Finally, the mad scientist's invention created an opportunity for the monsters to leave the film and invade the audience. We were now seeing a night sky with flashing lightening. Nothing else was happening. There were no monsters emerging from the screen, and we were starting to get restless. A low buzz of conversation was starting to escalate. Just as some of the kids were beginning to shout protests, a figure did emerge, but it wasn't from the screen, it was from the darkness at the end of the aisle. Some guy in a werewolf mask that matched the one in the movie was tentatively advancing into the dim light, waving his arms around and growling. I glanced at the other aisle and saw another masked figure lurching around. The auditorium was quiet. Deep in our hearts, we had all known that it would be a hoax. Steve was sitting to my left. I heard him mutter something, and then he jumped to his feet and yelled, "Let's get 'em!"

It was as if we had all been waiting for this moment. We jumped out of our seats and converged on the wolf man, punching and kicking furiously. Kids were piling onto his back and trying to grab his arms and legs while he flailed around. I managed to get a couple of good shots at his belly before being crowded out by others, and I saw Richard nail him in the face at least once. The poor guy was attempting to make it to the exit, and struggling for every foot. There were so many boys on and around him that he was obscured from view, but we could hear him yelling above their voices, "Damn it you kids, get off!" He was really running the gauntlet, and the pent up resentment of a hundred adrenalin fueled young males was being channeled into those punches and kicks. When he reached the door, it was suddenly over. There were a couple of final licks and then the wolf man, tattered and limping, managed to exit the auditorium.

The melee had only lasted a few minutes. We gradually stumbled back to our seats as our heart rates began to return to normal, and sat quietly for the rest of the show. Steve looked shell-shocked, so astonished at the turn of events that he had been immobilized. We were surprised when the film continued to roll to its conclusion, and even more surprised when the lights went on and no one came in to give us a lecture or take names. We had expected consequences, but evidently none were forthcoming. Most of the kids seemed tired and slightly dazed. As Steve and Richard and I slowly walked up the aisle, I wondered what had happened to the wolf man. I started to look for blood spots on the floor, but then decided not to. I didn't want to know. Richard was excited. He had really enjoyed himself. I felt the residue of exhilaration, but it was tempered by something that I couldn't define. Maybe the experience had been slightly scary after all. As we left the lobby and walked out into the bright afternoon, my uneasiness began to dissipate. We laughed and embellished our exploits. It had been a riot - Steve had caused a riot. Or had he? Would it have happened anyway? And who was the guy in the mask? I tried to imagine the story from the wolf man's point of view. I doubted that it would be anything like the story that we would tell our friends.

# 13

# Everything Right is Wrong Again

On the first day of seventh grade, I arrived at school alone. Walter B. Hill Junior High was much larger then Minnie Gant and much more densely populated. Five or six elementary schools had funneled their graduates into Hill, and all of us were being directed to the auditorium for an orientation assembly. I was searching for friends to sit with, and not finding any. This was partially due to the fact that many of the kids from Gant were attending Stanford Junior High because of "zoning." Some of my best buddies, including Mike, were not going to be by my side for this new adventure. It was another example of the callousness and indifference of adult authority. Kids who were good friends and companions could simply be removed from my world by some arbitrary turn of events. Suddenly, someone was "moving away," and that person was never heard from again. It reminded me of what I had heard about life in Communist Russia.

The auditorium was noisy, and newly minted seventh graders were filling seats and milling around in the aisles. As I felt myself being absorbed into the crowd, I heard someone call my name and saw an extended arm waving me over. With a sense of relief, I made my way through the traffic to find out who it could be. "Hey Bill, how ya doin?" a voice said. It took me a couple of seconds to recognize Jim Thresh, a kid I had known in my first few years at Gant. I remembered him from those days as a very cool kid, and could recall hanging out with him on overcast mornings, as we watched the construction of a new building on the school grounds. For reasons unknown to me, his parents had taken him out of Gant and enrolled him in a different school. It had been almost four years, and I was surprised that he had remembered me, but glad to see him again. I sat down next to him, and we had a good time jeering at the teachers and administrators who gravely informed us of our impending fate. As it turned out, Jim would become one of my best friends, and a frequent collaborator in sabotage.

It was soon evident that junior high would be very different from elementary school. For one thing, everyone seemed to be better dressed. Guys were wearing slacks and collared shirts or v-neck sweaters. Some wore Levis, but they looked new and pressed. The Levis had to be "decked," which meant removing the belt loops and the stitching on the back pockets. Desert boots were the shoe of choice for most of us. Trench coats were also a hot item. Sometimes it only took one person to start a trend. In eighth grade, one of my childhood friends showed up with baggy, low slung Levi cords, a striped short sleeved T shirt, and moccasins. His hair was longer than average, and his eyes looked like he had been swimming in highly chlorinated water. At first he was teased about the new look, but gradually more and more kids adopted his style. It was important to stay abreast of these developments

Many of the girls were obviously hell-bent on becoming women. Some of the ones that I had known at Gant had undergone amazing transformations. Girl Scout uniforms and pony tails had been replaced by fashionable attire and brand new hairstyles. They were all wearing nylons and many had makeup. Some were sporting substantial curves and trying to emphasize them. While I appreciated their efforts, I also felt that the indigenous female population had somehow achieved a sudden leap to a much higher level of maturity. They were certainly attractive, but I had a feeling that it might be risky to mess with them. They were not as easy to read as the guys, just as my mom was not as easy to read as my dad. It was a little intimidating.

Some of the boys could also be intimidating, and even though I was all of twelve years old, I soon found out that some of the rules that I had learned as a little kid still applied. Big kids were still to be considered dangerous until proven otherwise. A week or two after school started, I was standing in line to purchase ice cream. It was lunch period, and the area around me was swarming with other students. A boy suddenly crowded in front of me, and I immediately told him to get lost. He said something, and then a much larger guy behind me gave me a hard push and I fell. As I started to get up, a man who was obviously some kind of monitor intervened. He acted as if my behavior was an affront to the sanctity of the ice cream line, and wanted specific details about our altercation. He questioned the big kid first.

"Alright – what's this all about?"

"Well, Mr. Renz, I saw this guy," he pointed at me, "take a swing at my friend there, so I pushed him. I was just protecting my friend."

"OK, I get it," replied Renz. He turned and glared at me, clearly not interested in hearing my side of the story. "Come on, let's go."

"But that's not true," I said. "That guy's lying."

He gave me another hard look. I felt as if he had some kind of grudge against me, but I had never seen him before. By the time he got me to the administrative office, I was fuming. He took me to Mrs. Hanson, one of the vice principals, and related a wholly fictitious narrative to her before giving me another scowl and departing. She didn't seem to share his attitude toward me, and asked what had happened. I told her my story as calmly as I could, but at the end I said, "Those guys lied, and he didn't even care. He was already mad at me, like I started it. What's his problem?" She could tell that I was angry, and I guess she believed me, because she said something about how difficult it is to tell who is at fault in these situations. I didn't buy it, but it was useless to keep talking, so I held my tongue. She had actually been very understanding, and I had no complaint about how she had handled things, but Renz was a dick. If this was standard operating procedure at Hill, I was in for a rough ride. As it turned out, Renz , or "Gomez " as he was called behind his back, was known to be a dick. I made it a point to avoid him in the future.

We all quickly adjusted to having different classes with different teachers. Most of mine were pretty good, but there were a few that were tedious. I was happy to be in an art class for the first time, which I considered a luxury. There were not many specific lessons, but since I was free to draw whatever I wanted for fifty minutes, I didn't mind at all. As an added benefit, other kids started to realize that I had some skills in this area, and I began to get requests for commissioned work. Sometimes it was lettering the name of a girlfriend on a notebook for the princely sum of thirty cents, or creating an image for someone's project. My friend from Gant, Conn, hired me to draw a hillbilly shack complete with wash tubs, cracked windows, dangling doors, and an outhouse, for his language assignment, which required him to label everything in French. I also did a few custom illustrations on butcher paper for textbook covers, featuring Batman, and a series of renderings of Hell's Angels on motorcycles.

The only class that I actively disliked was Physical Education. Actually, I was fine with everything except the team sports. I didn't mind taking a lap, push-ups, calisthenics, or exercise in general. When we had to address the issue of physical fitness through a series of specific exercises, I was the school champ at holding the frog stand. But football, basketball, baseball – forget it. Fortunately, our teacher was an overweight slob who didn't supervise the games. He would organize the teams, assign a couple of students to referee, and then retire to his office. Most of the time I would simply refuse to participate, and chill out on the grass, watching the other kids argue over first downs and penalties. When I was designated as a ref, I was equally indifferent. On the rare occasions when my judgment was solicited, I would tell the players to figure it out for themselves. Sometimes they got angry about it, but I didn't care. I felt that I had arrived at an appropriate solution to an annoying problem.

Social hierarchies had been somewhat vague in elementary school, but they quickly became clearly defined in junior high. There was a group of "socialites" which consisted of athletic boys and attractive girls, and a group of "lowriders" which consisted of "bad" boys and attractive girls. The only substantial difference between the two, as far as I could tell, was the footwear. The lowriders almost always wore black leather shoes with pointy toes, which we referred to as "pixie feet." The strata between these two groups consisted of friends who were bound together by common interests, like music, or dope. Of course there was some overlap and shifting around within these groups and quite a few students who didn't fit into any of them. I had a couple of friends in each, which protected me from harassment, but didn't gain me membership. As far as I was concerned it was a good arrangement.

Rumors and gossip suggested that the socialites and bad

boys might be doing exciting things, like drinking, smoking, fighting, and having sex. I did a little field research with a couple of my lowrider friends, hanging out with them before one of the dances while they drank beer through a straw and smoked. I hated the taste of beer, and they didn't seem to like it much themselves, but they dutifully slurped down a couple of cans and claimed to have achieved a good buzz. They seemed to believe that the buzz was essential for maximum enjoyment of the evening's activities, but the ritual seemed stupid to me. Hoping to gain better insight, I invited them over after school and gave them some leftover cans of beer, and the few packs of cigarettes that remained from the days when my parents had smoked. We went out to the pool deck and I watched them drink and smoke for a while. It didn't look like they were having a good time, and I concluded that drinking and smoking were lame.

As far as fighting was concerned, I felt like I could fight if it was required, but it wasn't something that I would choose to do for pleasure. However, the possibility that kids my own age could be engaging in sexual activities was intriguing. I listened attentively when the subject was being discussed, but most of what I heard sounded less than credible. I was certain that some of the guys were making up stories to enhance their reputations, because I had learned from Hugh Hefner that it was uncool to boast about one's conquests. There were a few girls who were talked about, but I didn't know them personally. Maybe there was some fire behind all the smoke. Hopefully, I would find out.

As a junior high school student, I received good grades, did my homework, got along with almost everyone, and rarely found myself in trouble. But that was only because I had become slightly more cunning, at least most of the time. I still had authority issues, and now I was required to deal with an army of different teachers instead of just one. I had no problems with adults who knew their stuff, played fair, and had a sense of humor, but I could not respect an instructor who was deficient in any of those areas. I enjoyed testing some of them by attaching unsolicited drawings to the projects that we were given. In science class, we had to compile an organized notebook for each different unit of study, such as chemistry, biology, the human body, etc. The notebooks were turned in at the conclusion of the unit, and I always did a full color cover illustration as an added "bonus." For example, the chemistry notebook featured an obviously mad scientist drooling over his freshly assembled monster, amidst bubbling beakers and test tubes. The science teacher was a young guy, full of enthusiasm, who seemed to get a kick out of my drawings, so I liked him.

Mrs. Campbell, an English teacher, was another case entirely. She was also young, but seemed tense and humorless. Conn enjoyed baiting her by referring to her as Mrs. Camel. Any time we were required to write her name on some official school document, he would alter her name to Camel, and soon I started to follow his example. Initially she believed us when we told her it was merely a typo, but after a while, she became extremely annoyed. There wasn't much that she could do, especially when we would cheerfully correct it every time she took issue with us. Finally she chose to ignore our efforts, even though we kept it going all year. When we had writing assignments, I tried to find ways to provoke her. Once I included the word "damn" in an essay just to see how she would respond. She gave me an F and a note – "This is completely unacceptable." It was exactly what I had expected, and I took it home and showed it to my dad, who agreed that she ought to relax a bit.

For our big final project we were required to create our own magazines, and allowed to choose the subject matter ourselves. It was a perfect opportunity to do something outrageous, so I gave it some thought and came up with the first and only issue of *Sadist*. I spent a lot of time and energy on it because I wanted it to be excellent in every respect, except for the content. I did illustrations, articles on instruments of torture, ads for useful devices, even a short story and a poem. The cover was a full color rendering of one of my old standbys, a severed head, but this one was hanging from a hook, with the point projecting out of the mouth, and executed with a much higher level of skill than my grade school efforts. Most of my male classmates thought it was excellent, while the girls were alternately disgusted and horrified. When I turned it in, I anticipated another F, but Mrs. Camel surprised me with an A. I think that she was smart enough to realize that she had gotten the last laugh, and I was forced to admit to myself that maybe I had misjudged her.

Mike and I had retired from bean shooting, and instead came up with something that was an actual weapon. This was the Zambezi dart gun. It employed the same beloved chrome tubes that we had used for the beans, but replaced the beans with genuine Zambezi darts which we made ourselves. This involved fabricating a paper cone and trimming it to fit into the tube. Then we would insert a straight pin through the end of the cone with the point protruding. A drop of airplane glue on the inside of the cone held the pin in place. It was admittedly tedious work, but worth it. The real problem with the Zambezi dart gun was finding something to shoot. Targets were ok, but not very thrilling. So, one day I brought mine to school, planning on lodging a dart in someone's posterior. I went to my first class, and took my assigned seat next to a friend in the last row. He asked me to demonstrate the dart gun, and I decided to oblige him then and there. He drew a crude target on a piece of notebook paper, and held it up with both hands. I inserted a dart into the tube, aimed and fired. The dart struck one of his fingers and he let out a muffled yelp and dropped the target. The teacher looked in our direction for a few seconds as we assumed studious poses, and then returned to her lecture. I had drawn a bit of blood, and my friend became my ex-friend for a couple of days. I chalked the accident up to performance anxiety and put my chrome tube away. The Zambezi dart gun was a bit too dangerous for my taste.

When I was in the eighth grade, I received an interesting Christmas gift from my parents. It was an army green crew neck sweat shirt with the word "bullshirt" silkscreened in large white capital letters across the back. I thought it was great, and started wearing it everywhere. My parents enjoyed my enthusiasm, and my friends thought it was cool. I expected to get some interesting responses with it, and was surprised, and a little disappointed, when I didn't. Somebody finally dared me to wear it to school, and I eagerly accepted. My mom was slightly concerned when she saw me wearing the shirt the next morning at breakfast.

"You're not wearing that to school, are you?"

"Sure, mom, why not?" What could she say? She and my dad had bought it for me, and there had not been any stipulations as to specific locations or occasions for which it might be inappropriate. I could tell by the look on her face that she was trying to decide whether to intervene.

"Hmmmm . . . well, don't blame me if you get in trouble."

"OK," I replied. I almost reminded her that she and my dad had set the wheels in motion when they had given me the shirt, but decided it was better not to. She could become testy when provoked.

When I arrived at school, the shirt got quite a bit of attention, and approval, from my classmates. I had expected this, and I enjoyed it, but I was much more interested in reactions from teachers and administrators. At the beginning of each class, I made sure that the instructor got a good view of my back as I found my desk, hoping for a challenge, ready to say, "What do you mean?" with an innocent expression on my face. Not one of them took the bait. The shirt aroused no public controversy whatsoever, and public controversy was exactly what I craved. At the end of the day, I was alternately disappointed and impressed. The thought crossed my mind that perhaps I was not as clever as I thought I was, but it was quickly dispelled by the unerring common sense inherent in ninety nine percent of adolescent boys.

Jim Thresh and I were spending a lot of time together both in and out of school, and as I mentioned earlier, he was often a partner in crime. Jim had an uncanny knack for laying his hands on useful items. One morning, he showed up at school with a little round box. It was only about one and a half inches in diameter, and the label on the top was hard to read. I took a closer squint at it and made out the words, "itching powder" in poorly printed red lettering. I was immediately interested. The product and the packaging had the same wonderful sleazy aura that made the Nu-Pike so attractive to me, so I was enthusiastic, but a little skeptical.

"Does it really work?" I asked dubiously.

"Yeah – it works! Try some!" Before I could object, he dusted the back of my neck. And it did work! It was not a mild itch - I had to wash the area with soap and water to get some relief. Jim had made his point, so now it was time to share the joy. The bell rang, and off to class we went. When we entered the room, quite a few students were already seated, so it was easy to meander to our desks and drop some powder down the collar of a guy that we did not care for. As the lesson began, we watched this poor soul as he gradually became more and more uncomfortable. Soon he was squirming around, and trying awkwardly to reach an unreachable spot on his upper back. After about ten minutes, he abruptly got up and left the room. It was extremely unusual for a student to walk out of class without asking permission, and it created an air of uneasiness among the students and a lot of low-volume conversation. The teacher seemed surprised, but soon resumed speaking. Our victim did not return, and Jim and I realized that we had struck gold.

We used the powder several times during the next few days, with great success. I persuaded Jim to let me borrow it, and showed it to Conn. A quick demonstration on the back of his hand convinced him of its effectiveness. We then took it to our English class on a day when we were scheduled to go to the library. At the library we were free to roam around the shelves and browse. It was an excellent opportunity because other students, male and female, would be sitting at tables with their heads bent over books. When we arrived, the librarian spoke briefly and then left us to our own devices, so Conn and I began our undertaking – to itchify at least one student at every table.

We tried to look casual, and spotted for each other to make sure no one suspected anything, but after all, even Sherlock Holmes probably would not have considered the possibility of itching powder. One by one, we sprinkled them, always behind the collar, and one by one they started scratching. By this time, we had used up most of the powder, and we had to work very hard to keep from laughing. Our victims did not appear to notice that they weren't alone in their misery, each trying to cope with the problem in his or her own way. A couple of them walked around, squirming and embarrassed looking. Others remained seated, obviously in distress. One guy was muttering what sounded like some very naughty words, and finally decided to make his exit. Conn and I were, of course, delighted, and Jim was extremely amused when I reported back to him. I asked him if he could get some more of the magic powder, and he said he'd try, but it never happened. I looked for it in toy and novelty stores, even in the tiny ads in comic books, but I couldn't find it either. Since then I have often had that same experience – just when I find a great product, it is suddenly no longer available.

Jim and I were in the same Spanish class with Mr. Pursley. He was a decent instructor, but Jim was having a difficult time memorizing the inane dialogues that were purportedly teaching us important lessons, like how to say, "I don't like meatballs." We sometimes had to recite these dialogues for a grade, but were commonly given multiple choice written tests as well. Because I did well on these tests, we decided that I would "help" Jim by providing him with the answers. We were a couple of rows apart, so I devised a system for cheating. I would pretend to scratch my left ear, and the number of fingers that I used would convey whether the correct response was a, b, c, or d. Mr. Pursley always recited the questions from his desk, which was in front of the room on the right, so he couldn't see what I was doing. This worked extremely well for the entire year, and boosted Jim's grades considerably. He was happy, his parents were happy, and I felt good about helping a friend.

There were times when I was a spectator to misbehavior rather than a contributor. Conn was a great one for silently disrupting our algebra class with elaborate pantomimes involving the repositioning of an enormous genital organ. He would convincingly convey the huge size and substantial weight of the thing, as if he were desperately trying to achieve some degree of physical comfort at his desk. The humor was greatly enhanced by his ability to elude discovery by Mrs. Amer, our teacher, and still keep an audience of five or six in quiet hysterics. In addition to Conn, there was another kid named Roger in the class who was willing to provide entertainment, but in a different way. His modus operandi was to be grossly abusive to someone, and then form an opinion of that person's merits based on the response. I first met him in the seventh grade in P.E. I don't remember how it started, but he said some extremely rude things to me, and I fired right back. He was not a fighter, so the interchanges remained verbal, and after a while they started to get humorous. We were trying to outdo each other with the most elaborate insults that we could contrive. Ultimately, we were cracking up too much to remain enemies, and a truce was declared. Although I usually found him entertaining, he cultivated an image of aloof cynicism which could be very annoying. He thought that he looked cool smoking a cigarette.

Roger's antics in the class were sometimes hard to watch, because although they were funny, they were also cruel. He had a habit of picking on kids who were essentially defenseless, and targeting their obvious vulnerabilities. He sat behind one such kid, and constantly taunted him, sometimes tearing up pieces of paper and sticking them in his hair. The poor guy didn't realize what was going on most of the time, but when he did, it didn't seem to bother him. He just ignored Roger, which was probably the best way to deal with him. But another student in the class didn't handle the bullying quite as well. Roger began referring to him as the "handsome devil" for the most obvious of reasons. Then he began calling him H.D. for short. He would tease H.D. about preposterous romantic exploits, and the kid would say nothing, but it was evident that he was upset. One day, to my horror, Mrs. Amer addressed him as H.D. He looked stricken, but instead of realizing that she had gone way too far, she smiled and said, "Well, isn't that what your friends call you?" I couldn't believe that she could be so insensitive. I was willing to shoot beans at people or make them itch, but this was just heartless. I felt sorry for H.D., and wondered what it would be like to be subjected to such abuse. I decided that Roger was not such a great guy. And I had nothing but contempt for Mrs. Amer.

Junior high was a transitional period for many kids, and I was no exception. Most of us were caught in an awkward position between accepting that we were children and believing that we were adults. The most obvious incursion of adulthood into my life was an involuntary attraction to women. I say women, because this was different from the childhood crushes of my elementary school years. I was fully informed about the pleasures and possibilities of sex, and my interest was being refined into an almost obsessive focus by the combined efforts of the Freudian triad. My id demanded it, my ego was figuring out how to get it, and my superego was considering what the consequences might be if I got it. The whole team was on board. Once again, I found that I was collecting and analyzing data which might lead to a better understanding of this new and unexplored terrain. It wasn't just a world of kids and grownups anymore. I now had females to contend with.

Jim had a girlfriend named Mitzi, who was forever trying to get him to spend more time with her. She started enlisting me in various schemes to get him over to her house on the weekends. I did my best to help out, without compromising my friendship with Jim, and she appreciated my efforts. We would talk on the phone almost every night, and gradually became good friends. Sometimes we would see movies together or go for long walks and discuss her situation. She and Jim had a pattern of breaking up and reconciling every week or two, so there was always a lot to talk about. Although she didn't realize it, Mitzi was providing me with all kinds of insight into the intricacies of the female mind. She would concoct Machiavellian ploys to bend Jim to her will, and I was impressed by her single mindedness. I realized that Jim had no idea of how thoroughly he was being manipulated.

I had never considered it before, but now I was learning that a girl could be as subversive as I was, perhaps more so. Although I was engaged in a personal battle against adult domination, it was sporadic and reactive. She was actively and covertly pursuing a specific goal, like James Bond or Napoleon Solo. When I considered the possibility that I might be dealing with girls like Mitzi in the future, it seemed wise to be prepared.

Another girl named Michelle had a crush on a friend of mine, so she questioned me thoroughly on every detail of his dossier. I was happy to oblige, and although nothing came of it, we also ended up being very close. Michelle was similar to Mitzi in that she was constantly concocting elaborate plans to connect with a particular guy, but different in that the particular guy changed with alarming frequency. She trusted me enough to reveal a willingness to take risks that I would never have considered. Michelle was a "bad" girl in the sense that she ditched school, lied often and outrageously, smoked dope, and hung out at the beach (and probably elsewhere) with older guys, but she was actually very sweet. She sat next to me in geometry class, and would copy my answers during the tests. When she would call, which was often, my dad would answer the phone, and hand it off to me, commenting on the sultry quality of her voice. Once he asked me, "Who is that girl?" I told him that she was in some of my classes at school, and he just said, "Wow!" It was startling to me that my dad would take notice of a fourteen year old girl, and underscored my growing suspicion that women might be harder to handle than parents or bullies. I was beginning to doubt that a handy lizard would be of much help to me in the coming years.

As I progressed through the seventh and eighth grades, I maintained the outward trappings of a model student. I made both scholarship and citizenship each semester, and produced artwork for a yearbook cover and a talent show backdrop, among other things. I even played my bagpipes, reluctantly, in a talent show. Once in a while I got into a little trouble, but nothing major. When a student sent a postcard to our math class from Hawaii, the teacher asked us if we would like her to read it to us. I said, "No, thank you," and was sent outside, but I didn't mind. Really – who sends a postcard to the math class? One of the male vice principals would sometimes hassle me because I was cultivating the ghost of a moustache. There was a point where it became semi-legitimate, and he told me it had to go. It went, but not without some resentment.

When we took a battery of aptitude tests, there was one that involved visualizing various polygonal shapes from diagrams. I completed it in about fifteen minutes, and handed it in. The teacher told me that I couldn't possibly have finished, and that I had better go back and take another look at it. I found his remark insulting, but simply told him that I was sure that it would be fine, so he reluctantly accepted it. When we got the results a few weeks later, I had received a ninety nine percent score. He was very surprised and I was very smug, although I didn't allow myself to swagger. It was OK with me if they all thought that I was just another well behaved rule follower, but inside I still felt like I was waging a secret war with a bunch of adults who foolishly believed that they had everything under control.

# 14

## Crimes and Misdemeanors

It was that all-American sport, shoplifting, that started the ball rolling. I may have appeared to be an (almost) model citizen at school, but on my off hours I was developing a taste for anarchy. It began when I entered the seventh grade. One day after school, Jim and I had gotten off of the bus at my stop in order to purchase some candy at Paul's Market. Actually, it was no longer Paul's, as he had sold out to a couple of Asian gentlemen. I missed Paul and Al, the cashier, because they had always been very friendly. Al had once given me a whole quarter for my birthday – two comics and a candy bar in those days. The new owners were certainly good folks, but they were much more reserved, and I felt no loyalty to them. Jim and I made our purchases, and when we were outside, he pulled a Hostess Fruit Pie out of nowhere, and laughed. "Five finger discount," he said. I was impressed, and decided to try it out myself. I had seen other kids swipe things before, and had never been tempted, but this time it was different. I didn't perceive it as dishonest, but rather as another bit of sabotage against the adult world. Besides, it was fun. The next time we went to Paul's, I slipped a Snickers bar into my jacket pocket, and then purchased several other items without incident. I had concluded that the key to avoiding suspicion when stealing was either to buy something, or to ask the sales people questions, and it seemed to work. We continued to loot the place after school, and were never caught, but I believe that the owners wised up at some point, and just decided not to make an issue of it. They were Asian in a white, upper middle class neighborhood, and I'm sure that they didn't want any trouble.

Naturally, my success with small items at Paul's encouraged me to go after bigger game. Mike and I colluded to remove several items from the stores behind his house. Once we took a rolled poster of Steve McQueen on his motorcycle from Horace Green Hardware. I was on watch as Mike shoved the poster down his pants leg, and awkwardly hobbled out of the store. Another time we snatched an expensive jacket out of the Broadway. Eventually, the Broadway became my target of choice. I stole all kinds of clothes from them. My favorite gambit was to take several pairs of pants to a dressing room, usually Levi cords or 501s, and put on one pair under my own pants. Then I would emerge with the extras, find a sales clerk, and ask for help finding something that I knew they didn't have. When the clerk couldn't find it, I would say thanks and hand him the extra pants. It was always a lark at the time, but I was lucky. If I had ever gotten caught, it would have been a disaster. I knew a couple of kids who had been apprehended. They had impressed upon me the terror of facing irate store managers, angry parents, and sometimes the police, yet I remained undeterred. Chalk it up to the idiocy of youth.

Another activity that I thoroughly enjoyed was blowing things up. Firecrackers were illegal in California, but sometimes we got lucky and scored a few, smuggled in from Tijuana. We had always used them to destroy our plastic models when they became stale, but now we were much more creative. Our best innovation was the delayed fuse. We would get a pack of cigarettes from a machine when no one was watching, then light one up, tear off the filter, and attach the fuse of a firecracker to the unlit end. It would usually take about ten minutes to burn down to the fuse, and then "BLAM." With this system, we could plant our little bombs all over the Los Altos Shopping Center, and then kick back and watch the fun. We usually hid them in the large planters on the promenade that led through the mall, and then loitered casually outside Sav-on Drugs. When the crackers started going off, the shoppers naturally became jumpy and alarmed. Some would drop their bags, and a few actually ran. It was wonderful!

When we felt that the mall was no longer a safe place for us to indulge in pyrotechnics, we found other locations. There was a multi level parking lot near my house that had excellent acoustics, so one day we loaded it up with several firecrackers and a cherry bomb, then sat in the nearby park to enjoy the fruit of our labors. We had upgraded our explosives with Benson and Hedges cigarettes. They were advertised on TV as the" seven minute cigarette," but when they weren't actually being smoked, they would smolder for about twelve minutes before ignition. An older man was strolling past us when the first explosion sounded, and the reverb from the concrete structure greatly enhanced its volume. He turned to us and said, "Hear that, boys? That's a .38." As more firecrackers went off, he gave us a running commentary on firearms. When the cherry bomb blew, he exclaimed, "And a .45 - godammit – someone better call the cops!" Evidently someone had, because two black and whites soon arrived. We were already walking away as the police got out of their cars and began to investigate.

Our ability to create such mayhem was limited by the supply of explosives, and it was generally feast or famine. Sometimes we would go for months before Mike could get some from his cousin, and then we were very judicious in their deployment. Jim was another good source for crackers and cherry bombs, and he and I also used the delayed fuse technique. We would sneak out at around midnight, after our parents were in bed, and meet at a designated spot. Sometimes we would eat at the all night restaurant across Bellflower Boulevard while we planned our mission. Then we would set up the bombs at different houses in the neighborhood, placing them on porches and under windows. If we hustled, we could usually plant three or four, and each be home and in bed by the time that they started going off. The distant explosions were infinitely satisfying.

I loved rambling around at midnight. Although there was never much activity, it made me feel adventurous, as though I might stumble onto something special that couldn't be experienced in the daylight. The neighborhood was always extremely quiet, and most of the houses were dark. The air was usually cool and relaxing, and the limited illumination from the streetlights would cast unusual shadows everywhere.

On such a Friday night, Jim and I crossed Bellflower Boulevard at around one o'clock. During the day it was a very busy multi-lane thoroughfare, but at that hour there were no cars in sight, and we could dance all over the street. We entered a large field on the outer perimeter of the State College, and heard the faint strains of a solo electric organ in the distance, playing a familiar melody from an old black and white cartoon. As we moved across the field through the high grass, the music became louder, and clouds of ground fog came swirling up to our knees. We started running toward the music, but it suddenly ended, leaving us damp and out of breath. We never found out where the music had come from. The whole experience was simply a random confluence of unrelated elements, but the result was like a few moments in an episode of the Twilight Zone. It was exhilarating rather than frightening, however, and one of the few moments of my adolescence when I actually noted how good it was to be alive.

When we didn't have firecrackers, Jim and I found other ways to entertain ourselves. We would sometimes pick pomegranates from a tree at his house, and use them as ammunition. There was an alley in Park Estates that ran parallel to Bellflower. A low cinderblock wall separated the street from the alley. We would hide behind that wall in the dark, and hurl a pommie high into the air over the wall. It would either splatter on the street or nail a passing car. This was also a nocturnal activity, so there wasn't much traffic, but once in while we scored. On this particular occasion, we heard the distinctive sound of fruit on metal, along with a screech of brakes. We continued to enjoy ourselves, confident that we would remain undetected, but I soon noticed a pair of headlights at the far end of the alley. They were slowly heading in our direction, and then suddenly went out. We stood still for a few seconds, and then the soft sound of tires crunching on gravel reached our ears. "Run," yelled Jim, as he jumped the wall. I jumped it too, and started sprinting behind him down Bellflower.

We were pouring it on when I glanced behind me, and saw a large dark figure closing the distance. I knew that I couldn't outrun him, so I stupidly decided to stand and wait, ready for the worst. He didn't slow down or speak, smashing right into me and throwing me down in the street, yelling about his car. Now that he was close enough, I could see that he was not too much older than we were, but he was a big guy. I wasn't in a hurry to get up, so I let him curse as I surveyed my options. I noticed that Jim was walking back toward me. A true friend, he wasn't about to let me take all of the heat. The thought briefly crossed my mind that the two of us might be able to hold the dude off. But then I decided that the best thing to do was fess up and take the consequences. He had just about yelled himself out, when I said, "Sorry, man."

"That was a fucking stupid thing to do!"

"You're right, you're right. Really man, I'm sorry."

"You coulda caused a fucking accident."

"You're right. We really didn't think about that," I replied. He was quiet for minute as I finally got to my feet.

"Well, you caught us fair and square," I said, "Now what?"

He stared angrily at me for what seemed like a long time, and shot Jim a nasty look.

"You with this asshole?" he asked. Jim nodded. Another minute passed. The guy seemed to be weighing his options.

"Oh shit, come on," He indicated that we should follow him back to the alley. "Hell, I did some dumb shit stuff when I was a kid."

We followed him back up Bellflower and over the wall to his car, which was parked in the alley. Sure enough, there was a nice, big, juicy, red splotch on his windshield. We offered to clean it up, but he declined, and started to give us some final words of wisdom. Before he had said much of anything, he started laughing. "Shit, I sound like my old man. Get the hell out of here before I change my mind." We were happy to oblige. Again we had been lucky, but that put an end to hurling pommies.

Now we turn to smoke bombs. I don't remember who came up with them, but Mike and I would manufacture them sometimes when we couldn't get explosives. This involved wrapping tin foil around a pencil to create a long narrow tube. We would fill the tube with match heads, and then close the open end into a small aperture with a single head exposed. Upon ignition, a jet of thick grey smoke would come hissing out, forming a substantial and malodorous cloud. The smoke bombs were fun, but they were not very versatile. They were too big to use in the mall, and often failed to ignite with a delayed fuse. We did sometimes use them to create a fake UFO. We would cover a Frisbee with foil to make it look metallic, and then attach a smoker to the inside with tape. It took both of us to launch it – one to light the bomb, and one to throw the Frisbee. The smoke would trail out behind as it flew, and it actually looked pretty good around dusk. We would usually toss it across the street from a camouflaged position when a car went by. The sound of squealing tires was ample reward for our efforts.

I managed to avoid parental interference most of the time. As long as my dad didn't really know what we were up to, the firecrackers and smoke bombs were accepted with reluctance. But sometimes there were accidents. One evening when I was twelve or thirteen, I was cutting match heads for some bombs. I had purchased several boxes of match books, and had been trimming them with a wire cutter, which was much more effective than scissors. I would hold the match book over a large mixing bowl, and the heads would fall into the bowl as I cut them off. This process was taking place at a coffee table in the family room, while I sat on the floor. My dad was reading in his Eames chair, and uneasily glancing my way.

"So, what exactly are you doing?" he asked. He sounded suspicious, but not angry.

"I'm just making some smoke bombs," I replied, as if there were kids all over the country doing exactly the same thing. Maybe there were.

"This may not be the best place for that sort of thing," he said, but I could tell from his tone that he was too tired to make it a serious issue.

"Don't worry, it's OK. And besides, I'm almost done," He made a dismissive sound, and returned to his book.

The bowl was about half full, and I was close to

completion. There were enough match heads for around twenty bombs. I clipped another match book, and somehow the wire cutters set off one of the heads. I saw the flame as it fell into the bowl, and instantly there was a loud hissing accompanied by a huge cloud of smoke that billowed up to the ceiling. My dad jumped out of his chair, yelling, "Godammit!" as the cloud began to dissipate, leaving a sulphuric reek in the air.

"Get that crap out of here," he commanded. I started cleaning up as my mom entered the room.

"What's the matter?" she asked, beginning to notice traces of smoke and the smell of burnt matches. I quietly stowed my gear and left the room.

Jim made a beautiful ashtray for his father in one of the shop classes. It was evenly layered clear resin with a blue dye on top of each layer, neatly beveled and polished. When he showed it to me, I was knocked out by the professional quality of his work. Jim's parents were always friendly with me, but I felt that they treated him badly at times. His mom was always walking around the house in her one piece bathing suit, with dark glasses, high heeled sandals, and a drink in her hand. She would sometimes mention Jim's poor grades in an obnoxiously teasing manner, and his dad seemed very distant with him. I knew that Jim was hoping that he would like the ashtray. And he did – at least until he left his burning cigarette in it for a few seconds too long. The highly combustible resin suddenly responded to the cigarette with a blinding flash, and the ashtray vanished in an instant. As Jim told me the story, I wished that I could have been there to see it. His dad had been very upset, and took it as more evidence that Jim wasn't very bright, but I always preferred to believe that he had planned the whole thing.

Mike and I were becoming dangerously well informed

about gun powder. Mike had laboriously extracted black powder from hundreds of caps for one of our movies, so that we could film an explosion, and had figured out there were different types of powder, with different properties. We talked his father into buying some "smokeless" powder for us from the nearby Unimart store. I am still amazed that he was willing to do this, as it seems completely irresponsible, but nonetheless, he did. Maybe he was hoping that we would blow ourselves to hell. The smokeless powder wasn't entirely smokeless, but it opened up new vistas of opportunity for us.

The first thing that we did was to build a miniature cannon. This consisted of a short pipe with a screw on cap. We drilled a hole in the cap to accommodate a fuse from a firecracker, primed it with black powder for the explosive and smokeless for the propellant, and then sawed the head off of a thick bolt for a bullet. For a target, we set a galvanized trash can lid against the wooden shed in Mike's back yard, then positioned ourselves about ten feet away. I held the pipe, and Mike lit the fuse. There was a loud boom, and the bolt smashed through the trash can lid and embedded itself deep into the wall of the shed. We were staggered with the result of our experiment, and also intimidated. Maybe this was a bit too hazardous to mess with. The cannon was stowed in Mike's garage for the duration, as we turned to other, less risky applications.

Our next move was to build a miniature rocket car, using the smokeless powder as fuel. It was constructed with a simple metal frame of heavy wire which held a metal canister as the body and fuel container. Once again, a hole had been drilled in the top of the canister for the fuse. The tires were scavenged from a toy truck, and designed to spin freely on wire axels. The various components were soldered together for maximum durability, and the end result looked like a small, horizontal cylinder on wheels, We were confident that it would be spectacular as we took it out to the mall parking lot for a test spin. This was on a Sunday afternoon, so the huge lot was almost vacant because most of the stores were closed. Mike set the loaded car on the asphalt, allowing at least a hundred yards of turf for its first run, because we had no idea how far it would go. We lit the fuse and waited. At first nothing happened, and then there was a hissing sound that gradually increased in volume. The car abruptly took off, but it was out of control, flipping and veering all over the place. It managed to cover a good distance before the fuel ran out, but this was not the outcome that we had anticipated. So back to the drawing board we went.

We decided that the only way that we could make the car work properly was to run it on a guide wire. This required a fixture on the top of the canister through which we could run the wire, so we attached an inverted metal V frame, got some kite string for the guide wire, and tried again. The string had to be taut, and close enough to the ground so that the wheels made contact. We solved this problem by having me hold it at the launch point, while Mike's younger brother, Doug, held the other end. Once we had everything organized, Mike lit the fuse. Again, nothing happened, and then there was the hiss, and the thing blasted across the lot, straight and true, and fast! It raced toward Doug, showing no sign of slowing down, and at the last minute he yelled something, dropped the string, and got out of the way. The car did its tumbling routine again for a few seconds before burning out. This was more like it, but when we examined our little darling, we noticed that it was a mess. The metal V had been knocked off, the canister was dented, and one axel was bent. We had achieved our goal, but at what cost? Back to the drawing board again.

This time we abandoned the car concept altogether and settled on a rocket. It was simply the canister with two of the V frames on top for stability. We knew that we couldn't really launch it into the air – it was actually more like a jet propelled monorail. We stretched kite string across the parking lot, all the way from a telephone pole in the alley to a sign with a directional arrow at the Broadway loading dock. Again the fuse was lit, and we watched the now familiar prelude to take off. We had really packed in the powder this time, and when the rocket left its launch point, it was just a streak. And, it worked perfectly. Not only that, but it looked like it was going to make it all the way to the finish line! We were jubilant, until we heard the faint sound of breaking glass. Somehow, our rocket had crashed into the sign itself, shattering the glass and some of the light bulbs inside. At first we were surprised, but after examining the damage, we accepted it as an unexpected bonus, collected the remains of our rocket, and got out of there fast.

I loved the sound of breaking glass almost as much as I loved explosives, but there were not many opportunities to make such exquisite music. When I was younger, we would collect soda bottles from the vacant lots and building sites, but these were worth three cents apiece, and that was good money, so we kept them intact. Sometimes we would get lucky and find panes in the dumpsters behind stores in the mall, which were perfect for smashing. Mike and I found several large sheets of glass in the trash behind the Tire Center, and we had a great time busting them up. I didn't even mind a couple of sliced fingers. When we discovered the new construction areas at Long Beach State College, we hit the jackpot. The college was constantly being expanded, and we would periodically check it out, just to take advantage of any new developments. New dormitories were being built, so there were several large multilevel structures in progress. On Sundays there was no one around, so we combed through them. There were beer and liquor bottles all over the place, possibly from parties on

Saturday night. I picked one up, lobbed it over a wall, and was rewarded by the dulcet tones of glass on concrete. Mike and I collected a bunch of bottles, and had a great time throwing them high into the air and into the buildings. The distant sounds of crashing and shattering were symphonic. Many years later, when I heard Nick Lowe's song, *I Love the Sound of Breaking Glass*, I knew exactly what he was talking about.

When we had no pyrotechnical options, and there wasn't any glass to break, Mike and I would resort to less destructive ventures. One of our favorites was to buy a bunch of flashers from Horace Green Hardware, and share them with our neighbors. The flashers were little metal disks which would fit into any conventional light socket. We would walk around after dark and install them into outdoor garden floodlights, free of charge. The lights would then flash off and on at short intervals, creating a pleasantly psychedelic effect. Sometimes we would even replace the conventional bulbs with red or green ones. The flashers and bulbs were not expensive, so we could really create a festive environment for any house that had extensive outdoor lighting.

Steve Baker, the kid who had caused the matinee riot, was also a frequent partner in crime. He was not above doing some shoplifting or engaging in mindless destruction. We sometimes took records that we no longer liked, particularly Monkees forty fives, and threw them, or "hummed" them, like Frisbees. It was fun to watch them smash into pieces against the house across the street or in the street itself. We would sometimes go out in the early evening to throw a few eggs, water balloons, or firecrackers. Steve still had a habit of selecting specific targets based on highly subjective criteria which he never shared with me. Once he made his choice, he would focus all of his considerable energy on maliciousness.

This time he opted for a spiffy red El Camino belonging to the folks who lived across the street from my house. I didn't know anything about them, except that they didn't have kids, but Steve had decided the El Camino needed his particular brand of personal attention. I was not a participant in this vendetta, which involved the application of toothpaste, peanut butter, and eggs to the vehicle. Every time he struck, he would brag about it to me, and I began to worry that I might be blamed for his misdeeds. The El Camino was always parked across from my house, and after Steve's third or fourth attack, I started to wonder why it hadn't been stashed in a garage. Was a trap being set?

I talked the situation over with Mike, and we hatched a plan to write a fake notice to Steve, apprising him of legal action pending for his crimes against the car. We tried to make it look as professional as possible. Mike typed it up, and we forged a signature and sent it, addressed to Steve himself. We had no idea of what to expect, but I was not surprised when he called me several few days later. He told me that he had received the letter and confessed to his mom, but his mom had been a legal secretary, and his dad was a lawyer, so the illegitimacy of the document was quickly detected. Still, none of them knew who had sent it. I wrestled with my conscience for a short time, and finally decided to confess. Steve was more relieved than angry, and his parents were slightly amused, and glad that someone had ended his reign of terror. The vandalism ceased, and the owners of the El Camino never had a clue about the back story. Steve curtailed his destructive activities, but our friendship unraveled in the wake of the incident and we gradually drifted apart.

Conn was another excellent collaborator. He was extremely intelligent, and willing to put that intelligence to excellent use. One day he came over with an amazingly simple scheme to close down the Broadway elevators. He had noticed that the mechanism for opening and closing the doors was triggered by an electronic eye. The doors would not close until the eye registered that the space between them was clear. The eye itself was a little glass lens set inside the door frame, which could easily be covered with a cardboard disc and some double stick tape. We immediately set to work, cutting out several discs about the size of a quarter, and putting a small bit of the tape on each one. It was a short walk to the Broadway, only about twenty minutes, but we were so keyed up that it seemed to take us much longer to get there. When we arrived, we immediately entered and caught one of the elevators to the third floor. The store was pretty crowded, so we studied the situation for a while, in order to figure out how to apply the disc without being caught. Finally, Conn decided on a course of action. We got on the elevator and stood at the back. When it had descended to the second floor, we crowded out with the other passengers, and Conn just slapped the disk over the eye as he passed. It looked like he was merely trying to keep his balance while being jostled. We loitered around as if we were examining merchandise as the elevator began to fill up again. Someone pushed the button for the first floor and nothing happened. The button was pushed several times with no result. People started grumbling. A salesman was called over. A manager was called over. Conn and I were now just part of a group of spectators, waiting to see what would happen. Finally, a repairman showed up. We watched him as he got down on his knees and began to examine the doors inch by inch, and then discreetly departed, flushed with success.

Conn also discovered a way to make fake UFOs that was very clever. It required four plastic drinking straws, a plastic laundry bag, four birthday candles, and some scotch tape. One straw was inserted about an inch into another, creating a fifteen inch plastic tube. We made two of these, and then bound them together to create a cross. The laundry bag was attached with tape so that the straws would hold it open at the bottom, and the hole at the top for the coat hanger was sealed up. One birthday candle was attached with melted wax to each straw. When they were lit, the hot air would fill the bag, and it would ascend to the heavens. It was essentially a mini hot air balloon. When Conn explained it to me, I was not convinced that it would work. But we put it together, took it out to our driveway, and lit up the candles. I had to hold the bag up so that it wouldn't catch fire as it gradually inflated, and then, miraculously, it took off. We watched it as it drifted up and out of sight, wondering where it would go and who would see it. Beautiful! We later found that it was better to launch them after dark. The glow of the candles and their shifting reflections on the plastic bag looked very mysterious in the night sky.

There were certain occasions when it seemed appropriate to us to hang a dummy from one of the street lights. I don't remember what those occasions might have been, but I know we did this more than once, and with a sense of ceremony. Maybe it was Halloween. We would use some of my old clothes and stuff them with newspaper, using socks and gloves for the extremities. Shoes were too heavy because everything was held together with tape and staples. A paper bag for the head would finish it off, and we would hoist it aloft with a short rope and tie it off. These dummies looked pretty good at night, especially with the illumination of the lamp directly above the "head." We would leave them dangling, and by morning they would be gone.

Conn and I came up with another amazingly simple trick which produced magnificent results. We would soak a tennis ball with lighter fluid and light it on fire, and then kick it around in the street like a soccer ball. Of course, this took place after dark, so the ball looked like a little flaming meteor. With several friends involved, it was very entertaining to boot it back and forth for a while on a pleasant summer evening. We were so taken with the adaptability of lighter fluid, that it was only a matter of time before someone decided to soak the toes of his suede desert boots with it. We lit 'em up and watched him run around for a minute or two. All we could see were two blazing shoes romping around in the dark. It was hilarious! When the fluid had burned out of the suede, the fire started to dwindle, but we hosed the boots down anyway just to prevent singed toes.

Sometimes we were simply inspired to take advantage of the opportunity at hand. One day, Conn and I purchased a package of chocolate sandwich cookies at Paul's, and took the stairs up to the top of the multilevel parking complex across the street. We were soon bored with the cookies, and the view from three storeys up. What to do? Throw cookies at the folks who were unfortunate enough to come within range, of course. There were not too many viable targets, but we did our best. In most cases, the cookies smashed into the sidewalk and exploded into fragments, startling the unsuspecting victims, but I recall a beautiful strike on the gleaming pate of a bald gentleman. The cookie made hard contact, and fractured into several satellites which ricocheted into space at a high velocity. We ducked back just as he looked up and put his hand on the spot where he had been hit. It was stupid, and kind of mean-spirited, but funnier than hell.

How did we get away with all of this?

# 15

## The Picture Becomes Clearer

During my years at Hill Junior High, my dad and I settled into an uneasy détente punctuated by open conflicts. We had already had a few skirmishes, such as the one concerning the length of my hair. He had always insisted on my having a very short buzz cut, referred to back then as a "butch." This was common for young kids, but by the time I was in fifth or sixth grade, I wanted to have enough hair to comb. He griped about it, making comments about my "greaseball" friends, which seemed silly to me. All of my friends were neat and well groomed. This was another of those situations when I felt that he was being completely unreasonable. I didn't understand that it was really about his need to keep me under control. My mom once again intervened.

"Why are you making an issue out of this?" she asked him.

"I just don't like that look." was his reply.

"What look?"

"You know what I mean."

"Well, it's his hair. Why don't you just leave him alone? It won't hurt anything if his hair is a little longer."

My dad, in his usual reluctant fashion, allowed me to make my own decisions when it was time to visit the barber shop, but he couldn't resist making the occasional caustic remark. I was getting used to this behavior, and although I felt it was uncalled for, it wasn't a big deal. After all, I had prevailed.

As I got older, my use of the telephone began to grate on his nerves. By the time I entered junior high, I was often engaged in lengthy conversations concerning the burning issues common to middle school students. I would use the phone in the study during the evening, while my parents watched TV in the family room. The door would be closed to insure privacy, but sooner or later that door would open and my dad would begin his tirade. I couldn't understand why the fact that I was on the phone was so annoying to him. It wasn't the cost, because my calls were local, and it wasn't because he wanted to make a call. If that had been the case I would have gladly terminated my chat and handed him the receiver. I tried several times to get a reasonable explanation from him, but the best that he could do was, "There might be an emergency."

I asked if I could have my own phone. "No."

What if I paid for it myself? "No."

The only conclusion I could make was that he wanted an excuse to exert that damn parental authority, and yet he never forbade me to use the phone, or put an official time limit on my calls. Instead, he would badger me almost every night. Was he somehow enjoying the opportunity to harass me? I realized that I would have to endure his absurd conduct if I wanted to communicate with my friends via Ma Bell. I was now seeing a pattern in his behavior. If he was absolutely certain that he was right, he would not back off. And most of the time he was absolutely certain that he was right. But when he clearly couldn't muster anything close to a legitimate argument to support his position, he would mutter and grumble, then grudgingly retreat.

After I thought that the matter was closed, he would sometimes say something derogatory, just to remind me that he had made a concession against his better judgment. What I found strange about all of this was his reluctance to present an ultimatum, as if he derived some pleasure from ongoing disharmony. Years later, when I asked my mom if he had ever admitted to being wrong about anything, her reply was an emphatic, "No."

I have to give my mom credit for supporting me against my dad when he was being unreasonable. At the time, I simply believed that she was my ally, and I always appreciated her efforts on my behalf, but her interventions were probably sometimes calculated to undermine my dad's authoritarianism as well. She was never aggressive with him, but she had a way of making him slightly embarrassed about being so dogmatic, especially as he prided himself on being fair minded and logical. Sometimes her behavior smacked of insurrection. Although she knew that he hated the record *Big Girls Don't Cry*, she purchased it and played it. I don't recall any controversy, but I have no idea what was said behind closed doors. She was also more willing than my dad to take me and my friends to the beach or the movies, and she was very punctual. My mom and I got along well most of the time, but she had some quirks. Sometimes she would get upset about things that made no sense to me. I recall one night at dinner when she complained about our neighbors because they had left a big cardboard box along with the trash cans on the street in front of their house.

"But, so what?" I asked, "It's just a box."

She rolled her eyes. "It's a box for a color TV."

"OK, but it's still a box."

Now she was becoming annoyed with me. "They just want everyone to know that they bought a color TV!"

"But how do you know that?"

"Because I know."

"Yeah, but what else are they gonna do with the box? I mean where else can they put it?"

"Well, they didn't have to just leave it out there."

"But mom, why do you even care?"

"I just don't like it."

My mom was harder to read than my dad. He was always ready to proclaim his unwavering position on any subject, but she was more ambiguous. There was a song by the Monkees called *Pleasant Valley Sunday* which was an indictment of middle class values. She detested it. When I asked her why, she responded that she wasn't interested in what the Monkees had to say about society, as if it had been a personal affront. But a book or movie which addressed the same subject might receive an accolade from her a few days later.

Sometimes she said things to me that were insulting, but I was never sure whether it was intentional or inadvertent. Once I came home with yearbook pictures from junior high that were truly horrible. She looked at them, and instead of saying something about how bad they were, and how I looked much better than that, she looked at the photos and said, "You were such a cute baby. What happened?" Ouch! Another time, someone made a few complimentary remarks about one of my drawings, and she responded by saying, "Oh, that's not much. I'll let you know if he does anything good." A few years later, when I was a sophomore in high school, I had a girlfriend named Suzie. She was very attractive, and did some modeling for a local agency. I don't know how the subject came up, but my mom was asking me rather pointed questions about her. Then she said, "Well, she's only seeing you because she knows we have money." I was offended by her remark. Susie and I were only fifteen, and besides, I didn't know that we "had money," so how could she? Even if it had been true, why say such a thing? As poisonous as her remark had been, it did raise some other questions in my mind. I had never considered our financial situation, but now I was curious as to how we lived so well while my dad only worked a few days a week, and was off in the summer. Finally I made some discrete inquiries, and my mom reluctantly told me her story.

When her parents died, she and her sister each inherited some oil company stock. It paid a dividend, which I think was used by her aunt to help support the two extra kids. In 1955, when I was two, my mom received a phone call from someone who was buying up all of the stock from that particular company. He offered her five hundred thousand dollars for her shares, which was a huge amount of money at that time, and she gladly accepted. My dad had just finished his doctoral studies, and had applied for a job at Long Beach State College, which was a brand new school. He got the job, and they had the house in Park Estates built, which they paid for in cash. My mom took the rest of her money to Merrill Lynch, and invested very conservatively. Those are the facts. My theory is that the windfall had a devastating effect on my dad. My mom retained control of her money, and managed it well. For someone as egocentric as my dad it was probably emasculating, and maybe my mom felt that he could use a bit of emasculation. Of course it's just a theory.

In 1965, my dad purchased a trimaran. It was just like him to find a boat that was unconventional. He was always on the lookout for something unusual. For several years he had driven an Apollo, a custom crafted sports car so esoteric that no one had heard of it. The trimaran had three hulls, hence the name. I don't know why he suddenly became so smitten with sailing, but he did. He would spend hours at the Ross Boat Company cleaning and polishing the boat. He liked hanging out with the guys, who called him Doc, and cultivated a deep tan on his back. The Ross Boat Company consisted of a couple of weather-beaten wooden shacks and several docks. It was situated on Alamitos Bay, so he could sail around in calm water at any time. He obviously wanted us to participate in his new hobby, and would try to talk me and my brother into joining him on the weekends. I tried it a few times, but I didn't derive much pleasure from doing chores at his command. My mom tried to participate as well, but she didn't love it either. In a last ditch effort, my dad signed all of us up for sailing lessons. After one or two lessons, my brother, my mom, and I decided it wasn't for us. He went through his usual routine of expressing his annoyance through random remarks, but it had no effect other than to make us annoyed with him. He joined the Long Beach Yacht Club and found some camaraderie there, devising a system for calibrating race results and sometimes racing himself. Sailing kept him occupied for several years. He later traded the trimaran for a highly specialized racing catamaran, and even designed a prototype for yet another racing cat. Then it was over. He cited the intense migraines as the reason, but the migraines had long ago become an excuse to avoid things that he didn't want to do. I don't know what had changed, but he was soon back to his "snoozing on the couch" routine. He traded in the catamaran for a Cal 20, and left it docked at the yacht club.

I had continued with my bagpipe lessons, and was now becoming quite proficient. My dad had found a beautiful set of Robertson pipes, and purchased them for me. He told me that he had gotten them from a Pipe Major who could no longer play, and that they had been custom made and presented to him by his men upon his retirement. All of the fittings were made of chased silver with elaborate Celtic patterns, and the pipes themselves were African Blackwood. When Jamie MacColl, my teacher, first saw them, he immediately wanted to buy them. It was like buying a Rolls Royce for a student driver, but I didn't know any better. I was now known at school and around the neighborhood as the kid with the bagpipes, and was called upon to play publicly from time to time. In the seventh grade, I was asked to participate in a talent show which was actually a silly play. I had a couple of walk-ons which interrupted the story, and was told, "Not now, Angus," each time. I never got to play an entire tune, and I realized that, for most people, the pipes were just a novelty item.

My dad, however, was very serious about them. He had not only sought out Mr. MacColl, who was regarded as the best piper and instructor in Southern California, but he had somehow located and acquired a fantastic set of pipes for me. The next step was to get me into a band, so one day he told me that we were going to a practice session for the Clontarf Irish Pipe Band. That night we drove a few miles to an elementary school where the practice was held, and I met the band members, who were all adults. They were a friendly bunch, and made me feel comfortable immediately. I was asked to play a tune, which I did, and just like that, I was in the band.

It was interesting to be the only kid in an adult environment, especially because no one condescended to me. It turned out that I was one of their best pipers, and when we later went to events that required a trio or quartet, I was always asked to play. In some ways it was a great experience. Hugh Davis always had good jokes, some quite off-color. Grant Ryan was a cool guy who later bought a bar, named it "The Hundred Pipers," and set up our practice sessions in the basement. Wayne Kerner, Grant's good buddy, was a professional sign painter and artist, so we had common interests. The Pipe Major, Dennis Brooks, was a scholar of Irish history and music. He played the Uilleann pipes and several other similar instruments. All of them supported the I.R.A.

My dad enjoyed taking me to practice. During breaks he would get involved in discussions with the members, expressing his sympathy with the Irish rebels. He made it known that he was a doctor and professor, and was pleased when they also started calling him Doc. That seemed to be his preferred nickname. I was not so pleased, because I had to learn a bunch of new marches in addition to what I was working on for Mr. MacColl. My dad was also quite excited about the prospect of parades. He had a kilt custom made for me, to match those of the other band members, and managed to find a sporran and all the other accoutrements. I didn't protest, although the idea of marching around on a hot day didn't appeal to me. I remember those parades vividly. Initially, I was a bit proud to be a twelve year old kid among genuine men, but that wore off quickly. The parades usually took place on hot, smoggy days, and ran for a couple of miles. Playing and marching in the sun, while trying to dodge piles of fresh horse shit, was even worse than I had anticipated. I had a very heavy set of pipes, and the silver mounts of the drones would gradually dig into my left shoulder as I walked. I didn't complain until the day that we had to do two parades, back to back. I was uncomfortable and exhausted, but my dad didn't appear to be very sympathetic.

During the summer between the eighth and ninth grades, my dad and Mr. MacColl conspired to have me compete in the annual Santa Rosa Highland Games. A family trip was planned around the event. We would drive up the coast, see Hearst Castle and some other points of interest, stay in San Francisco for a few days, then arrive in Santa Rosa in time for the games. The trip went well. The highlight for me was San Francisco. It was the Summer of Love, so there were plenty of hippies to gawk at as we drove through the Haight Ashbury district. When we arrived at the Games, my band mates and Mr. MacColl were already there. I was competing in the novice march, with a large number of other young players. Mr. MacColl helped tune my drones (very important) and in due course my number was called. I played *Captain Norman Orr Ewing*, a four part march which was a popular competition tune, and came away with a second place trophy. Everyone was proud of me, but I was not very excited. I felt like I had done what was expected, and now I should be able to relax. I was not on fire to enter more competitions. I was much more interested in playing drums.

I had gotten a pair of drumsticks from Hugh, the drummer in our band, and could not refrain from practicing the single stroke roll. I was completely preoccupied with perfect timing and would replay the instrumental version of *Goldfinger* over and over, trying to match an eight stroke fill near the end of the song. I nailed it fairly quickly, and was now eager to get a drum set so that I could really rock and roll. I never thought of what I was doing as practicing. It was fun and exciting, and I didn't need a timer to remind me that I had to continue - I wanted to continue. I had never felt that way about the pipes. It was obvious that I was much more motivated to be a drummer, and my dad was not very happy about it.

I continued with the pipes, going to the lessons and practices, but I was beginning to rebel. When it was decided that I should enter another competition, I declined. My dad was annoyed, but there was nothing that he could do about it. Mr. MacColl wanted to start teaching me the classical music of the pipes, Piobaireachd, which is significantly different from the marches and reels that are commonly played. Piobaireachd (don't bother trying to pronounce it) consists of a theme and many variations on that theme. It is played slowly, and seems to go on forever. I was flattered by his confidence in my abilities, but bored stiff with the music. Still, I gave it my best shot – for a while.

Then two incidents occurred which signaled the end

of my piping "career." The first took place when my parents hosted a dinner for some friends. We were all seated at the large dining room table, and had just finished an excellent meal, when my dad turned to me and said, "How about a tune?" I was taken completely by surprise.

"What?" I replied, not sure that I had heard him correctly.

"How about a tune, son?" He said again, looking around the table with a smile, as if he were the Laird of some great estate.

I knew that I wasn't going to perform at his whim. I felt like a trained monkey.

"No, thank you, "I said it quietly but firmly. I don't know how this appeared to everyone else at the table, but the tension between me and my dad was palpable. He looked at me for a few moments, aware that we had an audience, and then abruptly said, "OK, then," and started a conversation with one of the guests.

Later there was a discussion about my reluctance to play for him, and I told him that it had been unfair to spring his request on me without any warning. Besides, I was not comfortable playing under such circumstances. It felt too much like I was showing off. He didn't apologize, but instead made it clear that he was disappointed in me. I didn't care.

The second incident was much worse. It was a Saturday morning, and we were about to leave for Mr. MacColl's house. I was ready to go, and waiting by the side door. I could hear him cursing in another room, but I had no idea what it was about. Finally, he came striding out, obviously in a foul temper. I opened the door and stepped outside, heading to the garage as he started shouting.

"Come on, come on, hurry up! We're going to be late!"

I could feel my old friend, the fury of the innocent, explode inside me.

"Why are you yelling at me? I was ready – you're the one who's making us late!"

Wham! He slapped me, hard, across the face. I was absolutely stunned. He had never hit me before. I couldn't process it. I felt like I was completely removed from reality as we got into the car. I didn't speak to him at all. I was on automatic pilot for the rest of the morning, blankly going through my tunes with Mr. MacColl. Even on the way home, when my dad said something to me in a tentative voice, I ignored him completely. I was waiting for him to apologize, but he never did. I don't think that I ever really got over it. His action was so unfair and so unwarranted that I couldn't let it go, but an apology would have made a big difference. Although he never did anything like that again, it colored my perception of him forever. Now I knew who I was dealing with. I knew that I had had enough of pipe bands, parades, and Mr. MacColl, but I didn't ask him if it was OK to quit. Instead, I told him point blank that I was done. It was the first time that I had openly challenged his authority, and he didn't take it well. I was prepared to hit back if he struck me again, but he didn't. He was angry and disappointed, but I was too old to be forced to continue, and he knew it. I, on the other hand, felt that I had won a significant victory. But the war wasn't over.

# 16
## After the Fall

When I awoke, the first thought to enter my mind was, "Man, I really fucked up!" I was flat on my back in a hospital bed. I attempted to move a bit, and found everything in order. There were no casts or bandages in evidence. I had a slight dull pain in my right wrist, and, when I attempted to get up, a severe pain in my upper right leg. I closed my eyes for a few moments, trying to recall what might have happened, but there was nothing there. I knew my name, and every other pertinent detail of my life, but there was a big blank when I tried to determine what event or events had brought me to such a sorry state of affairs. The room was designed to accommodate two patients, but I was the sole occupant. Daylight was filtering through the windows, and I guessed that it was mid-morning. I didn't know how to call a nurse or doctor, and I certainly wasn't going anywhere, so I waited and dozed off from time to time, certain that someone would soon show up and explain everything.

Eventually, I heard the door open, and a doctorish looking man entered, accompanied by my parents. He sat on the corner of the bed near my feet, and smiled. "Well, young man," he said," you're looking pretty healthy this morning. You were very lucky."

"I don't feel lucky," I replied," What happened?"

My mom said, "You fell off the roof. Don't you remember?"

"No. I'm not even sure what day it is. Can we go home?"

"Well, not quite yet," said the doctor, "You've had a concussion, a pretty severe one, so we need to keep you here for awhile to make sure everything is OK. Besides, you have a broken cheekbone that we need to fix and another chip in your right wrist. You're going to be here for a few days at least."

"The only thing that hurts is my leg. Are you sure it isn't broken too?"

"It's not broken, but you have some nice bruises." He paused, "Well, I'll leave you now, but a nurse will check on you in a bit, get you something to eat if you want." He got up and left, and I was alone with two very concerned looking parents.

My mom told me that I had gone outside to play basketball. She had heard the ball bouncing around for a while, and then a big thump. She was just about to come out and check on me, when I showed up at the side door, acting kind of dizzy, with blood all over my face. She said that she kept asking me what had happened, but all I could say was, "I'm not delirious," so she immediately got our neighbor to drive us to the hospital. The neighbor was our good old enemy, the father of Mary and owner of Garcon, who turned out to be a pretty good guy in an emergency. During the drive, I kept reiterating that I wasn't delirious, and when my mom explained where we were going, I understood that it was just to find out "what condition my condition was in."

Later, my parents concluded that the basketball had gotten stuck behind the backboard, and that I had climbed up onto the roof to get it. Somehow I had lost my balance and fallen. I couldn't remember any of this, but it seemed like a reasonable explanation. I was surprised that I had fallen from the roof because, despite repeated warnings, I had been climbing up there and running around for years. One time I had even played my bagpipes on the roof.

I was in the hospital for a week. I had surgery for my cheekbone that left a tidy little scar near my right ear. I also had a splint on my right wrist. My leg was sore for a few days, but that subsided. I was told to stay in bed as much as possible while my concussion was monitored. There wasn't much to do but sleep, eat, read, and watch TV. My friends couldn't visit because they were all fourteen like me, and no one under sixteen was allowed in. They did call, and send a lot of cards and notes, so I didn't feel abandoned, and my parents came every day and brought books and magazines. My memory of recent events returned, piece by piece. I recalled an item that I had received for Christmas, and then Christmas came back. It was always a specific detail that triggered the restoration of an entire event. By the time I left the hospital, I was up to date, but I never recovered the day of the fall or the fall itself. Finally, the doctors gave me a clean bill of health on the concussion. I was very wobbly from having spent so much time in bed, but I managed to get to the wheelchair, and from that into my mom's car. Going home!

It was spring of 1968. The end of my last year of junior high was fast approaching. I was back at school, now with distinction of being the kid who fell off of the roof. I had been prepared for some ridicule. After all, it was kind of stupid to fall off of a roof, but everyone had been very friendly and supportive. In fact, I even seemed to be getting more attention from some of the girls. I had always gotten excellent grades, but because I had been out for a couple of weeks, I was behind in some classes, and for some reason, not very inclined to worry about it. I didn't think about my accident much, and never had a sense that I might have been killed, but on some level I knew that I wanted to have more fun. Maybe it was a typical response to being laid up for a while. I certainly learned nothing from my fall, because I was less inclined to follow rules than ever. I can't honestly say that there was a direct cause and effect relationship between accident and attitude, but a couple of friends commented, rather ambiguously, that I seemed to have changed a bit.

I finally persuaded my dad to get me a drum set. I'm sure that this was due in part to post-accident sympathy, because my dad was not excited about the drums. He was usually snoozing on the family room couch, and I'm sure that he was dreading the racket, but he had painted himself into a corner by endorsing the bagpipes, which were just as loud. My mom was kind enough to arrange lessons for me, and she cheerfully taxied me to and from the teacher's house. This may have been another understated dig at my dad, as well as a declaration of support for my interest.

As soon as I sat down with the complete drum set, I felt at home. I learned the lessons quickly, and would practice to records in my bedroom, which was at the opposite end of the house from my parents' room. I spent hours playing those drums, going from the Tijuana Brass, to the Beatles, to the Who. Mike also got interested and took lessons, and we would take turns playing to various records that we liked. We even got psychedelic, with flashing colored lights inside the bass drum, and cheap incense from Sav-on. Steve Baker, Roger, and I formed a band and performed for a school dance as the "Dented Fender." The pipes were work, but this was fun. I was becoming obsessed with the drums, and indifferent to school and homework.

I was also becoming obsessed with the idea of having a girlfriend. Michelle, my hot little "bad girl" buddy, had sent me some very incendiary notes while I had been in the hospital.

"I lead a pretty bad life, but without you I wouldn't

have a life to lead. Oh . . . Bill, I love you so much. I never really told you how much you mean to me. Ya know how I got jealous when you started calling Mitzi? And ya know how I'm always asking you who you like? Well, to make a long thing short, I think this shows you that I really love you!"

I was very excited about these revelations, but when I attempted to follow up on them, she started backpedalling. I should have been prepared for it because she had expressed the same feelings for a bunch of different guys in the time that we had been friends, but that didn't make me less disillusioned. I was already dealing with a breakup, and I hadn't even had the relationship! We remained friendly, but I retained some bitterness. It was my first exposure to the emotional turmoil that was an inevitable element of most romantic relationships, and it was different from anything that I had ever experienced. Life was complicated enough already – what was I getting into?

I attended a party soon after my recovery. It was a Saturday night, and I knew most of the kids. The parents of the girl who was hosting the event were stashed away somewhere, and there was music, and food, and swimming. Several of the lowrider guys had climbed the backyard fence in order to decide whether the bash was worth a crash. They signaled for me to come out, so I conferred with them about who was there and who wasn't. They were slightly drunk on beer and smoking cigarettes, trying to be bad and cool, but not inclined to cause any trouble. I went back inside and mingled a bit, but it wasn't very exciting. The living room was dimly lit and couples and singles were scattered around. There was a girl on the couch looking at a large book of photos. I didn't recognize her, but she was attractive, and I was intrigued by her interest in the book. I sat down near her and asked what she was looking at. She looked up at me and responded, "It's a book about Ireland," and soon we were comfortably engaged in conversation. I moved closer and cautiously put my arm around her, and she responded by settling into me a little. It was the first time that I had ever made such a move, and I was amazed at the result. It was pretty heady stuff!

Her name was Mary Kay, and we were both surprised that we had never met before, or had any classes together. She played the violin, and was very serious about it, and I told her about my drums and bagpipes. She had known that there was a kid at school who played the pipes, and she had also heard about some guy who had fallen off of a roof, but she didn't seem to hold any of that against me. After a very pleasant hour or so, she looked at her watch and told me that her mother was going to pick her up in a few minutes. "I have to go," she said, "but Emily is having a party next Friday. You should come." I told her that I would, and we said goodbye. As I walked home, I could hardly believe what had happened. Did I actually have a girlfriend? My mind was racing. An amazing vista of dazzling possibilities opened before me. Only one thing was certain - it was going to be a very long week.

Friday finally arrived, and I headed over to Emily's house. She lived in my neighborhood, so it was an easy walk, and a last opportunity to review all of the thoughts that had been bouncing around in my head since last Saturday. It was pleasant to be out after dark. There was very little traffic, and everything was cool and quiet. The streetlights provided soft illumination at regular intervals, and there were many tall trees which cast feathery shadows on the street. I felt good, although I was a little anxious about meeting Mary Kay again. I had no idea what to expect, but there wasn't much time to think about it now. I walked up the path to Emily's porch, paused for one last moment, and rang the bell.

The door opened, and I was welcomed inside by several friends. There was a large crowd of kids, standing and sitting in groups. The rise and fall of various conversations, mixed with bursts of laughter and music from the record player, filtered through the house. The lights were low, and it was difficult to recognize anyone from a distance, so I wandered around, looking for Mary Kay, and drifting in and out of brief discussions with people that I knew. I had been there for about twenty minutes when I felt a gentle tap on my shoulder, and when I turned around, there she was. I was thrilled that she had gone out of her way to find me, and even more thrilled when, after a few minutes of small talk, she suggested that we go out to Emily's back yard.

The yard was nicely landscaped, with trees and paths and patio lights, and there were plenty of shadowy areas that looked inviting. Mary Kay seemed to have an itinerary in mind as she steered me away from the lights, and I could see no reason to interfere. We were now face to face and relatively isolated from the other partiers. I knew that something was about to happen as she leaned in and looked up at me. I closed my eyes and our lips met. It was my first genuine romantic kiss – a milestone! But there was more. Arms were enfolding, lips were parting, tongues were exploring! Mary Kay clearly had an excellent set of kissing skills, and I did my best to follow her lead. It was intoxicating! I lost track of time and my mind emptied itself. I felt immersed in a sea of exquisite physical sensation, and was quite willing to float there forever.

When we finally came up for air, Mary Kay gently suggested that we should go back inside. At that point, I probably would have walked off of a cliff if she had suggested it, so I followed her into the house. I felt slightly dizzy, and probably had a stupidly ecstatic look on my face. I seem to remember getting several inquisitive glances from my buddies as we passed them on the way to the buffet.

We had a couple of snacks, and mingled for a while, holding hands and silently proclaiming our new status as boyfriend and girlfriend. Emily's parents were nowhere to be seen, so we decided to explore the house. It was clear to me that we were looking for a quiet place to resume our previous activities. We found a bedroom which was unoccupied and sat on the bed. The lights were out, and there was no need to turn them on. Soon we were back in action. At some point, I got up and closed the door. It is indicative of my state of mind that I didn't consider the implications of our behavior. It seemed perfectly natural for us to be alone and undisturbed, so I was taken by surprise when Emily's mother opened the door and politely but firmly told us that we should join the other guests. We were slightly embarrassed, but only slightly, and got some teasing from kids who had seen us disappear earlier, but none of it mattered. The future looked bright ahead.

Mary Kay and I began spending our lunches together at school, meeting between classes, and talking every night on the phone. We went to school dances and parties, and sometimes managed to get together on Saturday afternoons. We walked and talked, but mostly we kissed, and I was totally infatuated. I consulted Mike and Jim and Mitzi and Michelle, and they all agreed that the next step was obvious – I should ask Mary Kay to go steady with me. So I purchased a little gold chain necklace, had it wrapped up in a box, and prepared myself for the big day. I felt confident that she would say yes, so I brought the package to school and popped the question when we met at lunchtime. I was expecting her to be as happy and excited as I was, but she wasn't. She opened the box and looked at the necklace, then told me that it was very sweet but that she couldn't go steady with me. But if it was alright with me, she would wear the necklace, and we could still be together. I was disappointed and confused. I didn't understand why she had turned me down. But I hadn't really lost anything except a little pride. I still had a girlfriend, and summer was coming.

Everything was fine for another week or so, but then I began to hear rumors that the reason Mary Kay wouldn't go steady with me was that she had another, older, boy friend. I was not happy to contemplate that possibility, although I knew how many idiotic rumors circulated throughout the school. After all, there had been whispers that Mary Kay and I had "gone all the way" at Emily's party. So I was willing to give her the benefit of the doubt. But one day she showed up at school without my necklace. I waited to see if she would say anything about it. Maybe her parents had told her not to wear it, or she had lost it. She never said a word. I thought that she might have simply forgotten to put it on that morning, but the next day it was still gone, and it never reappeared. Did she actually believe that I wouldn't notice? Or was she telling me something by not wearing it? I thought of all I had learned from Mitzi and Michelle, and tried to figure it out. Although I could have simply asked her what was on her mind, I didn't see the point of bringing it up. If she had been deceitful already, why should I expect her to be truthful now? I was boiling with anger and disappointment, but rather than confront Mary Kay, I simply cut her off. It was probably not the best course of action, but I had never been in such a position before. It was disconcerting that something so simple and beautiful could become frustrating and complicated in such a short time. My friends seemed to agree that I had done the right thing, but some were persistent in trying to get us back together. Mary Kay was apparently willing to make amends. She wrote a note to me and had it delivered at school;

"Since you never give me a chance to talk to you, I

decided to write and tell you how I feel. All this stuff going around isn't worth the time at all. We should just forget it all and be friends. Everybody says that they think that you think that I hate you. Well, I don't. Not at all! Just because I won't go steady with you has no reflection on the way I feel about you. I still like you and I still want to be friends with you.

If I have really caused you misery I'm very sorry. But I just wish you would act more like a man about all this and stop making everyone feel sorry for you. I really see no reason why you should hate me.

PS - I still want to go to the prom with you."

It didn't make any sense to me. The fact that she wouldn't go steady with me seemed to be a clear reflection of the way she felt about me. I hated the lingering confusion and despondency that I endured in the wake of our breakup. This was not at all like a typical skirmish with authority, where the good guys and bad guys were clearly delineated, and the transgression was obvious. Uncertainty continued to haunt me for a long time, and I kept reviewing the details to see if I had missed something important. I did not want my disappointment to get the best of me, and I certainly did not want to be perceived as the loser in this conflict. There was only one appropriate course of action, and this required a different kind of courage and defiance. I did not take Mary Kay to the prom.

I was soon to be part of the Walter B. Hill graduating class of 1968. There were a few events being planned, including the graduation ceremony itself, so when I received a message to report to Mrs. Hanson's office, I anticipated that it would have something to do with providing some artwork for one of them. I had done the yearbook cover, designed the background mural for the talent show, and won ice cream for my homeroom for some dumb emblem, so it seemed like a logical conclusion. I liked Mrs. Hanson. She was obviously nobody's fool, but she was also fair minded and had a sense of humor, so I didn't expect any trouble. I knocked on her door, and she invited me in and offered me a seat.

"Hi Bill," she said, "I have a project that I'm involved with, and I need someone to help me out. I was wondering if maybe you could be that someone."

"Well, maybe," I cautiously replied," what is it?"

"Well, we're going to have an assembly next week, and I need someone to take questions from the audience and read them to our guest speaker. Are you OK talking in front of an audience?"

"Yeah, I guess so. But why me?"

"I'm pretty sure that you could do a good job, and besides, for this assembly I think it would be better to have a student on stage than one of our instructors. The assembly is about drugs, and we're showing a movie, then we have an expert to talk about the consequences of using drugs, and answer questions. Do you think you could do it?"

I thought about it for a minute. I wasn't very excited by the prospect, but, as I said, I liked Mrs. Hanson. And I didn't have any problem with public speaking. "I guess so, yeah, OK," I said.

She got up from behind her desk and walked with me through the office door. "Alright, thank you, Bill. We'll talk again before the assembly, and I'll go over everything with you."

I considered myself fairly sophisticated on the subject of drugs. I had gradually broadened my perusal of *Playboy* to include the stories and articles, and particularly Hugh Hefner's editorial, the Playboy Philosophy. Here, Hef expressed very liberal views on sex and drug use, but they were tempered with warnings about the law, and about the real risks to both physical and mental health. There was no overblown rhetoric, and Hef backed his opinions with citations from people like Masters and Johnson, and other well respected authorities on these subjects. I was impressed by his information, and his rationality, and I was curious about Marijuana, but so far I hadn't tried it. I knew that there were a few kids who were into drugs. There was a group of glue sniffers that gathered under the bridge after school, with their plastic bags and tubes of model cement, and there were smokers like my grade school buddy, whose academic performance was abysmal except when we were forced to learn the metric system. The problem was not widespread at our school, but in the wake of the "Summer of Love" there was hysteria among parents, law enforcement, and federal and state authorities. Between hippies, Hell's Angels, rock and roll records with suggestive lyrics, and the looming threat of nuclear annihilation, adults had plenty to worry about.

The day of the assembly arrived, and it appeared that the entire ninth grade was packed into the auditorium. I had been assigned a seat in the front row, so that it would be easy for me to get to the stage when the question and answer session began. The students were noisy, and there was a general air of derision in the room. Everyone knew that the school administrators were taking the presentation very seriously. That in itself was enough to generate skepticism and hostility from several hundred fourteen year olds, but there were also enough smokers and sniffers to incite ridicule if the show became too hyperbolic.

Mrs. Hanson walked out onto the stage, which had been set up with a podium and microphone on each side. She quieted the crowd and introduced the guest speaker, allegedly some kind of professor and "drug expert" who looked and sounded like a caricature. I immediately thought that he was an idiot and, judging by the muttering and whispers from the audience, I was not alone. He gave a brief introduction to the film that we were about to see, then shuffled offstage. The lights went out, and the movie began. As soon as Sonny Bono appeared onscreen, all credibility vaporized. Even kids who had no interest in drugs knew that Sonny and Cher were out. We were listening to Cream, the Beatles *White Album*, and Iron Butterfly. The most interesting music on the radio was totally psychedelic, man. Sonny Bono? No way!

We were subjected to earnest anti-drug sentiments from Mr. Bono, intercut with footage of police raids and "drug users," for what seemed like a very long time. The kids laughed and hissed, generally proclaiming their disdain for such junk. When it finally ended, there was a round of furious applause that underscored our contempt, not just for the movie, but for the assumption that we would "buy it." When the lights went back on, Mrs. Hanson and the expert returned to the stage and stood together behind one of the podiums. I responded to a prompt, and took my place behind the other podium, where a pile of handwritten questions from students waited for me. Mrs. Hanson explained to the audience that I was going to read the questions, and that the expert would answer them. There was some giggling, and a gentle admonishment from Mrs. Hanson to be "polite to our guest." She then left the stage, our guest stepped up to the microphone, and the farce began.

I asked several questions which I can't recall, but I do recall that every response ended with the same dogmatic warnings about the evil of any and all drugs. The film had specifically targeted marijuana, so most of the questions and answers concerned the wicked weed. Thanks to Hef, I knew that there was credible research to indicate that the claims being made by Mr. Bono and our expert were hugely inflated. I didn't mind hearing a reasonable argument based on accurate information, but this was merely propaganda, and dishonest as well. The audience was growing more and more hostile, and so was I.

"I'd like to ask a question of my own, if that's ok," I said, as if I were sincerely seeking enlightenment.

He looked confused. "Well, I don't know." He glanced back to where Mrs. Hanson was standing, hidden from the audience, behind the curtain.

"Well, these are student questions and I'm a student."

I saw Mrs. Hanson nod, and he turned back to me, regaining his composure, and replied, "OK, sure, of course you may."

The students had quieted down, and I felt relaxed and confident. I was gonna nail this jerk.

"So," I said, "Let's say you had a serious disease, and the only thing that would cure it was marijuana. Then would it be OK to use it?"

He didn't hesitate. "No – these are bad drugs! No one should use them under any circumstances!"

I turned to the audience and raised my hands in a gesture of futility, but I was smiling. The students yelled "Go Fogg" and laughed. The expert did not look happy – his presentation was not going well, but I couldn't believe that he did any better at other schools. He talked for a few more minutes, but I wasn't paying attention and neither was the audience. After it became clear that no one was interested in hearing anything more from "the expert," Mrs. Hanson came out and wrapped it up. As I left, I realized that there might be some unpleasant consequences for me, but I felt that I had done the right thing, and was ready to defend myself. Sure enough, I was again summoned to Mrs. Hanson's office, but when I arrived, she looked like she was trying to hide a smile.

"Look, Bill," she said, "I know you didn't like our guest, but that wasn't very courteous, don't you think?"

"I'm sorry, but c'mon, that guy was an idiot," I protested.

"Everyone knew it. Besides, I just asked him a question."

"Yes, I guess that's true." She was openly smiling now. "But it was a little uncomfortable."

"Look, I'm sorry if I messed things up for you, but really, he was terrible."

I could tell that she agreed with me, even if she couldn't allow herself to say so. We both smiled. "So I guess you won't be asking me to do anything like that again," I volunteered.

She laughed, "No, probably not."

I could tell that everything was alright. I liked Mrs. Hanson even more now. She was cool. And I found that I had gained a very high approval rating among my peers, who now assumed that I was a pot head. I tried to explain to a couple of people that I wasn't, that I just couldn't tolerate the condescending tone of the whole affair, but no one believed me, so I gave up. Years later, I read that Sonny had considered the film a bad career move because it made him look "square." I, on the other hand, looked much more tuned in than I really was, but that was OK. I decided to roll with it. Anyway, junior high was almost over, and I was much more interested in what high school would be like.

# 17
## High School My School

On the last day of junior high, after a graduation ceremony in which I was given a trophy (wow) for best artist, there was a huge party. It took place at the home of classmate who lived in Park Estates, a gala affair with a live band. Mitzi and I arrived together, and then separated as she went looking for Jim. I mingled with friends, and had some food, keeping an eye out for Mary Kay in order to avoid a chance encounter. As it began to get dark, the band started up with *Sunshine of Your Love*. I was hoping to connect with a girl that I was interested in, and when I finally found her, we danced a bit, then sat in the deck chairs and talked for a while. I managed to get a few kisses out of her before she had to leave. As far as I was concerned, the party was progressing beautifully. Things gradually started winding down at around ten. Another girl, Brenda, asked if I would escort her to the spot where her older boyfriend was picking her up. I walked her to the location, and waited with her until she saw his car in the distance. She gave me a little peck on the cheek, and sent me off before he arrived, in order to avoid any trouble. As I headed back to the party, I was feeling terrific. Girls! A sense of optimism was beginning to override my caution. Maybe this was a taste of what high school would be like! When the party officially ended, I ran into one of my lowrider friends. We were in the mood for mischief, so we took the wagon wheel that was propped up against a fake well in a nearby front yard. The wheel was big and heavy, but we muscled it into the street and got it rolling. We ran with it until we had achieved a suitable pace, and then let it go. As we veered away and cut down a side street, we could hear the wheel end it's odyssey with a charming crash. It was a perfect ending to a delightful evening.

That was a good summer, made additionally exciting by the anticipation of high school. We went to the beach, rode our bikes, bought new clothes, and psyched ourselves up. I was still acting as a go-between/referee for Mitzi and Jim, which meant that Mitzi and I would often get together when Jim was unavailable. I was invited to a party with Mike and his friends, so I asked her to come with me. It was an opportunity to meet some new kids who would be joining us at Woodrow Wilson High School. I only knew a few of the partiers, and Mitzi didn't know any of them, but it didn't matter. She was attractive and gregarious, and everyone seemed to like her. There were about twenty of us in the back yard, congregating in small groups around the pool, when the girls who were hosting the event, Robin and Pam, announced that they needed a volunteer – a candidate for hypnosis. None of us believed that they could pull it off, so we talked Mitzi into being the guinea pig. She was a good sport, but skeptical, and gave us a smile of farewell as the hypnotists led her to a small sheltered area on the far side of the yard.

Initially we waited for their return, but as the minutes passed, we turned back to our conversations. No one was surprised when the three girls came back after what seemed to be a long time, and announced that it hadn't worked. Mike and I asked Mitzi what had happened, but she didn't have much to say, and then Pam asked her if she would like to kiss Mike. She said yes, so Pam instructed her to do it, and she did. Everyone

216

was now studying the situation with extreme interest. Mike was a handsome guy, so there was some question as to whether it would require hypnosis to achieve such a result. Pam told her to really kiss him, and she really did. Mike was obviously enjoying himself, and the crowd was encouraging them, but we still were not entirely convinced – until Pam pointed at me and exclaimed "He just pinched you!" Mitzi swiveled around, absolutely livid. For a second I just stood there admiring her thespianism, and then she slapped me so hard that I almost fell into the pool. I was dazed, and the inside of my cheek was bleeding. No one said a word. Robin and Pam looked as if they hadn't expected such a dramatic turn of events, and quietly led her away. When they returned, Mitzi acted as though nothing had happened.

"You don't remember anything?"

"No, why, what did I do?" She sounded absolutely sincere.

"You slapped Bill really hard in the face!"

She looked around, and then looked at me. My face must still have been red where she had struck me.

"Oh no, I couldn't have." She looked more closely. Did I?"

"Yeah, you really did," I said. I wasn't mad, just bemused. In fact, I was starting to feel sorry for Mitzi. She really had no idea of what she had done, but everyone confirmed my story. She looked stricken, and then she started crying and apologizing to me. I reassured her that it wasn't her fault, but she was very upset. It took me about a half hour to calm her down. We then tried to rekindle our sociability and rejoin the party, but the mood had darkened, and Mitzi was obviously still embarrassed, so we departed. I reviewed that evening many times over the next few weeks, and remained convinced that the hypnosis was real, or maybe surreal. The episode went a long way to confirming my hypothesis that getting involved with girls could be dangerous, but despite my painfully acquired wisdom on the subject, there was no way around the fact that I desperately wanted to get involved with girls. Fortunately I had the advantage of attending a school with a huge student population, at least half of which was female.

A few weeks after school started, Mitzi introduced me to Susie, the gal that my mom later claimed was after our money. She was chic, and a lot of fun, but she was regularly unavailable due to modeling jobs, and after a month or two I got tired of being put on hold. We had a blow out about it at one of the school dances, and I decided that, even though I really liked her, the highs weren't a big enough compensation for the lows. I started seeing another girl, but she expressed concern that Susie and I might still really like each other, which engendered a new and different set of conflicts. Once again, I elected to opt out. I was now often engaged in battle on two fronts. With my dad, I was fighting defensively, trying to hold my ground against his dictatorial policies. With the girls, I was on the offensive, with the tantalizing fruits of victory looming before me.

Jim and I were planning to go out for swimming and water polo. I was looking forward to swimming, because I was the neighborhood champ, and had won a couple of races for the Yacht Club team. I didn't know anything about water polo. Workouts were scheduled for the last two weeks of vacation, so we rode our bikes to the pool on the first day to try out. The water polo coach was Paul Zack. He had been on an Olympic team, and conveyed an aura of no-nonsense aggressiveness. His motto was, "Gentlemen, I don't like to lose." We did some drills, and listened to him tell us about the game for a couple of hours. It wasn't bad, so Jim and I decided that we would stick with it. The second workout was similar, but on the third day, Zack was absent, and the swimming coach was there, along with the entire team. He announced that we would not be doing drills, but instead would have a regular swimming workout. I had no idea what was in store, but after an hour of laps, I felt sick and exhausted. I turned to a varsity swimmer next to me and asked if this was an unusually hard workout. "Nah, about average." he replied. We continued for another hour. I was barely moving by the time we finished, nauseated and blurry eyed from the chlorine. Jim was a more experienced swimmer than I, but he was also re-examining the degree of his commitment. The bike ride home was agonizing. But the next morning we decided that we couldn't give up so easily, so we reluctantly returned to the scene of our misery, and gradually learned to endure it.

The advantage to being on the team was that I made a lot of new friends very quickly, but the downside was that it was another team sport. I was on the C team, which consisted of sophomore beginners, so there was not much pressure. The B team was mostly juniors, and the Varsity team was a group of hulking, Tarzan-like seniors, although we had some very talented sophomore players who were soon promoted. The workouts were either before or after classes, sometimes both, but I was able to keep up, and I began to enjoy the vitality of being in good physical condition.

We began the season by wearing sneakers during the workouts, which was very strenuous, but when the coach finally allowed us to remove them, we felt fast and strong. However, I never learned to love water polo, and I was never very proficient as a player. My philosophy was, "get rid of the ball as soon as possible," although I did score a goal once or twice. When swimming season started in January, I was much happier. I ended up specializing in the butterfly, and did well for the C team even though my form was not elegant. Initially, I won my events, but was disqualified for breaking my kick at least twice. The coach was not happy with me, and to solve the problem, he had me bind my feet together with a giant rubber band during workouts. I didn't enjoy this, but it did solve the problem.

I found that the coaches were quite pragmatic in their approach to problem solving. Ear infection? Pour alcohol into the offending orifice! Severe cramp? Swim it out! This was real he-man stuff. When one of us wasn't performing at an acceptable level, Zack, or Zubbo, as we rechristened him, would yell," C'mon, show some hair!" I never adopted that particular phrase, but its implications were clear. Sometimes he would break a clipboard in frustration or anger, and even though I was a part of the team, I regularly felt like an outsider witnessing a fascinating sociological experiment. Once, on the day of an important swim meet, we were each given a pill. When I asked the coach what it was, he said, "vitamins." And when I didn't immediately swallow it, he became irritated and told me to take it. I didn't like this turn of events, and mentioned it to my parents afterwards. I'm pretty sure that my dad made a phone call about it, because the coach was frosty with me for several weeks.

The water polo games and swim meets were scheduled at various schools throughout Long Beach and surrounding areas. When we took the bus to another school, there was a festive air to the proceedings. We had one guy who would play Jethro Tull songs on his flute, a couple of others who had good jokes to tell, and the coach would loosen up and act like "one of the guys." When we reached our destination, Jim and I would leave the pool area and go on a shoplifting spree. We had team sweat suits with elastic closures in the legs, so it was easy to swoop into a store and toss candy, and Hostess pies and cupcakes into our pants, then waltz out. Eventually we recruited several other guys to join us, and we would bring back a load of junk food for our varsity guys, who repaid us by threatening anyone who wanted to fight us. It was a good system, but if we had been caught it would have been a huge scandal.

I would usually spend break times and lunch with a girlfriend or a small group of classmates or teammates. Jim and Mitzi were still together, and they would sometimes provide an entertaining spectacle with their fights. I recall one instance when Mitzi got so angry with him that she knocked him off of a railing that he was sitting on, and into the bushes. That girl could really pack a wallop! There were a few other students who could be counted on for amusement. One of them would chew up some cookies during lunch, and then pretend to be sick, spewing them all over anyone in his vicinity. He was also kicked out of class for excessive (and deliberate) flatulence. In general, however, the students at Wilson, as they had been at Gant and Hill, were well behaved and well groomed. There was a formal dress code that forbid things like short skirts and pants for girls, and untucked shirts, sandals, and facial hair for guys. I got tagged for an untucked shirt a couple of times, which was not a major issue, but facial hair was something else. The school administrators were trying to hold the line against the Hippie phenomenon, so when the vice principal caught me with an unshaven face, he was angry and unequivocal.

"What's the idea, Fogg? You know the rules!"

"Yeah, but I don't get why this is such a big deal."

"Well, it is – so you can either shave right now, or I'm sending you home!"

What an idiot, I thought, imagining a razor and shaving cream in one of his desk drawers. "Are you serious?" I asked, somewhat contemptuously.

"You bet I am, mister!" The conversation wasn't progressing as it should have, I suppose. He was getting even louder and redder.

"OK, then I'll go home. Thanks," I said cheerfully. I stood up and walked out of his office without a backward glance. I was glad that he had made it so easy. I was getting a little better at controlling myself in confrontations, and I had figured out that an explosive outburst was likely to get me into more serious trouble. Although I couldn't always keep a lid on my temper, I had learned that it was better, and more satisfying, to outsmart 'em if I could. Maybe I was maturing.

Well, maybe not. The quality of education was not consistent at Wilson. It is true that I had some good teachers there, but most were mediocre, and some were truly wretched. It was incredible that an instructor could take a fascinating subject like biology or chemistry, and turn it into utter tedium. I was usually bored and frustrated. I was also much less interested in achieving good grades in every subject. I had been doing it for years because my parents, particularly my dad, expected it. By now I felt that I had amply demonstrated my abilities, and I was starting to resent putting so much time and energy into subjects that didn't interest me. I was willing, even eager, to commit all of my resources into meaningful activities, but it seemed like it was time for me to start determining what those activities should be.

My biology teacher could have been a poster boy for incompetence. His name was Wardle, and his physiognomy suggested that there might be a walrus lurking in the branches of his family tree. He would deliver the most enervating lectures with a confidence that was completely unwarranted, or sit at his desk while we worked on a lab project of no discernable value. Our class grades were based on quizzes that were given five or six times during each quarter. At the end of the quarter, he would consult every student and recheck his grade book to make sure all of the quiz grades were correct. It was an excellent opportunity to mess with him. Every quarter I would doctor one or two of my test papers to indicate a higher grade. It was easy for me to duplicate his writing and check marks. I would make sure that it looked like I had achieved an A- or B+, and when he showed me the grades that he had written down, I would tell him that they didn't look right.

"What do you mean?" He would ask.

"Well, I saved all my tests. Can I go get them?"

"Alright, but hurry up. I have to get this done today."

I would come back with the quiz papers for that quarter, including the fakes, and hand them to him.

"I guess you're right - it looks like I made a mistake here . . . and here. Sorry about that."

"OK," I'd say, "Thanks for fixing it."

I did this to him every quarter, and each time I acted more upset. The fourth time, I essentially accused him of deliberately recording my grades inaccurately.

"You do this to me every quarter, and I'm getting sick of it. I don't see anyone else having this problem. What's going on?"

He apologized profusely, no doubt afraid that I would report him for unfair grading practices. He had complained to the swimming coach about me once for reasons that I didn't understand, so there was a legitimate reason for acrimony between us, and I probably could have made things difficult for him if I had been vindictive. But I wasn't. I just couldn't take him, or any school that would employ him, seriously, and felt compelled to address the issue in my own way. I finished the course with a very good grade.

The chemistry teacher, Dr. Voisard, was another disaster. He actually looked like a mad scientist – a mummified little man with giant, thick, black framed glasses and a dingy lab coat. He immediately had us doing elaborate calculations to determine the molecular weights of various compounds without giving us a clue as to why. I was interested in learning about chemical reactions – like explosions – but we never touched on anything other than calculations. In the lab we had to execute dismal exercises which were somehow supposed to relate to the class work, but I usually mixed whatever was at hand just to see what would happen. The only time that I ever saw Voisard smile was when he mixed some hydrogen sulfide and slowly shuffled around the room, whisking the rotten egg odor into the face of each student with a piece of cardboard.

Another aspect of high school life that I detested was the mania that surrounded football. The cheerleaders, pep rallies, and assemblies grated on my sensibilities. I couldn't fathom why anyone with a lick of sense would want to participate in such juvenile activities. It was the same with the fraternities and sororities. One of my friends was invited to join a major fraternity, and he told me what he had endured for "Hell Night." I couldn't believe it, and although he was a great guy in many ways, I found that I no longer respected him as much as I had before. The sports and the clubs seemed to bring out the worst in people. On one of the very few instances when I was persuaded to attend a football game, I saw some serious fights break out. Even the parents who attended our water polo games and swim meets were sometimes embarrassingly abrasive. This was referred to, apparently without irony, as "team spirit."

My dad was insistent that I continue with advanced math studies, so I didn't have room in my schedule for many electives, but I did manage to secure an art class in the tenth grade. The teacher was a gruff, burly woman named Tressler, who was not well regarded by most of the students, but I liked her. She actually taught us a few things about color and perspective, and she was very encouraging to me about my work. Drawing and writing were almost always stimulating for me, as opposed to the odious tedium of equations and rote memorization. I couldn't envision myself going into any kind of career that would require mathematical skills or a huge repository of stale facts. My dad never had a serious discussion with me about what my future would hold. To his credit, he would frequently say, "find something that you love to do, and it will work out." But then, paradoxically, he would give no support to the things that I loved to do, and instead tried to force me to do what he wanted. When it was time to select my eleventh grade classes, there was only room for one elective, and my dad insisted on another math class. I wanted art, but he was adamant. It was some kind of calculus, I think, and I hated it. After several weeks, I again confronted him on the subject, and again he refused to reconsider.

"OK," I said, "but if you don't let me switch to art, guess what? I'm gonna fail math. "

He was incensed, and for once at a loss for words. Finally he responded.

"You can't do that!"

"Yes I can, and I will," I replied calmly. I had never even come close to failing a class in my life, but I didn't care. I wasn't going to be forced to follow his agenda. He was checkmated and he knew it. He walked away without further comment, but his posture told the story. In a few days I found the signed request for a class change on the kitchen table. I hoped that he would finally accept the idea that I needed more autonomy, and lighten up a bit, but my dad was not one to accept defeat gracefully. Although he could still often be a nice guy, he seemed to keep finding reasons to be angry with me, and the hostilities escalated.

# 18
## The Wages of Sin

I met Lesli in my tenth grade history class. Perhaps it would be more accurate to say that I noticed her, because I don't believe that we spoke to each other until the second semester. The teacher was a young man, Mr. Koons, whose appearance and personality suggested a genealogical link to Jerry Lewis. I was not a big fan. I don't recall the specifics of our initial conversation, but there is a strong likelihood that we shared our respective opinions of the class and the instructor. She referred to him as "Snooky." I liked her irreverence and sense of humor. She was cute, smart and easy to talk with, and I decided that I wanted to get to know her. I asked if I could visit her on Saturday, and she said, "OK."

It was a rainy weekend in February, so I got my mom to drop me off at Lesli's house, which was not too far from us. She lived in a small duplex unit with her mother, who was away at work that day. It was a perfect scenario for me, as we really couldn't go anywhere due to the storm, and we were totally on our own. The "getting to know you" conversation gradually turned into a steamy make-out session. When my mom came back to pick me up, I knew that Lesli and I would be spending a lot of time together. And we did. Fortunately, the February storms passed, and I was easily able to ride my bike over to see her on Saturdays. I had been a little embarrassed to have my mom involved in my itinerary, but I was still too young to drive and parental assistance was sometimes required to get to movies and other destinations.

We soon developed a routine of meeting between classes at school, and having lunch together. The history class was the only one we shared. I usually had to work out for a couple of hours after school, but sometimes the coach would work with the varsity swimmers first, and I would have an extra hour before reporting to the pool. On those days, Lesli and I would look for a quiet place that would accommodate our notions of romance. We were extremely lucky in this respect, because the school was directly across the street from a huge park with lots of hiding places. There were also a few forgotten nooks and crannies in the school itself, which was a grand old structure that dated back to 1925, with a rebuild in 1933 after a huge earthquake.

One time we climbed some stairs to a neglected sundeck above the gym. We found an unlocked door which opened to a storage closet full of beat up, old, canvas lounge chairs with folding wooden frames. The canvas was faded, and the wood dry and grey, but we managed to find one that was intact, and proceeded to set it up. I tested it to see if it would collapse, but it seemed perfectly solid, so I sat down, and then Lesli joined me. We were well into our first kiss of the afternoon when the folding lounge folded. It wouldn't have been much of a crisis except that when we stood up, I found that the whole thing was attached to the tip of my left middle finger, which was caught between two elements of the frame. The pain didn't register for a few seconds, but when it did, it was fierce. Lesli was wavering between sympathy for me and hilarity at the ridiculousness of the situation. I managed to extricate my finger, which was rapidly getting ugly, and we left the sundeck, sadder but no wiser. I had a black fingernail for the rest of the semester, which is prominently featured in a photo of the two of us in formal attire for a spring dance.

The park had its hazards too. There were a few employees who wandered around doing nothing in particular. Lesli and I were good at finding places to hide, but once in a while we would be discovered in various states of dishevelment. Fortunately, we were never rounded up and turned in. I imagine that finding students in similar situations was a commonplace occurrence, and probably one of the few exciting aspects of the job. We continued our activities nonetheless, and simply made it our priority to find better hiding places. The one consistent problem was that I had to work out after being with Lesli. If I had been participating in any other sport besides swimming, everything would have been fine, but my Speedos could not hide the evidence of my recent activities. I either had to "cool off" for a few minutes before exiting the locker room, or endure a cold shower, but either way I was usually a few minutes late getting into the pool, which did not endear me to the coach.

By April we were spending almost all of our free time together. There were school sponsored dances on Friday nights, with live bands that played all kinds of Top Forty tunes. These took place at the Bruin Den, a utility building in the park near the school. Lesli and I would meet at the dance, hang out with our friends, and gyrate through a few songs, then escape to the aptly named Recreation Park. On Saturdays and Sundays we would take long walks, or ride the bus to the Lakewood Mall. Sometimes I could talk my mom into dropping us off and picking us up for a Saturday night movie in downtown Long Beach. There were several old time theatres there with perfect balconies for passionate teenagers. But best of all were the days when Lesli's mom was at work, because then we could have the house to ourselves.

Lesli got along well with my parents and friends. She seemed to get along well with everybody. I had met her sister, who lived a block away with her husband and son, and they were friendly, but I could feel some tension from her mother. On the surface we were cordial, but I knew that she regarded me with skepticism. She was a formidable woman who seemed grimly determined to keep things in their proper order. As a single working parent, she probably had every right to feel that way, especially with the added difficulty of a free-spirited teenager to manage. The nature of Lesli's relationship with this woman was shrouded in mystery. According to Lesli, she was actually a step mother, but I never got a straight answer about their history together, and didn't press it. Although there were some occasions when she was involved in our activities, I always felt that it was best to avoid her if possible, and that was easy because she was at work most of the time.

I spent much more time with Lesli than I ever had with Mary Kay, and most of it was terrific. This time I felt like I had something more than just a girlfriend – I was involved in a relationship! Lesli was warm and upbeat almost all of the time, but she would sometimes tell me about other guys in a way that seemed calculated to inspire jealousy. I was not sure why I needed to know details of her past relationships, but felt compelled to listen when she chose to divulge them. One of her former boyfriends lived a block north of her on the same street, and a good friend of hers, Dave, lived a few houses south. Dave had apparently occupied the same intermediary position between Lesli and the boyfriend that I had held between Jim and Mitzi. I didn't have an issue with any of this until Lesli confessed to having a makeout session with Dave in the nearby park. Now I had an issue – a big issue! Why had she done it? No clear answer. Why did she have to tell me about it? No good reason. I was angry, but in the classically idiotic tradition of lovers everywhere, I directed my anger at Dave, even though I knew that nothing would have happened without solid initiative on Lesli's part. I walked, or maybe stomped, down the block to his house, and rang the doorbell. There was a screen door in front of the regular door, and when Dave answered the bell and saw me, he kept the screen door closed, sizing up the situation very quickly.

"I understand that you and Lesli had a little session in the park." My tone no doubt indicated that it was not intended to be an objective statement.

"Um . . . yeah, I guess we did."

"You wanna come out here and discuss it?"

"No, thanks."

His response caught me by surprise. I had anticipated some sort of physical altercation that would give me a chance to vent my anger and feel heroic. Now I was left with nothing to do. It was depressingly anticlimactic.

"Well . . . see that it doesn't happen again!"

"OK." We stared at each other for a few moments, then I turned away and he closed the door. That was it. I wasn't satisfied, but at least I had made my point. Lesli was appropriately contrite, and harmony was restored. I hadn't really wanted to break up over her indiscretion, but I was getting that same slightly queasy feeling of insecurity that was becoming so familiar. It made me disinclined to ask her too many questions, and continued to underscore my belief that I had better be careful, because girls could be hazardous to my health.

On a Saturday evening, I was lying on the floor in front of the TV waiting for Jim to show up. When the doorbell rang, and my brother let him in, I was still on the floor. I recall Jim standing near me and saying, "Hey man, let's go," when I suddenly realized that I had no energy. I felt unable to get to my feet, and my mouth was bone dry. I told Jim that I didn't think that I could go out that night, and he took off. I had no idea why I was so lethargic, and chalked it up to the accumulated effect of too many workouts. When I managed to get up and get to bed, I fell into a solid sleep, but the next morning I felt worse, and my throat and tongue were sore. I thought that it might be some weird kind of cold, but when I explained the symptoms to my mom, she decided that we should check with the doctor on Monday. When we arrived at his office, I again described my symptoms. The doctor checked me out and determined that I had mononucleosis. Mono!

We all knew about mono - it was the "kissing disease." I didn't know anyone who had contracted it, but there were various stories and theories floating around – none of them good. I was worried. Had I gotten it from Lesli? Had I given it to Lesli? As soon as we got home, I called her up and told her what was going on. I would have to stay home for several weeks, rest, and take some medicine. It had been strongly hinted that I should curtail any "extracurricular activities" with her. My prospects for the near future looked dismal, but Lesli seemed undismayed. She felt fine, and she would come over to see me. She wasn't worried about getting sick, and was ready to bring me soup and nurse me back to health. It was very sweet.

After two weeks of convalescence, my appetite was back and I felt much better. I was still under house arrest however, and starting to get very restless. Lesli and I talked on the phone almost every night, and we were both very eager to resume our amorous exploits. On the following Saturday, my parents went somewhere with my brother, so I took a chance and rode my bike to Lesli's house. I felt perfectly healthy as I pulled up to her door and rang the bell. I had called and she was expecting me, so it was a joyful reunion on the porch. She suggested that

I park my bike in the alley "just in case," so I cruised around the block and locked it to a telephone pole, then walked back to the front door, and we went inside. We immediately ensconced ourselves in Lesli's bed, and soon our clothes were strewn around the room. We had progressed way beyond mere kissing, but were confidently cautious about the possibility of pregnancy. It was all very exciting. I had no feelings of guilt, and Lesli didn't seem to either, but we did worry about getting caught or found out, especially by her mom.

I was soon declared fully recovered, and Lesli and I picked up where we had left off before my illness. I never could determine how I had become ill – Lesli never had any symptoms, nor did anyone else that I knew. But I was glad to be officially healthy again. It was spring in Southern California and the weather was fantastic, which seemed to enhance our delirious teenage version of love. Lesli was a great one for sending me notes, frequently embellished with stickers, photos, and drawings, in handwriting that seemed to reflect her free-spirited personality. Some of them capture the wide-eyed, gee-whiz quality of our affair;

"Bill! This just happens to be an extremely important, extra super special note for you alone! In case you haven't yet guessed, this is cuz today we are actually four months old! I simply have to tell you that these past months with you have been the very, very, VERY most far out- of- sight ones in my whole entire life!"

"Since rabbit's feet are supposed to bring Good Luck, I hurried down to get you one - you see - with me being near you when you start driving, you'll need all the luck ya can get!"

"What I'd really like to get ya, things like; sunshine for your sad moods, blue, blue skies, and extra special grass that's so-o-o-o green and soft, and happy days together, but you just can't buy things like that! I loves ya!

Yep, everything was wonderful - until Mothers Day rolled around. We knew that Lesli's mother would be very busy that weekend because she worked for a florist, and Mother's Day weekend was traditionally the primo time of year for bouquets and arrangements. In fact, she was already cranky about the long hours that she would be putting in at the shop. But we were anything but cranky, because we knew that we would be extra safe in the house that weekend. So we made our plans. Lesli would call me as soon as her mom left for work, and I would jet over on my bike. We would spend the morning in bed, and then head off to the beach to meet our friends. Perfect!

I rode to her house, and locked my bike in the alley. It was around nine when Lesli let me in the front door. Her room was small and cozy, especially with the dim light from the drawn shades. We had the radio on at a low volume, enjoying Dylan's *Lay, Lady, Lay* and *Pinball Wizard* by the Who. The morning air was cool on my bare skin. By eleven, we were both feeling lazy and relaxed, and starting to consider heading for the beach, but all of that changed in a heartbeat. The front door was creaking open! I grabbed my clothes from the floor and jumped into Lesli's closet, closing the door as quickly and quietly as possible. All I could think about was getting my clothes on without making any noise. The closet was full of hanging garments, boxes on shelves, and shoes on the floor. It was also dark, and I could barely see what I was doing. I got my boxer shorts on with some difficulty – there was hardly any room to move, but I felt a little more secure. If the door opened, at least I wouldn't be completely exposed. I was now sweating with panic. The moisture caused the fabric of my clothes to stick to my skin as I dressed, but I finally managed to get my t shirt and jeans on. I found my shoes, and some socks that might have been mine or Lesli's, but there was no way I could get them on without rustling around and bumping into things. I took a few deep breaths to see if I could slow my heart down, and tried to concentrate on escape.

I could hear voices from somewhere in the house, but I couldn't understand what was being said. It sounded like a normal conversation, so perhaps our little tryst was as yet undiscovered. Time was crawling, so I don't have any idea how long it was before Lesli cracked open the closet door. I noticed that she had somehow managed to find her bathrobe. She whispered, "My mom is in the kitchen. I'm gonna try to keep her there. I'm opening the window for you, so wait a little, then go!" She looked brave but worried as she left. My heart was racing again, and I still had no sense of time. I thought about staying in the closet until midnight, and then leaving when her mom was asleep. Perhaps she would soon go back to work, and everything would be OK. There was no clear course of action. I had no idea why she had returned to the house, or what she would do. Maybe she already suspected that we were up to no good. I pushed the door open a bit more and listened. I could still hear them talking. It was time to go.

I took another deep breath, quietly pushed the closet door open, and slowly peeked out. I could see out the doorway and down the hall to the front door. The coast was clear. I bolted around the bed, shoes in hand, to the window, dropped the shoes outside and scrambled through. I'm sure I must have made some noise, but I was full of adrenalin and way beyond caution. I ran through the side yard outside the window to a gate that opened onto the alley, fumbled the gate open, and got to my bike. Almost there! The combination lock held me up for a few seconds, and then it was open. I jumped on, still carrying my shoes, and raced down the alley. My head was clearing a bit, and I realized that Lesli's mom might get her car and track me down, so I took a circuitous route, only pausing in a secluded area to put on my shoes. It was then that I realized that I had left my bathing suit and towel in the closet. I doubted that Lesli's mom would find them, but even if she did it wasn't conclusive evidence of anything. I decided to go to Mike's or Jim's, so we could collaborate on an alibi. My panic suddenly transformed itself into exhilaration. I had gotten away! What a story! But it wasn't over yet. Maybe I should remain on guard until I talked to Lesli. After all, I had no idea what might have happened after my escape. The exhilaration faded. Maybe Lesli was in trouble. There were too many thoughts and emotions racing through my head. Finally I just headed home with a feeling of exhaustion. When I arrived, everything seemed normal. My mom said, "What happened? I thought you and Lesli were going to the beach." I mumbled something about the plan not working out and went to my room. So far I was safe – Lesli's mother hadn't called my parents. Now all I could do was wait.

Lesli called me that night. Her mother was back at work, staying late to handle the Mother's Day overflow. I asked her what had happened.

"Nothing, really," she said, "I don't know why she came home. It was weird."

"What do you think?"

"I don't know. She might be suspicious - she's always suspicious. But I don't think she really knows anything. I was afraid to ask her why she came back."

"Well, did she say anything about it?"

"No," she replied, "We just talked like everything was normal."

"Has she ever done this before?" I asked.

"Maybe. I can't remember."

"Did you hear anything when I left?"

"I don't think so. I don't know. This whole thing is kind of creepy. I found your towel and stuff in the closet."

"I guess we better cool it for a while," I said.

"Yeah – I guess."

So we cooled it, at least as far as Lesli's bed was concerned. But there were plenty of other places where we could heat things up. And besides, summer vacation was rapidly approaching, and we would have much more free time to spend together.

When school ended, we settled into a pleasant routine. Lesli had to take a summer class in math. She was extremely intelligent, but numbers were not her strong suit, and I was probably at least partially at fault for distracting her from her studies. It was a morning class, so I would meet her at around noon, and we would either walk to the beach, or head to her house. Yes, we were up to our old tricks again. Lesli's mom had said nothing to indicate suspicion, and it had been over a month since our "close call," so we were feeling stupidly confident. The luxury of being alone in Lesli's room on a hot summer day, with the music on and the lights off, was too seductive to resist. I turned sixteen that summer and got my driver's license, which gave us much greater mobility, at least when my dad would allow me to use his car. As June stretched into July, and July to August, we frolicked in the bed and on the beach, went to movies, took long walks, and made elaborate plans for the future.

On a lazy mid-August afternoon, we were in our favorite spot, engaged in our favorite activity. Lesli decided to go to the kitchen for a snack. I heard her say, "That looks like my mom's car," and then came the sound of the door locking. She hurried back into the room. "Get in the closet," she whispered. At least I had been smart enough to stash my clothes in the closet, even though I had been dumb enough to assume that we were safe. Lesli put something on and scurried away, while

I quickly dressed. I could hear yelling, and pounding on the front door – evidently, Lesli had locked a deadbolt from inside, and her mom could not get in. The noise stopped. I knew that this would be bad. Everything was quiet for a minute, and then I heard something nearby. It was the sound of the bedroom window being opened! There was some muffled thumping as Lesli's mom evidently climbed through the window, and a louder crack accompanied with muttered profanity. Her shoes were loud on the hardwood floor, as she rapidly strode from the bedroom through the house to find Lesli.

"Alright, where is he?" Loud and threatening.

No reply

"I know he's here!" Louder and more threatening.

"In the closet." Lesli sounded totally defeated, but I couldn't think about that now. I had only a few seconds to prepare myself. My heart was so loud that I couldn't concentrate. What would I say? What would she do?

The closet door swung open. Lesli's mother glared at me, her eyes level with mine, face flushed, small beads of perspiration between her nose and upper lip, and a fresh bruise on her forehead. The light from the window behind her accentuated the wild wisps of her hair that had come undone. I was paralyzed.

In the coldest, most measured tone possible, she said, "Don't you think that's about enough of this?"

It sounded like a statement more than a question, so I wasn't sure how to respond, or even if I should respond. Finally I mumbled, "I guess so."

She backed away just enough so that I could exit, but I had no idea what to do. Lesli was standing nearby, looking horrified. Her mother gave me another hard look and said, "Don't you dare leave this house. I'm calling your parents." They left the room, and I could hear Lesli's mother scolding her in a hushed but angry voice as she made the call. All I could do was wait, and speculate on the horrible and imminent future.

After what seemed like an eternity, the doorbell rang and I could hear the voices of my parents. Lesli opened the door, and they walked into the living room. I realized that it was the first time our parents had ever met. My mom and dad faced Lesli's mother, waiting for her to speak. "Get your son out of here!" she commanded, and then launched into an almost evangelical tirade about sin and immorality. She actually sounded unhinged, yelling about "fouling your own nest" and "breaking faith." I started to wonder why she had decided to trap us, instead of having a serious talk with Lesli about her concerns, and that Lesli's life at home might be a lot worse than I had thought. My mom and dad didn't interrupt. They looked a bit surprised, as if they had expected something different. Finally she slowed down enough for my dad to say, "Look, we're really sorry about this. We'll take him home." He indicated that I should follow and we headed for the door. I glanced at Lesli and saw the tears, but I could also see that she wasn't completely crushed. We knew better than to try to say anything to each other, but we also knew that it would be impossible for anyone to keep us from ever seeing each other again. As my parents got into the car, I told my dad that I had left my bike in the alley. "OK," he said, "But you go straight home. We have some things to discuss." I walked back to the alley, got my bike, and rode home as slowly as possible.

For me, the aftermath was strangely subdued. My dad asked me if Lesli was pregnant, and I assured him that she wasn't. He then told me that he thought it was best for me to leave her alone for now. I couldn't quite decipher his attitude. He didn't really seem angry, although he treated the situation very seriously. Ironically, a few weeks earlier he had quietly given me access to his stash of condoms, "just in case." I thought that he may have been a little proud of the fact that his son had scored, but also a little embarrassed about being proud. My mom seemed more worried about Lesli than anything else. Her mother had put on quite a performance, and both my parents were obviously unnerved by it. There was nothing for me to do but wait.

A few days later I received a letter. Lesli was under tight restriction, but had managed to have a friend smuggle it out and take it to the post office.

"Billy – This letter is probably a royal mess – I'm sorry, but it'll have to do. Bill, stop shaking! I loves ya, so with all of our put together love, we can both really and truly make it! I can't put everything down I feel – if only someone I knew here could take me in as a foster child then I could see ya. Bill I love ya and need ya so very much – take good care of yourself – in two years we can be extra OK again!"

Lesli did end up in a foster home nearby. She acted as if she regarded the whole thing as an adventure, but she may have been disguising her true feelings. I couldn't believe that her mom would be so vindictive, and my parents were shocked. We managed to see each other at a couple of the school dances, but it was not the same. I felt guilty but relieved, and guilty again about feeling relieved. This hadn't been a mere breakup. Our relationship had been shattered by forces beyond our control. I was shaken by what had happened, but I never believed that we had done anything wrong. Our wonderful affair had met an undeserved fate.

# 19

## Extracurricular Activities

Most of my free time during high school was devoted to girls, even though my affairs with Lesli and Mary Kay had ended in tragedy. My best friends, Jim and Mike, were likewise preoccupied, so although we still got together, we were not causing as much mayhem as we had in previous years. There were many serious conversations about our various triumphs and defeats with the opposite sex, and also a fair amount of scheming and tactical analysis as we planned our romantic campaigns. Did I say romantic? Sorry -it was really all about sex.

In 1968, when I entered high school, the "Summer of Love" had already taken place in San Francisco. The social values of the Fifties were still hanging in there, although they would soon be eroded by a new outlook. There were a few "bad girls" and an occasional pregnancy, but, for the most part, having a girlfriend and dating was an elaborate and emotional struggle for sexual intimacy that was often unconsummated. It was very exciting, but also fraught with real peril, especially for the girls.

My school was huge, so it was easy to be unaware of what was going on in other cliques, but within my circle the dissemination of gossip regarding breakups, makeups, and new couples was endless. I was a year away from getting my driver's license, so spending a few hours at the local drive-in was not yet an option. Fortunately, our school held dances almost every Friday night at a recreational building in the park. The lighting was always suitably dim, and there was minimal adult supervision plus a live band. Jim and I would meet our girls there, and we would dance and mingle for an hour or two, then leave the building to generate some steam on the damp park lawn. At around ten or eleven, the dance would end. We would escort the girls to wherever their parents or friends were picking them up for a ride home, and then walk back to Park Estates. The walk took us through the Recreation Park Golf Course.

At night the course was closed, but there was a road through it that provided a nifty short cut. It was chained at each end to prevent cars from entering, but we simply hopped the chain. We also took this route in the mornings to get to school, and would swipe errant golf balls on the way. There was a shed along this road that housed the golf carts, and the door was secured with a latch and padlock. I noticed that the latch was screwed into the door, and realized that we could get in by just unscrewing and removing it, padlock and all. So, one Friday night, we brought a screwdriver with us, and hid it next to the shed on our way to the dance. When we returned several hours later, we recovered the screwdriver, and proceeded to break into the shed. There was a two storey clubhouse nearby, with a café and pro shop, but the lights were all out, and the doors were locked up. We felt safe, but it still seemed like a good idea to be quiet and cautious.

We got into the shed without any problem. It was dark, but we could see well enough to select a cart and locate the correspondingly numbered key hanging from a hook on the wall. We rolled the cart out of the shed, and then closed the door and replaced the latch and lock, which didn't make much sense. Maybe we thought that the cart would not be missed, or maybe we were just trying to be considerate thieves. Jim jumped into the driver's seat, and started up the cart. It wasn't very loud, but the noise seemed amplified by the surrounding silence. I got in as he hit the accelerator, and we rode onto the course.

The vehicle was obviously not designed for speed. When Jim floored it, we were probably doing about fifteen miles per hour downhill. We zigzagged around on the grass, and experimented to see if the cart could be easily rolled. We were pretty far out on the course, and having a good old time, when I looked back and saw lights in the distant windows of the clubhouse. I alerted Jim, and we agreed that it was time to flee the scene, so we aimed the cart downhill at the nearest tree, and leaped out. As we ran to the outer perimeter of the course, we heard the faint sound of the collision. There was no evidence of any activity behind or around us, but we weren't taking any chances. We jumped the fence and shot across Pacific Coast Highway to the safety of Park Estates and home, congratulating ourselves on another great evening. We had spent time with our girlfriends, dancing and necking in the park, and topped it off with a bit of delinquency. It was just like dessert after an excellent meal. Yessir - life was good indeed.

Of course, there were those off hours when the girls were busy or otherwise indisposed, so we would fall back on pyrotechnics to keep us sharp. Jim and I were still taking our nocturnal excursions. The Sambo's restaurant across Bellflower was always open and we often had a snack there. Jim had managed to scavenge a couple of cherry bombs, so one night when we had finished our food and paid the bill, we went into the men's room and flushed one. It is my belief that the fellow who designed the cherry bomb had intended it specifically for this purpose. Otherwise, why create an explosive device that would still perform perfectly when fully immersed? It was big enough to be loud and destructive, but small enough to glide through standard plumbing. If cherries had come with instructions, they could have simply stated, "Light and flush," and every kid in America would have known exactly what to do. Even without instructions, it was fairly obvious.

We tried to be creative with the second bomb. A few days later, we were at my house and my parents were out. We decided to attach a lead fishing sinker to the bomb, and lob it over the back yard fence and into Steve Baker's pool. We waited until dark, then went out, lit it up, and tossed it. There was a little bloopy splash, and a few seconds later a huge, bright, silent flash sent water high into the air. When we returned to the house, the phone was ringing. I picked it up, and Mrs. Baker was on the line. She was a sweet woman, and very polite.

"Hello, Bill, this is Dorothy Baker calling."

"Oh, hi Mrs. Baker."

"Hi. Look, we just saw something really strange out in the back yard, and I wondered if you noticed it."

"No, I've been inside watching TV. What was it?"

"Well, I don't know, but it looked like a big flash of light in the pool."

"That's weird. What do want me to do?"

"Maybe you could just check your back yard and see if there's anything there?"

"OK – I'll take a look. If I see anything, I'll call you back.

"Alright. Thank you."

Jim and I went back out, and I turned on the deck lights so it would look as if I was diligently scouring the yard. I left them on for about ten minutes, and then switched them off. I called Mrs. Baker and told her that I hadn't seen anything. There was just the barest hint of a giggle in her voice as she thanked me, suggesting that she hadn't been fooled at all. Mrs. Baker was pretty cool.

At about this same time, I decided that I wanted to try smoking some of the dreaded marijuana. I had read extensively about pot in Playboy and the Free Press, and despite the dire warnings from Sonny Bono and other equally respected authorities, I didn't think that it was necessarily a first giant step on the road to perdition. I consulted with Jim on the matter, and he was confident that he could get some from the older sister of a friend. The plan was to sneak out and meet at around midnight on Friday. We had selected a quiet, secluded spot to light up. I was bringing some food because, according to my research, we might get hungry. By Wednesday, Jim had the dope, and by Thursday he was busted. The older sister had been caught by her parents and forced to name names. Then her parents called his parents and all hell broke loose. Jim was beyond restricted – he was under house arrest. He was also a standup guy, never mentioning me as the instigator of the crime. I had been lucky again, but the episode soured me on the risks associated with illicit drugs, and I never got involved with them again.

We were all anxious to drive, and therefore willing to take some ill-advised risks in order to savor the thrill of operating a motor vehicle. Mini-bikes and go-karts were common, yet questionable, ways to scratch that itch. Neither was street legal, but in our quiet suburb there was always a kid who had one or the other. I had tried out a friend's mini-bike, and had ended up with a nice deep gash on my left shin. My few attempts at riding a motorcycle were problematic as well, so I was not as enraptured by these devices as some of the other kids were. Jim was more interested than I, despite the fact that he had once found himself barefoot on a mini with no brakes, headed straight for a cinderblock wall. It didn't turn out well - he left the soles of his feet on the asphalt, and was laid up for quite a spell. Jim had an older friend named Jay, who raced speedboats and motorcycles, and was nice enough to let Jim hang around while he worked on them. Unfortunately, he crashed his motorcycle into a tree, head on, and didn't survive. Another guy I had known during the days when Gary, the bad boy, had been my mentor met a similar fate. His name was Scott McKenzie, and he had been one of the few big boys who treated me like a friend. I had lost contact with him, and was dismayed to learn that he had also died on a motorcycle during his high school years. In fact, every motorcyclist that I've ever known has had at least one serious accident.

Getting behind the wheel of a car without a license was not as dangerous from a physical standpoint, but it wasn't without hazards. During the ninth and tenth grades, Jim was sometimes able to "borrow" his family's station wagon. On nights when his parents took the other car and went out for the evening, we would drive around Park Estates, too worried about getting caught to really enjoy ourselves, but acting like we were having a ball. It seemed like a huge risk for Jim, given his father's attitude about such things - maybe it was Jim's way of striking back.

Mike was also interested in cars and motorcycles, and his father was not at all like Jim's. I would sometimes find the two of them in the garage on a Saturday morning, his dad working on their Forty-nine Chevy, with tools strewn all over the place, hands black with grease and the inevitable trickle of bright red blood, alternately starting and revving the engine, then turning it off and diving back under the hood. It bored me to tears. Mike's dad bought a Nash Metropolitan, and Mike was allowed to drive it in the mall parking lot on Sundays, when most of the stores were closed and the lot was deserted. The Metro was an object of much derision, because it was a silly looking little "woman's car," in two tone pink and white. Mike and his pal, Wayne, would take turns burning the hell out of the engine, transmission and tires, while I sat in the back seat. It was fun to hear the car squeal and see the white smoke from abrupt starts, stops, doughnuts and brodies, as they bullied it through a brutal workout. I felt some sympathy for the Metro. It always provided good entertainment, but never garnered any respect. When Mike got his license, he was not keen to be associated with it, especially on dates. It spent most of its golden years at the curb.

At sixteen, we could go down to the DMV and take the tests for a driver's license. I had taken classes at school to prepare for these tests, and arrived early on the morning of my birthday, well prepared. I passed everything easily, and was processed and photographed. Minors were photographed in a black and white profile shot at that time, which made it fairly easy to create fake licenses, but now I was getting a real one! I left the DMV with a temporary – the genuine article would arrive in the mail. This was a milestone, and I was anticipating a new frontier of dates and drive-ins. When I got home, the first thing that I did was ask my dad if I could use his car. He finally gave me permission to use it for a couple of hours, while adroitly managing to convey his reluctance. This was to be his modus operandi until I managed to get my own vehicle. It was one of the few remaining opportunities that he had for leveraging some control over my life, and he never let me forget it.

"Hey, dad, can I use the car?"

"Well, I was planning to run a few errands."

"OK, when are you gonna do that?"

"I hadn't decided."

I still hadn't gotten a solid yes or no. "Well, what do you need to do?"

"What do you need to do?"

"I was gonna go to Los Altos with Mitzi."

Long pause and audible sigh, "Well, I guess I don't

need it right now. "

"So it's OK?"

"I guess so."

I can't recall a single instance when he simply said yes or no. When he seemed especially obdurate I would say, "Look, if you don't want me to use it, just say so. I get it – it's your car." But he would just work through the standard dialogue, making it abundantly clear that he was bestowing his largesse upon me. It was extremely annoying, but I put up with it because I wanted that car.

The car in question was a 1968 AMX. Again, my dad had chosen something sporty and unusual. It was white with a big red racing stripe, two reclining seats, and lots of power. It was almost as if the designer of the car had deliberately set out to create the perfect vehicle for a sixteen year old boy. I was not inclined to race or speed, but the car, by its very nature, gave me the appearance of an aggressive delinquent to adults, and a smooth operator to my peers. This was fine with me. The reclining seats were custom made for drive-ins, whether we intended to view the film or indulge in other activities. My dad, despite his irritating demeanor, was quite generous in allowing me to use the AMX, so it was usually available for dates during my junior and senior years. Had he actually anticipated my needs in selecting this particular car? I'll never know.

Now that we were legal motorists, we discovered new opportunities for disrupting the tranquility of suburbia. Mike and I had formed a little ad hoc committee on fire extinguishers, and decided that there was a particular type of extinguisher that could be re-purposed to meet our immediate requirements. This was a tank that could be filled to a certain level with water, and then topped off with compressed air from a filling station. When properly loaded, it would fire a strong jet of water more than twenty feet. We did some "shopping," and finally found what we needed in the same multilevel parking lot that we used for explosives. At this time, Mike was driving a VW van that his dad had bought. We simply rolled into the unsupervised lot, pulled the extinguisher off of the wall, and rolled out. We tested it scrupulously, refilling it several times, checking the accuracy of the pressure gauge, and the range and force of the spray, then took it out for a trial run. It performed magnificently! We would slowly cruise around, looking for a likely target, usually a kid around our age. Then we would pull over and ask for some directions as politely as possible. When our quarry was a few feet from the passenger window, the request for help would suddenly metamorphose into an act of aggression. "Care for a swim?" I would inquire, as I thoroughly soaked our victim in ice cold water. Sometimes other friends would join us and ask for a turn at the hose. Once we pulled into the local Tastee-Freeze for some soft serve ice cream. We were sitting in the van, enjoying our cones, when we noticed a carload of girls parked nearby. We seemed to be getting disdainful glances from the driver, who sported a huge and elaborate beehive of carefully lacquered hair. We considered the situation languidly, and when it was evident that the girls were preparing to depart, Mike fired a perfectly aimed jet through the driver's window which absolutely destroyed her coiffure, turning it into a sopping, stringy mess. He started up the van, and we slowly drove past the distraught females, waving a cheery goodbye.

On the home front, I was spending most of my time drumming. I had one friend in particular, Rhys, who was a guitarist, and as much of a fan of the Who as I was. On the weekends, we would retire to my room in the back of the house, crank up my stereo, and play along with the entire *Tommy* album. When *Live at Leeds* was released, we added that to our playlist. I really have no idea how loud we sounded to my parents and the neighbors, but it could have been pretty noisy. If Rhys wasn't available, I would play by myself, and sometimes turn around to find several of my friends watching through the bedroom windows. My dad didn't complain much, but sometimes he would insist on some quiet so he could nurse a migraine on the family room couch, with an ice bag on his forehead. Once I asked him why he didn't lie down in his bedroom, which was more insulated than the family room. I thought it would be more comfortable for him, but he retorted in his usual exasperated tone that it was "even noisier back there." I didn't believe him, and it struck me that perhaps he wanted everyone to be aware of how much he was suffering.

When he wasn't suffering, my dad found enough energy to hassle me about the length of my hair. This gradually escalated into a full- fledged war, but initially it was a series of consistent, minor but aggravating, confrontations. My hair was not very long, but a little bit of extra around the ears and the back seemed to be a red flag for every adult I encountered. In the eyes of my dad, my coach, and the parents of friends and girlfriends, long hair was the emblem of those damn Hippies, who were determined to destroy the status quo. I had always hated getting my hair cut. No matter how many precautions were taken, and in those days barbers would wrap a tissue snugly around the neck and clip a sheet-like cover over that, I always ended up with an irritating itch under my collar. Now I not only hated getting clipped, but liked the longer hair as well. So, when I was forced to deal with the issue, I would get as little hair removed as possible. It was technically a haircut, and would get me off the hook for a little while, even though it didn't meet the desired standards of my oppressors. The fact that I was getting so much static about this issue just ratcheted up my defiance level.

My dad had another habit which was extremely offensive. Sometimes I would sleep late on Saturday and Sunday mornings. It seemed perfectly normal to me, and was common among my peers. After all, I had attended school all week, done homework - well, some - and participated in vigorous workouts every afternoon, and even some mornings. On most Fridays there was a polo game or swim meet, and a late evening out with a girlfriend. A couple of extra hours of slumber were appropriate under such circumstances. And yet there were times when my dad would barge into my room at around ten, angrily exhorting me to, "Get up, get up!" It was startling to say the least. I would ask why, and he would say something about laziness and then storm out - this from the champion snoozer of Park Estates! There was no reason for it other than his need to assert himself.

On one of my late night excursions with Jim, I forgot to latch the door when I returned home. My dad evidently noticed this, and rousted me with even more vitriol than usual.

"Come on, wake up!" I was a light sleeper, but it still took a few moments for me to assess the situation...

"What?" I said, not understanding what he was so wigged out about.

"Did you go outside last night?"

"What?" I wasn't connecting the dots.

"You heard me – did you go outside?!"

"Yeah. So?"

"Dammit – you're not supposed to go outside after I lock up!"

"Why not?" I was angry but calm.

"What were you doing?" He had adroitly sidestepped my challenge.

"I couldn't get to sleep." He continued to glower at me.

There was no way that I was going to tell him what I had really been up to. "So I took a walk around the block. Look - what's the big deal?"

"You're not to go out after I lock up!"

"Why not?"

"Because I'm telling you!"

"But I don't get it - what's the problem? I just took a walk." I had him - he didn't have any real reason to create such a fuss, and he knew it. This was simply persecution, and I wasn't going to take it lying down, even though I actually was lying down. I was starting to enjoy myself. He was visibly disconcerted, and I was feeling collected and confident.

"You'll do as I say!" Domestic totalitarianism was his last resort.

"What are you gonna do? Lock me in? If I need to take a walk, I will."

He was absolutely steaming, but also at an impasse. We stared at each other for what seemed like a long time, and then he stomped out, slamming the door. For the first time, I felt like the tide of battle might be turning. But it was going to be a long war.

# 20

# Once In Love with Amy

In late September of 1969, the fall term had just begun. It was my junior year, and I had been promoted to the B team in water polo. This was not a significant achievement. Almost all of the juniors had been promoted. We were milling around outside the gym after school, preparing to board the bus for an away game and wearing our red and gold sweats. Other students were passing by, and several girls were loitering in a group on the sidewalk. One of them was a knockout, and I asked a teammate who she might be. "I'm pretty sure her name is Amy," he said, "and I heard Derek is after her." I took a long look at Amy, and decided that she and Derek wouldn't be a very good match. A few minutes later, we were headed to our game.

Later that evening, Jim and I wound up at the world famous Bruin Den, usually referred to as the "canteen," where the school sponsored dances were held. By the time we walked in, there was a sizeable crowd, and the band was playing Creedence Clearwater tunes. We met a few friends, caught up on things, and checked out the clientele. The canteen was always dim. It was a large open space with a linoleum floor, probably illuminated by three or four sixty watt bulbs. Because of the poor lighting and the large number of kids dancing and kibitzing, it could be difficult to locate a particular person at any given time. But I wasn't looking for a particular person at that moment, just checking out the couples on the dance floor. The band took a break for a minute, and the dancing couples reconfigured into singles and groups. Amy was suddenly in my line of vision, talking with a couple of other girls. Even at a distance, her attractiveness was obvious. I realized that I wanted to get a closer look, so I walked over with as much insouciance as I could muster. I had never been shy, so by the time I was near enough for an introduction, I knew what I would say. She turned to look at me with an innocent and mildly curious expression, and I remember thinking, "Wow, she's really beautiful," as I tried to maintain my air of nonchalance.

"If you're Amy" I said, "rumor has it that a certain individual named Derek Lonigan is looking for you."

"Oh . . ." This, apparently, was not good news. I gave her a few moments to consider her options.

"Maybe we could dance while you're deciding what to do. I know Derek, and he'll probably leave you alone if he thinks you're with someone else. If you want him to leave you alone.

"Well, I guess he's a nice guy, but . . . thanks for the warning,"

"My pleasure," I said, realizing the truth of that statement. Now she was smiling. The band started playing again, so I had to shout, and she leaned in toward me. "Would you care to dance?"

"OK, "she replied. "I feel kind of dumb asking, but what's your name?"

So we danced through the night, and we held each other tight – wait – no we didn't. Actually, we danced and tried to talk, but the canteen was too noisy for much conversation. When we finally stepped outside, and she told me that it was almost time for her to leave, I was disappointed, but encouraged by the fact that she had stayed with me all evening.

"Do you feel safe now? I asked.

"Ummm . . . I guess so – from what?

"Derek."

She laughed. "Oh yes, very safe. I forgot all about that. Thank you."

"OK then." The clock was ticking. "Look – I'd like to offer my services again. Maybe next weekend?"

She appeared to be thinking it over. Then I got another smile. "Well, I guess I might need protection."

"Can I call you?"

"OK," She asked around for a pencil and a scrap of paper, wrote down her number, and quickly handed it to me. "I have to go now", she said, as she started to walk away. "Bye."

I smiled and waved, elated over what had unexpectedly turned out to be a delightful turn of events. Gradually, the elation settled into a sense of overwhelming optimism. I went back in to find Jim, so that we could walk home together. I was looking forward to telling him about what had happened. I still had Amy's phone number in my hand, and decided to put it in my wallet for safekeeping. I unfolded the paper, and there was the number and her name, as if I would forget it. I liked her handwriting.

Resisting the temptation to call her immediately, I waited until Monday night. The football game on Friday, loathsome as it was, seemed like a safe bet for a first date and that is what we settled upon. I drove the AMX to her address, a nice looking house with a well-tended front yard, across the street from an elementary school. It was already dark, and the porch light was on, so I took a breath, walked up to the door, and rang the bell.

There was a delicious moment of anticipation, and then Amy answered the door, looking lovely. She invited me to come inside, and I knew that I was about to meet the parents. Her mother was friendly and polite, but her father was not very welcoming. Without saying anything that could technically be labeled impolite, he managed to convey his disapproval quite eloquently. After a couple of cursory questions and an admonition to have Amy home by eleven thirty, we escaped. As we drove to the game, I asked if her father might have had a rough day. She told me that he was actually her stepfather, and not to worry - he would thaw out eventually. The fact that she had used the word "eventually" was encouraging.

We sat together in the crowded bleachers and ignored the game. I held her hand and got a little reassuring squeeze in return. When the game was into its second quarter, we decided to take a walk. The park was across the street, and the air was sweet and cool. Everything was very quiet after the noise of the football crowd. I put my arm around her and we slowly wandered among the trees and shadows, still talking, gradually revealing a little of ourselves to each other. Her father was a doctor. She had a horse and usually rode on the weekends. Her family had moved to Long Beach last year, and she still didn't know too many people. We were surprised that we had never met before at school, because we had a couple of friends in common. She was everything that I wanted her to be – a bit shy, but very sharp, and funny. We were walking more slowly now, and talking less. I turned to face her, and we both knew what was going to happen. There was no awkwardness or hesitation. It was just a slow, soft, gentle kiss. Well, maybe several. And my world had suddenly been irrevocably altered.

Soon we were officially a couple, meeting each other for lunch and between classes. I found myself spending even less time listening to teachers, and instead writing notes and drawing pictures for Amy. We developed the habit of leaving messages for each other in the flat file drawers that we were allotted for art class, because we had the same art instructor, Mr. Milroy, but at different times. Milroy was a good guy. Somehow he found out that Amy and I were together, and he had an unobtrusive way of letting us know that he liked the idea. On the other hand, Zubbo, the water polo coach was not so supportive. Amy had a history class with him, and when we would linger by his classroom door before the bell, he would sometimes tease us. He started to refer to me as "Grub" because my hair was longer than he liked. He would ask Amy what she saw in me, and then shake his head and go back into the classroom. He did all of this with some humor, but there was also an edge to it. He was probably only twenty three or four, and couldn't figure out why such a stunning young woman would want to be involved with a punk like me. It was sometimes a mystery to me as well, but I certainly wasn't going to take any chances by questioning her on the subject.

In my Spanish class I sat next to Dave, Lesli's "friend," who was turning out to be a very entertaining guy. Our differences had been put aside, and since he was also on the polo and swim teams, we had much in common. We would play word games, passing a sheet of paper back and forth, and ending up with hilariously obscene results. We would also use our newly acquired language skills to translate drivel like the theme song to *Mr. Ed* into Spanish. This made the time pass more quickly, but I was merely waiting for the thrill of seeing Amy's radiant face through the little window in the classroom door.

Sometimes at lunch we would hang out with friends, but we preferred to ignore everyone else and find a spot where we could be alone. Usually this was a semi-isolated stairwell. We would sit on the steps, have some food, hold hands, and talk about whatever seemed important at the time. Sometimes we would see each other after school, but not often because I had workouts. When she could, Amy would attend the polo games and swim meets, but her father ran interference on some of them, especially if they were not at Wilson. He didn't seem to be thawing out.

I looked forward to every weekend because we could spend longer periods of time together, but Amy usually had some difficulties negotiating with her father when it came to seeing me. He never told her that we couldn't go out together, but he would set up conditions and restrictions that seemed solely calculated to make things difficult for us. I was always polite to him, but only because he was calling the shots. I really wanted to smash his face. He would complain to her about my hair, and once told her that she couldn't see me unless I had it cut. As I've said, there was nothing remotely controversial about my hair, just a few extra curls around the edges. But I was really becoming obstinate about cutting it because of the consistent harassment from my dad and the coaches. After this dictum, Amy's younger brother saw me at the Forty-Niner Days carnival, and told her dad that I was still untrimmed. It is a testament of my feelings for her that I finally allowed myself to get clipped – but just enough to meet minimum standards and shut down her dad.

Amy was not very comfortable with compliments about her beauty. She seemed to be self conscious about it at times, as if it were a liability rather than an asset. She once responded to a comment that I had made by saying, ''I hope that's not the only reason you like me.'' Of course there were many reasons why I was crazy about her, and I enumerated them, but I was surprised at her reaction. She told me that there were times when guys would come up and put an arm around her in the hall at school, which she found to be distressing and embarrassing. My first impulse was to find those guys and destroy them, but she wasn't keen on that either. I was also sometimes surprised at her attitude when her father was being difficult. She would get upset, but she was always reluctant to criticize him, usually saying that he was just being protective. I couldn't stand the guy, although I tried not to complain about him. He was the only real problem in an otherwise perfect relationship.

Well - it wasn't really perfect. We had some disagreements, and some tense moments, but I had learned that these were the inescapable side effects of involvement with females. The one falling out that I recall with clarity involved a date that she had with another guy. This was partially due to her father's consistent reiteration that he didn't want Amy to get "too serious" with me. It was also an opportunity for her to test her commitment to our relationship. I was very angry about it, but I wasn't going to interfere. She went on the date, and reported back to say that it had been miserable, and that she had thought about me for the entire evening. This was good news, but I would rather have not been subjected to such a case study.

One evening when I arrived to pick Amy up, her mother answered the door. Behind her I could see the short hall leading to their living room, and on the floor Amy and her father appeared to be engaged in some kind of playful wrestling match. They stopped immediately, and Amy got up and came to meet me while the father disappeared. I sensed that she might have been embarrassed to be seen in such an unusual situation. Later in the car she explained that sometimes he would tickle her like that, and it was just silliness. I thought it was odd and inappropriate, but decided not to ask questions. It was the only time that I ever saw her father smiling.

Amy and I were both huge music fans. There were great concerts at the Long Beach Arena, so we would drive down there on a Friday or Saturday night, buy tickets right before the show, and see all kinds of great bands. Usually there were four or five acts on the same bill, and we saw Grand Funk, Chicago, Doobie Brothers, and the Moody Blues among many others. We would also listen to records together in her room sometimes, after a date. She had an excellent ear, and pointed out Paul giggling as he sang *Maxwell's Silver Hammer* on the Abby Road album. I had never noticed it. She also liked to hear me play my drums, especially to Beatles songs like *Strawberry Fields* and *Rain*.

When it was announced that the Who would be performing at the Anaheim Stadium, I was totally stoked. The tickets were expensive at five dollars apiece, and had to be purchased at the Ticketron in the Broadway basement. I scraped together enough money, and was among the first at the Broadway doors on the day that the tickets went on sale. When the doors opened, there was a mad dash through the store and down the stairs to the basement. Fortunately, no one was killed or injured, and I managed to score two tickets.

Amy and I were very excited about the concert, which was a daytime festival-style event. My dad was willing to let me take the car, and everything was lined up, but two days before the performance, Amy's father announced that he would not let her go. When she told me, I was angry but not surprised. She said that he didn't want her around hippies and drugs, although he had never objected to any of the other concerts that we had attended. I asked her if I could talk to him, but she didn't want to risk it. In desperation, I asked my dad if he would intervene, in order to assure him that there was no need to worry. He was good about supporting me under certain circumstances, and he made the call, but Amy's father refused to come to the phone. Amy wasn't the kind of girl to disobey her dad, either overtly or covertly, so on Sunday, Mike and I went to the concert. The Blues Image and Leon Russell were also on the bill, and both gave excellent performances. The Who played all of *Tommy* and more. It was a spectacular show, and I was sorry that Amy had missed it, and even sorrier that she hadn't been by my side. I now officially hated Amy's father.

Amy kept her horse, Ace, at a local stable, and she spent a lot of time riding him, grooming him, and doing whatever horse aficionados do. Sometimes we would go out there together, and at other times I would meet her there, flying under her father's radar. We managed to go on a few rides at night, and I would sit behind Amy with my arms around her, while she piloted Ace along the trails in the moonlight. Pretty cool.

We had all kinds of other cool things to do together, as well. There were parties and the canteen to go to if we were feeling social, and other places if we wanted solitude. After dark, the beach was perfect for kisses and conversation. I had an oversized coat that my dad had given to me, and it was big enough so that I could zip us up together in a warm, intimate bundle when the weather turned cold and we wanted to be near the water. We also went to the drive- ins, steamed up the car windows, and ate a lot of late night pizza. At Knott's Berry Farm I had a small plaque engraved with our names, and we stuck it on the dash of the AMX. Sometimes we would double up with Amy's best friend and her boyfriend to visit Ports o' Call or Disneyland.

Whenever it was time to wrap up a date, I would unwillingly take her home, where we would linger and kiss each other on the front porch for as long as possible. I was definitely infatuated - much more so than I had been with Mary Kay or Leslie, and it was important to me to communicate my feelings. There was a good sized pearl that I had gotten at Sea World in an oyster, which had been languishing for several years in my little combination safe bank. It struck me as a perfect token of my esteem, so I had it set on a thin silver chain at the local jeweler and presented it to Amy. In return, she bought me a ring. Once she met me at lunch with some rawhide lace and told me to write down seven secret wishes. She made seven knots in the lace, and then tied it tight enough around my wrist so that it couldn't fall off. She had made one of these for herself, and wanted to share the experience with me. It was one of many little intimate bonds that we had created in the six months that we had been together. It was now spring - summer vacation and senior year were not far away, and we were anticipating great times ahead.

Amy called me one evening at the beginning of April. It was immediately obvious that something was wrong. She sounded as if she had been crying.

"We're moving!" she told me. I didn't understand what she was talking about.

"Wait – what do you mean? Who's moving?"

"We are – my family!"

"No, wait, that can't be right," I was speaking calmly, certain that I was missing something. "Is this some April Fool thing?"

"Bill – no! I'm serious! My dad told me tonight. I guess they didn't want to say anything before, but now . . ." She couldn't finish.

"Amy, wait a minute – you mean that your family is moving away? That's crazy!" I wasn't willing to believe it.

"That's what he said . . ."

"Well, where?"

"Florida - Gainesville!"

"Florida! That's insane!" I was thinking maybe some place within driving distance – but Florida? "When the hell is this supposed to happen?"

"This summer . . . after school's out!"

It was no joke. Amy was moving to fucking Florida! In a few months she would be gone!

We had always tried to find ways to spend more time together, but now there was desperation in our efforts. Every time her father interfered, we were angrier and more depressed. We tried to concoct some plans to thwart, or at least postpone the inevitable. Could Amy at least stay in Long Beach with a friend for the summer? No, no, she had to help with the move, get registered at the new school, etc. We fantasized about other possibilities, but they remained just that – fantasies.

It was nearing the end of the swimming season, and there was a major event coming up. Our teams were very hot, and this was a chance to win our league in the C, B and Varsity competitions, so the coach was taking everything very seriously. I was not. Amy's imminent departure was all I could think about. As the big meet approached, we were told to shave arms, legs, heads, faces, anything to lessen the resistance as we raced through the water. This was standard practice for swimmers when the stakes were high. I recall showing up for a light workout just before the meet, and seeing lacerated shins and forearms, testifying to a lack of experience with the razor. I followed through on the arms and legs, but I didn't cut my hair or shave my face. It wasn't much, but under the circumstances I felt that I had to retain some token of self preservation, however trivial. I don't think the coach noticed because he was frantically tallying points and clocking our times. When I won my events, shaggy and unrepentant, and stood on the blocks with the hairless competitors who had copped second and third place, I began to feel like I had recaptured a little bit of my soul.

Later that afternoon, I learned that our B relay team had qualified for a slot in the CIF championships. This meant that, although the regular season was over, I would have to continue working out for this one event. I didn't want to give up valuable afterschool time that I could spend with Amy, and even though we had qualified, I knew that we would never win anything in CIF against the best swimmers in the state. I asked the coach if he could find someone else to take my slot, and he said OK. On the following Monday afternoon, the coach asked me why I wasn't poolside and ready to work out. I reminded him of our agreement.

"I never said that!" was his response. "You suit up and get out there!" He was angry.

Well, I was angry too. I changed and walked out of the locker room to the pool area. As I approached, he turned to address the entire team.

"Fogg doesn't want to swim on the relay for CIF," he said in his most derogatory tone. He singled out a couple of swimmers who could match or beat my time. "Would you be willing to take Fogg's place?" One of them said that he would. Then he turned to me. "OK Fogg," he sneered, "you can go."

If his intention had been to humiliate me in front of my teammates, it didn't work. I just looked at him for a moment, turned around, and walked out. He had confirmed my disgust for his lack of personal integrity, and my antipathy for sports in general. I didn't give a fuck for the team. I wanted to spend more time with my girl before zero hour, and I had succeeded in getting it – end of story. I was completely fed up with all of the interference in my relationship with Amy. The arbitrary exercise of a modicum of authority by people who had no sense of justice was maddening. I was truly beginning to understand the dynamics of armed insurrection. But I had no time for any of this. I felt like I had no time at all.

Our last few weeks together passed in a blur. We continued to do our favorite things, but it was all colored with depression and inevitability. Our last day together was bright and hot. Amy was driving the family station wagon, and I was lying on the front seat with my head in her lap, listening to *Suite: Judy Blue Eyes* on the radio. We had been attending to last minute errands, cruising around, and not talking much, just savoring the pleasure of being together and hoping that the moment would not have to end. When she finally had to take me home, and we couldn't delay our parting with another long kiss, I got out of the car, walked to my door, and turned around for one last look. The car was slowly backing out of the driveway, and she was leaning forward. I could see her shoulders shaking. Then she was out of the driveway, into the street, and gone.

"Dear Bill,

This year has gone by way too fast for me. Before I met you it was a complete drag, then it just raced by while I enjoyed your company and your love. You are a beautiful person, and you will be in my heart and soul forever. No one can take the memories away, even if they do separate us physically. It seems that we were made for each other, blueprint and all. You can't truly love someone if there are things about that person that upset you. Nothing about you upsets me, so I know that my feelings are well-based. There is no "fine print" in our love contract, no catches or exceptions. The only things in it are true emotions and complete understanding, and like you said, instinctive behavior.

You are all I want in a man (people will insist on calling us girls and boys, but it isn't quite true.) I love you, Bill. Must there ever be an end? Amy"

# 21
## Childhood's End

I was heading into my senior year with an Amyless summer stretching before me. I had no real interest in anything, except to indulge my misery, and play my drums as loudly as possible. I had actually cut back on the kinds of activities that could have gotten me into trouble, although not out of any sense of guilt or responsibility. I just had less energy for such things. I wasn't blasting innocent bystanders with the fire extinguisher, or setting off bombs in the neighborhood after midnight, or at least I was doing that stuff much less frequently. I wasn't drinking, smoking, or doing drugs, and I hadn't been responsible for any pregnancies. Amy and I had not indulged in the same kind of flamboyant affair that had caused difficulties with Lesli and her mom. Despite my general disengagement with the educational process, I had gotten good grades, and I had also performed well for the swim team. But none of that seemed to matter. I was consistently being perceived as a difficult case by coaches and parents. Fate was conspiring against me. Everything was upside down.

My chronic recalcitrance kicked back in, but now it was tempered with a tiny slice of insight. It wasn't a conscious decision, but I now realized that I didn't have to fight back every time I was confronted with the idiotic fascism that so many adults exhibited. Instead, I could simply do what I felt like doing, while making it clear that I was not at all concerned about the consequences. This wasn't a fully articulated philosophy, but I instinctively knew that I no longer cared about trying to follow the conventions of behavior within my little suburban hierarchy. Of course, the first manifestation of my resolution was a refusal to shave, or cut my hair. My dad railed, but so what? I didn't bother to argue with him, instead reveling in my gradual transition from clean-cut, all-American boy to bearded hippie miscreant.

Amy and I were sending each other letters at least once a day, sometimes twice. I would call her each Sunday and rack up some solid long distance charges on the phone bill. There was a certain satisfaction in maintaining our relationship against all odds, but that didn't fill the empty hours, so I decided that I would stop moping and mount a two pronged attack on my dilemma. Prong number one – get out and have some fun. Prong number two – devise a plan to see Amy.

As the summer progressed, I actually began to enjoy myself a bit. Lesli and I had managed to salvage a bond of friendship from the shambles of our affair. She was doing domestic chores for a woman named Miss Burdick and being paid minimum wage for her efforts. When I started looking for ways to make some money, Lesli arranged an introduction, and I began helping to shift various items from one place in Miss Burdick's rambling beachside abode to another. Miss Burdick was a fascinating character. She was around eighty years old, and would have made a good substitute for Margaret Hamilton in the *Wizard of Oz*, although she was actually a very nice lady. I enjoyed helping her out, and she seemed to have no issues with my appearance. I picked up a few other low level jobs and started saving my money. As yet there was no specific plan in my mind, but I knew that cash would be required for whatever I decided to do. I spent most of my free time at the beach, drifting around on a little catamaran with Dave and some other friends. We met a group of girls who were vacationing at the bay, and soon sorted ourselves into couples, sailing, swimming, and sunning almost every day. When the girls returned home to Palos Verdes, which was only a thirty minute drive from Long Beach, we continued to get together fairly often.

There were several practice games for water polo scheduled for the end of the summer. I showed up with my long hair, and a neat, but fully developed beard and moustache. The entire student body at Wilson High School had voted to eliminate the dress code, so I was not violating any statutes, but Zubbo was not about to have a hippie on the team. I was given an ultimatum to clean up before school started or else, but I was allowed to play in the practice games. The first one was fairly casual, but the second one, a week later, was a disaster. Zubbo couldn't attend, so the father of one of my team mates took over as coach. As soon as the game started, he began arguing with the referees, and yelling at the players. This continued to escalate until it became acutely embarrassing. I hated every minute of it, and I decided that I didn't want to play polo any more. When Zubbo returned, I asked him and the swimming coach if I could continue working out, and stay on the swim team, but withdraw from polo as an active player. I thought it was a perfectly reasonable request, especially as I was not much of an asset for polo. By now I should have known that my "reasonable" request would be greeted with outright hostility. Zub looked like he might consider it, but the swimming coach was adamant.

"No, Fogg – everybody plays! And cut that hair this weekend!" Angry again? OK, fine.

I acted as if I was considering his input very carefully,

then replied in a complacent voice, "Well in that case, I quit." I smiled. "See you later." It was gratifying to see the confusion on his face as I walked away. I don't think he had considered the possibility that I would not comply with his demands. I had no misgivings whatsoever, even when he would make cutting remarks to me afterward, in the hall at school. When I started wearing a headband, I would hear "How are things on the reservation, Fogg?" I always smiled and made eye contact before answering, "Great . . . I mean really terrific!" I was certain that I was having a much better time than he was, and I took some pride in the fact that my example had led to at least two other defections from the team.

It was not surprising that the art instructors had a different perspective on things. Mrs. Tressler actually complimented me on a headband that I had made, and Mr. Milroy sponsored some highly questionable drawings that a couple of friends and I had produced in his class. I met a guy named Gerald that year in art, and it turned out that he shared my interest in comics and monsters. We started doing a series of bloody, violent images with a perverse sense of humor. I drew a dog dragging a severed human arm as part of a set entitled "Bad Vibes." Another drawing showed a nude man crashing head first into the sidewalk, his head a gory explosion, with a maverick eyeball rolling on the concrete. A caption read, "As her husband entered the room, he leaped from the window." Gerald did a beautiful pencil rendering of Hitler's face with a sharpened stake entering his mouth and exiting the back of his head. He called it "Revenge of the Jewish Pole Vaulter." Mr. Milroy thought that they were great. He arranged a special section of the school's annual art exhibit just for us, and we filled a wall with gross mayhem. I was amazed that we got away with it, but evidently Mr. Milroy went to bat for us. Our work created some controversy, and probably confirmed the feelings of other school authorities that I was a bad influence.

Because I was no longer on the polo and swim teams, I was required to enroll in a regular gym class. The other two defectors, my old friend Jim and another good guy named Frank, were in the same boat. We ended up together, trying to contrive ways to get through the class with as little participation as possible. Fortunately for us, the instructor seemed to have a similar attitude about his job, and would usually leave us alone as long as we appeared to be engaged in some activity that could loosely be construed as "physical."

We devised a game called sitball that we could play in one of the handball courts. The game required three players and a sentry. The players would sit on the ground, one on the right, one on the left, and one in the center, each about ten feet from the front of the court. The object was for one player to gently roll the ball against the wall so that it would angle off and roll back to another player. If the recipient was forced to do anything more than casually extend an arm to capture the ball, it was a point against the person who had initially rolled it. The object was for the participants to maintain a high level of inertia. A solid game of sitball would be literally and figuratively pointless. The sentry was to keep an eye out for the gym teacher. The opening bars of the Monkees' theme song. "Here he comes . . ." would signal the imminent arrival of the teacher – our cue to pretend that we were engaged in a strenuous handball tournament. We spent many relaxing mornings honing our sitball skills, and when I switched to an afternoon gym class for my last semester, I passed the legacy on to a new generation of sitball enthusiasts.

This afternoon gym period provided my last brush with the psychopathology of athletics. Because I was now a master of designated inactivity, I rarely needed a shower at the end of the class. I was usually inclined to walk or ride my bike home, and then shower. It seemed stupid to take a shower in the less-than- stellar facilities provided by the school, and then take another at home, but of course, some knucklehead administrator had made it a rule. The standard routine was to hose off, then get a towel from the lackey in the towel cage, dry, dress, and present the damp towel to the lackey at the exit, as evidence that protocol had been observed. At first I went to get a towel without showering, but the student in charge, a particularly obnoxious dimwit, refused to give me one. Boy, he had me there. I couldn't see any point in explaining my theory of the School Shower Paradox to him, so I went back to my locker and changed into my clothes, and then headed for the exit without the required towel. One of the coaches was vigilantly performing exit duty, and he immediately caught me with his icy stare.

"Where do you think you're going?" Long hair brought out the worst in these guys.

"Home, why?" I was just as polite as can be.

"You're not going anywhere without taking a shower first!"

I patiently presented him with the School Shower Paradox, but he wasn't buying it. I was also observing the usual reddening face and increasing volume of Challenged Authority. It no longer angered me. I was enjoying his performance.

"Go back and take a shower!" As if this would be his final word on the subject. Well actually, I guess it was.

"See you later," I said as I walked past him. I thought that his head was going to explode, but it did not. The next day, he tried again, but I ignored him. After that, he would indicate his feelings about me, which seemed to border on hatred, with a glacial demeanor. I tried to flash him a smile now and then. He seemed to need some help with his attitude.

I was finding all kinds of new ways to subtly challenge the status quo. I don't believe that I was as concerned with issues of fairness as I had been in the past. Now it was simply a source of personal amusement. When it was time to have the all-important Senior Picture taken, I showed up at the photographer's studio with my long hair and beard, and a fox fur coat instead of the usual suit and tie. I had anticipated resistance, but the photo was taken without comment. I thought the result was merely funny, but it got a lot of attention when the yearbook came out. One girl, who had rejected an overture from me earlier in the year, actually seduced me because of that photo. It seemed ridiculous, but I happily went along for the ride.

My friend Rhys and I were still jamming to the Who, but we also engaged in such whimsical activities as enjoying a pizza on the median strip of Bellflower Boulevard while surrounded by speeding traffic. My destructive impulses had diminished, but I still got a kick out of tweaking the rules. I persuaded a girlfriend to drive with me through the Jack in the Box pick up window in the nude, after having found a sense of personal liberation in driving the racy AMX around late at night without clothes. Sometimes I would ditch school with a friend and go body surfing, or take a long ride on my bike.

Classes seemed even more irrelevant than ever. I was still enrolled in an "advanced" curriculum, and this included a course titled Humanities which was taught, for lack of a better term, by one Dr. Aubrey Harter. Harter was a pleasant guy, but he had lately adopted some new kind of all-embracing approach to education. Anything that we did or said was beautiful, as far as he was concerned. He had a long white beard which was probably intended to signify enlightenment, but I was not convinced. I still had my movie camera, so my friend Dave and I put together an absurd little eight millimeter film for a class project, complete with soundtrack. It featured objectionable blemishes, dinosaurs, and naked buttocks, and when Harter pronounced it to be "beautiful," we knew that it was time to transfer out of his class.

By the time Christmas vacation arrived, I had a box full of letters from Amy, a nice chunk of cash in my savings account, and a plan. I had decided to fly to Gainesville and get a room in a local motel without giving her any advance notice. Then I would call on Sunday as I usually did, and we would figure out a way to meet somewhere. I did not want to deal with the anxiety and complications that might arise if I tipped her off, and I believed that it would be a perfect Christmas present, based on the content of her letters. My parents didn't raise any objections when I told them what I was doing. My mom gave me the impression that she thought it was kind of a cool idea, but neither of them shared my confidence that it would work out perfectly. I contacted a travel agent, organized the itinerary, and paid the tab. Now it was all delicious anticipation. I took a bus to the LA airport on Saturday morning, and flew to Jacksonville, where I spent the night. On Sunday morning I took a flight in a small airliner to Gainesville. As the plane descended to the runway, I was enraptured by the realization that I would soon see Amy after what seemed like an eternity of separation.

I took a taxi to my hotel from the airport. Gainesville didn't look much different from Long Beach as far as I could see. The day was humid and overcast, much like a summer morning in southern California. I arrived at the hotel, checked in, and collected my thoughts in a clean, simple two bed room. I had never had such an intense sense of euphoria. It was early afternoon, and the room was quiet, except for the low volume soundtrack of familiar city sounds. I sat on one of the beds, savoring the reunion that I had scripted for us. A phone was on the night table. This was it! I picked up the receiver. The hotel operator answered, and I asked to make an outside call. It was the first time that I had dialed Amy's new number without the area code. I could hear the ringing, and then her mom answered.

"Hello?"

"Hi . . . it's Bill. Could I talk to Amy?" I was trying to sound calm, but the circumstances were so different, and the stakes were so high, that I had no idea if I was even close.

"Oh . . . hi Bill. Just a minute, I'll get her." She had picked up on something. As she handed the phone to Amy, I could hear her say, "It sounds like he's right next door."

"Hi." There she was, no longer thousands of miles away.

"Hi Amy," I was giddy, on the verge of laughing.

"What . . . where are you?" She was genuinely puzzled, and a bit concerned.

"I'm here."

"What do you mean, here?"

"Here. In Gainesville"

This was the moment when she was supposed to immediately understand what to do - continue to have a quiet conversation with me, arrange a rendezvous, and find an excuse to leave the house while making a casual remark about how good the phone connection had been. Instead, she blurted out, "Mom – he's here!"

So much for my script! There was flurry of muted conversation – now her father was involved. My plans were unraveling so quickly that I didn't know what to do. It felt like eternity before Amy's voice came back on the line. She sounded distressed, and so subdued that I could barely hear what she was saying.

"Why did you do this?"

I was nonplussed. "I wanted to see you. . . I thought you would be happy . . . I mean . . . what are you talking about?"

Silence.

"Look, Amy – I just want to see you."

273

I could hear her talking to her parents again. I waited vacantly. I felt numb.

"My dad says I can come and see you, but not for long."

"Don't you want to see me?"

"Yes, but . . ." she didn't sound convincing. "Where are you . . . I mean where are you staying?"

I gave her the address and hung up the phone. This was all wrong. How could she have told her parents? I thought about all of those letters expressing her heartfelt desire to be with me. What the hell? Now I was almost dreading her arrival. It could have been a minute or an hour before I heard a gentle tapping on the door. I got up slowly and opened it, realizing that it had suddenly become evening. There was the same lovely girl, softly illuminated by the hotel lights. I had been waiting for months just to be near her. But our reunion was exactly the opposite of what I had expected - a brief, almost impersonal hug, tears, an overall sense of distance and unease. She wouldn't kiss me, didn't seem to want to look at me. The beard and long hair made me look like a different person, even though I had sent photos, and she had liked them. Her father was angry, her mother was nervous. It seemed that I had just destroyed her happy little world instead of coming to the rescue. I don't remember the dialog. Everything was now a dismal blur. She did not stay long. I was crushed. A feeling of bitter lassitude overcame me, followed by a slow surge of the old familiar fury. Fuck her! I started making the necessary phone calls to get myself out of there as soon as possible.

When I arrived at home, my parents were compassionate enough to leave me alone, although it must have been obvious that my romantic adventure had taken a turn for the worse. There were several letters and a Christmas card from Amy that had arrived during my absence. "I wish we could be together by a warm fire, sharing our presents and love for the holidays.

Maybe someday . . ." I tore them up and tossed the pieces in the trash. Another letter appeared a few days later. She had written "I'm so sorry!" in huge letters, explaining how she had been so surprised that she hadn't known what to do. Her parents had relented the next day, and had given her permission to see me again, but when she drove to the hotel, it was too late - I had already left. I was unmoved by her apology. When my friends called to find out what had happened, I did not have much to say.

"So, Bill . . . how was Florida?"

"Cold."

1971 - a new year, a clean slate. I was still numb and angry, but I was also resolved - no "poor me" bullshit. There were a lot of cool girls out there, and some of them were beginning to embrace that free love spirit that was a cornerstone of the hippie philosophy. During my final semester at Wilson, I was the frequent beneficiary of that philosophy. I had a key to the Cal 20 that my dad kept docked at the Yacht Club, and it was an excellent place for an intimate evening. The boat was small, but it had a cozy interior space, big enough to accommodate some pillows and sleeping bags. A radio and some snacks made it perfect, and I spent many happy hours there, rocking on the water. I was getting more attention from the girls, but it was probably due, at least in part, to my appearance, and assumptions about my possibly illicit activities. There were not many guys with long hair and a beard at school, so there was undoubtedly some curiosity and interest based on that alone. I didn't care- anything that would give me some leverage was ok with me.

My hair kept getting longer, and my wardrobe more eclectic. My favorite item was a purple fake fur coat that Rhys had excavated from a Salvation Army store. He was kind enough to allow me to borrow it, and when he left for

Australia, we shipped it back and forth for a couple of years. I was automatically assumed to be part of the small but fervent stoner community at Wilson. When Jim and I would walk down the hall at school together, I would get tagged for being high. I was always perfectly straight, but Jim, who looked much more conservative than I did, was usually tripping on windowpane. It was kind of funny, but I was surprised that reasonably intelligent people could be so dogmatic in their beliefs. My dad was still harping on my appearance, but his tone had shifted from anger to reproach. During one of his harangues, he remarked with humiliation that his friends referred to me as his "hippie kid." He obviously found their remarks embarrassing, but I had no sympathy. Instead, I was completely offended

"You should stand up for me!" I was yelling at him. "Just because I have long hair doesn't mean I'm a bad guy. I'm your son. And anyway, if they're saying things like that, they're not your friends. Who cares what they think?" I expected more from him, and he knew it. He didn't yell back, but he didn't apologize either. Some of my misgivings about my dad's character were confirmed a year or two later when I went to Bogota, Colombia to teach English for the summer. When I returned, he had a neatly trimmed beard of his own! I gently teased him about it, and he became extremely irritated. He wore a beard for the rest of his life and never said a word about our previous conflicts on the subject.

On the other hand, the parents of the girls that I dated never made an issue of my hair or attire. After my experience with Amy's father, I had been apprehensive about the reception that I would receive from other fathers, but they were uniformly pleasant to me. I have no idea what might have been said when I wasn't around, but I was always made to feel welcome by parents who could have been justified in worrying about entrusting their daughters to some hippie. I had a steady thing going with a wonderful gal named Nancy who was a year younger than I was. Her dad was a Navy Captain, and they lived on the base near downtown Long Beach. I expected the worst when I went there for the first time, but her mother and father were great, and later on they allowed her to take a couple of weekend trips with me, once to San Francisco and another time to Catalina Island. It was reassuring to know that not all adults were as close minded as my dad.

The last months of my high school career were very pleasant. I had a good group of friends, a couple of girls who were fun to hang out with, and no immediate concerns regarding classes, obligations, or relationships. My little clock radio would awaken me each morning with *What is Life* by George Harrison or *Morning Girl* by the Neon Philharmonic and the sun would etch a bright rim around each window shade. I would contemplate a day of interesting possibilities, and climb out of bed feeling curiously optimistic, even though strange things were happening in the world. Rock stars and politicians were dying at an alarming rate, students were flipping out at colleges and universities, and Manson murders were still a hot topic. None of this was affecting me in a direct way, although I did have a tenuous link to one of the Manson girls, who was a cousin of Mike's girlfriend.

The final events of my senior year were the prom and the graduation ceremony. I circumvented the prom by spending the evening at Shelly's Manne Hole, a great jazz club in downtown LA, with a couple of friends and our dates. We had dinner, enjoyed some excellent music, and ended up at a local graveyard telling each other spooky stories. I was equally unenthusiastic about attending the graduation ceremony for the class of 1971, but this was ultimately unavoidable. It was made bearable by good company and the knowledge that this was the last act of submission that I would have to perform in the interest of public education. The process was tedious because we had a huge graduating class, and it took place outdoors on a very hot afternoon. I can't say that I had any feeling of accomplishment when some administrator finally handed me my diploma, just relief that the ritual was officially over. That evening, several of us met at the beach. We had decided to camp out and watch the sunrise, so we got a fire going, charred some hot dogs, and sat around discussing what we would do for the summer, and what college might be like in the fall. A young woman opted to share my sleeping bag for a while, and a pleasant time was had by all. I slept well, and was awake before dawn, gritty and bedraggled, but glad to be near the ocean, waiting for the sun to appear.

I'd be lying if I said that I had an epiphany. I should have - it would have been the perfect time and place for one – but I didn't. There were various thoughts floating through my mind, and they would sometimes collide and fragment into other thoughts, but that was about it. I was considering majoring in art at Long Beach State College simply because I wasn't interested in anything else that they had to offer. I had no particular career goals other than playing drums in a band of some kind. I would soon be required to register for the draft, and I had mixed feelings about that, which were absolutely not grounded in an understanding of the reality of armed combat. I had finally achieved virtual autonomy at home, and my mom was actually supportive of my musical inclinations. My dad and I could have a civil conversation as long as we avoided certain topics. As far as romance was concerned - did I say romance? I meant sex - I was having a wonderful time. Even my first dose of VD hadn't been a big deal - just a couple of shots and a short period of abstinence.

I was almost eighteen, dangerously close to certifiable adulthood. I thought that I had everything figured out for the moment, but I knew, based on past experience, that life was bound to become more complicated, and soon. I had started off as a bit of a hell-raiser disguised as a good kid. Now, I was no longer so readily inclined toward destructive mischief. Of course, if some firecrackers came my way, I would probably not be philosophically opposed to having a little fun with them. But a future of art, music, and girls beckoned, and it was much more enticing than the possibility of freaking people out with firecrackers. And I obviously didn't look like anyone's idea of a good kid now. The long hair, beard, and "hippie" apparel marked me as a member of the evil counter culture, even if I didn't share many of its values. Maybe I was essentially the same person that I had always been, despite the superficial changes in my behavior and appearance. Anyway, the jury was out on any absolute judgment. That was the kind of assessment that some angel or devil might make much later on. According to the doctrine of my Born Again acquaintances, a single point on the cosmic ledger was all that stood between the biggest asshole in heaven and the nicest guy in hell. Hopefully, it would be some time before my particular case was adjudicated, so there wasn't much point in trying to figure it out now. The sun was coming up, and the water looked inviting. The future was an open book with infinite possibilities. Well . . . almost infinite. Good kid, bad kid – the labels were clear. But the reality, a huge range of subtle shadings between the two extremes, was not so clear.

There was only one thing that I knew for sure.

Good or bad, I wasn't a kid anymore.